高职高专“十二五”经济管理系列规划教材

外贸单证实务与实训

曹　康　唐艳红　主　编
李　婕　王　欣　副主编

電子工業出版社
Publishing House of Electronics Industry
北京 · BEIJING

图书在版编目（CIP）数据

外贸单证实务与实训 / 曹康，唐艳红主编. —北京：电子工业出版社，2014.8
高职高专“十二五”经济管理系列规划教材
ISBN 978-7-121-22635-9

Ⅰ. ①外… Ⅱ. ①曹… ②唐… Ⅲ. ①进出口贸易－原始凭证－高等职业教育－教材 Ⅳ. ①F740.44

中国版本图书馆 CIP 数据核字(2014)第 047677 号

责任编辑：王莞朕
印　　刷：北京虎彩文化传播有限公司
装　　订：北京虎彩文化传播有限公司
出版发行：电子工业出版社
　　　　　北京市海淀区万寿路 173 信箱　邮编 100036
开　　本：787×980　1/16　印张：13.25　字数：282 千字
版　　次：2014 年 8 月第 1 版
印　　次：2018 年 8 月第 7 次印刷
定　　价：29.00 元

凡所购买电子工业出版社图书有缺损问题，请向购买书店调换。若书店售缺，请与本社发行部联系，联系及邮购电话：（010）88254888, 88258888。
质量投诉请发邮件至 zlts@phei.com.cn，盗版侵权举报请发邮件至 dbqq@phei.com.cn。
本书咨询联系方式：（010）88254199，sjb@phei.com.cn。

前　言

“外贸单证实务与实训”课程是高等职业院校国际经济与贸易专业和商务英语专业的核心课程。本课程不仅要求学生掌握常规的外贸基础知识和理论，更重要的是培养学生实践动手能力，为此我们编写了本书。

本书基于外贸单证工作流程，分为认读合同、申请开立信用证、审证和改证、缮制商业发票与装箱单、缮制订舱委托书和办理运输手续、缮制出境货物报检单和办理报检手续、缮制与申领原产地证、出口货物报关流程和报关单的填制、缮制投保单和办理保险、缮制附属单据、缮制汇票、单据审核、交单收汇与单证归档，以及业务综合技能训练14个项目。除项目14外，每个项目都包括学习目标、工作任务、操作步骤、知识扩展、能力实训、能力扩展栏目。

在教学过程中，教师可以让学生扮演外贸单证员，依据学习目标，尝试独立完成每个项目中的工作任务；可根据学生完成工作任务的情况，进行相应的示范操作；在示范操作过程中，对相关知识进行讲解；最后让学生在规定的时间内完成对应的能力实训和能力扩展练习，从而达到提升外贸单证操作能力的目的。

本书由曹康和唐艳红担任主编，李婕和王欣担任副主编。曹康对全书进行了统稿。参加编写的人员有：王欣（项目1、11）；曹康（项目2、3）；孙晓荣（项目4）；倪莹莹（项目5、9）；李婕（项目6、8、10）；田玉（项目7）；唐艳红（项目12、13）；王娟（项目14）。

在本书编写过程中，参考了许多专家的教研思路与经验成果，在此表示感谢。此外，由于编者的学识水平、实践经验有限，书中难免存在疏漏和不妥之处，恳请读者与专家批评指正。

编　者

目　录

项目 1

认读合同

学习目标

知识目标： 掌握合同条款的主要内容。
能力目标： 能够根据交易磋商内容起草合同，能读懂合同的内容。

1.1 工作任务

大连思念纺织品进出口公司（DALIAN SINIAN TEXTILES IMP.&EXP.Co.,LTD.）是一家专门从事纺织品出口的外贸公司，与波兰普利希纺织品公司（POLISH PULICI TEXTILE GROUP Co.,LTD.）有着多年业务交往。2012 年 5 月，外贸业务部小张与波兰普利希纺织品公司经过多次磋商后，签订了一份关于女士针织衫的出口合同，合同号为 PG1061。在双方建立关系之初，已经就“一般交易条件”达成协议，其中规定：除双方另有协议外，价格按 CIF 价格核算，其中保险按 CIF 发票金额另加 10%投保一切险；按照中国人民保险公司 1981 年 1 月 1 日的保险条款办理；付款方式为信用证方式。根据以往的工作经验和公司业务分工，业务部经理王小明将该笔业务的后续工作交给单证员蔡平完成。在本业务中，蔡平首先需要熟悉该业务的磋商内容和合同内容。

任务 1 熟悉业务磋商的往来函电。
任务 2 理解贸易合同的主要条款内容。

1.2 操作步骤

1.2.1 第一步：熟悉业务磋商过程中的往来函电

首先，出口方单证员蔡平要熟悉业务磋商过程中的往来函电，如图 1-1 所示。

(INCOMING) MAY 21: PLEASE QUOTE US CIF GDANSK OF ART No.11574, 11575, 11576, 11577 AND THEIR AVAILABLE QUANTITY SEPERATELY FOR JULY SHIPMENT.

(OUTGOING) MAY 22: WE WOULD LIKE TO QUOTE AS FOLLOWINGS: 11574 2 000 PIECES CIF GDANSK EUR 6.60 PER PIECE; 11575 2 500 PIECES CIF GDANSK EUR 5.60 PER PIECE; 11576 2 500 PIECES CIF GDANSK EUR 8.80 PER PIECE; 11577 2 000 PIECES CIF GDANSK EUR 8.10 PER PIECE. JULY SHIPMENT AND IRREVOCABLE L/C AT 30 DAYS AFTER SIGHT, REACHING US 45 DAYS BEFORE THE SHIPEMENT.

(INCOMING) MAY 23: 11574 2 400 PIECES CIF GDANSK EUR 6.40 PER PIECE; 11575 3 000 PIECES CIF GDANSK EUR 5.20 PER PIECE; 11576 3 000 PIECES CIF GDANSK EUR 8.50 PER PIECE; 11577 1 600 PIECES CIF GDANSK EUR 8.00 PER PIECE, VALID 25TH, 2012.

(OUTGOING) MAY 25: 11576, WE ARE SORRY THAT WE CAN ONLY SUPPLY YOU 2 400 PIECES IN JULY BECAUSE OF KEEN DEMAND. AND THE LOWEST PRICE ARE AS FOLLOWINGS: 11574 2 400 PIECES CIF GDANSK EUR 6.50 PER PIECE; 11575 3 000 PIECES CIF GDANSK EUR 5.50 PER PIECE; 11576 2 400 PIECES CIF GDANSK EUR 8.50 PER PIECE; 11577 1 600 PIECES CIF GDANSK EUR 8.00 PER PIECE. REPLY HERE 26TH MAY, 2012.

(INCOMING) MAY 26: WE ACCEPT YOUR OFFER DATED MAY 25, 2012. PLEASE SEND US THE S/C.

图 1-1　业务磋商过程中的往来函电

1.2.2 第二步：进一步熟悉该笔业务的合同内容

出口方单证员蔡平根据磋商内容，进一步熟悉该笔业务的合同内容，分别阅读了合同的约首、本文和约尾三部分内容。

1．约首

约首一般包括合同名称、合同编号、签约日期、签约双方当事人名称与地址，以及双方订立合同的意愿和执行合同的保证等。本业务填写的约首如图 1-2 所示。

<table>
<tr><td colspan="2" align="center">SALES CONTRACT</td></tr>
<tr><td colspan="2" align="right">No.: PG1061
Date: JUN.9,2012</td></tr>
<tr><td>THE SELLER:
DALIAN SINIAN TEXTILES IMP.&EXP.Co.,LTD.
53 ZHIGONG STREET, DALIAN,P.R. CHINA
Tel:+86 0411 54345659
Fax:+86 0411 54345659</td><td>THE BUYER:
POLISH PULICI TEXTILE GROUP Co.,LTD.
UL. KILIŃSKIEGO 57,OSTROWIEC ŚW. POLAND
Tel:+48 41 2651326</td></tr>
<tr><td colspan="2">THE SELLER AGREES TO SELL AND THE BUYER AGREES TO BUY THE UNDERMENTIONED GOODS ON THE TERMS AND CONDITIONS STATED BELOW.</td></tr>
</table>

图 1-2 约首

2．本文

本文是合同的主体部分，主要包括：品名、品质、数量、价格条款，尺码明细，包装条款，装运条款，保险条款，支付条款，检验条款，索赔条款，迟交货和罚金条款，不可抗力条款及仲裁条款。本业务填写的本文依次如下。

（1）品名、品质、数量、价格条款如图 1-3 所示。

COMMODITY&SPECIFICATION	QUANTITY	UNIT PRICE	AMOUNT
LADIES'S KNITTED CARDIGAN		CIF GDANSK	
ARTICLE No. 11574	2 400 PCS	EUR 6.50/PC	EUR 15 600.00
11575	3 000 PCS	EUR 5.50/PC	EUR 16 500.00
11576	2 400 PCS	EUR 8.50/PC	EUR 20 400.00
11577	1 600 PCS	EUR 8.00/PC	EUR 12 800.00
TOTAL	9 400 PCS		EUR 65 300.00
TOTAL CONTRACT VALUE: SAY EUROPEAN DOLLARS SIXTY FIVE THOUSAND THREE HUNDRED ONLY. MORE OR LESS 5% OF THE QUANTITY AND THE AMOUT ARE ALLOWED.			

图 1-3 品名、品质、数量、价格条款

（2）尺码明细如图 1-4 所示。

ARTICLE No.	S(PCS)	M(PCS)	L(PCS)	XL(PCS)
11574	600	800	500	500
11575	500	1 000	1 000	500
11576	600	800	500	500
11577	200	800	400	200

图 1-4　尺码明细

（3）包装条款如图 1-5 所示。

PACKING: Each piece in a polybag,40 pieces to one export standard carton. Shipping Marks:

POLISH
PG1061
GDANSK
C/N：1-UP

图 1-5　包装条款

（4）装运条款如图 1-6 所示。

PORT OF LOADING: DALIAN　　**PORT OF DESTINATION**: GDANSK
TRANSHIPMENT: ALLOWED　　**PARTIAL SHIPMENTS**: ALLOWED
TIME OF SHIPMENT: BEFORE JULY 30, 2012

图 1-6　装运条款

（5）保险条款如图 1-7 所示。

INSURANCE: To be effected by the seller for 110% of full invoice value covering all risks as per CIC of PICC dated 01/01/1981.

图 1-7　保险条款

（6）支付条款如图 1-8 所示。

PAYMENT: By irrevocable L/C at 30 days after sight, reaching the seller 30 days before the shipement month.

图 1-8　支付条款

（7）检验条款如图 1-9 所示。

INSPECTION: The seller shall have the performance and qualities, specifications, quantities of the goods carefully inspected and issue inspection certificate before shipment.

图 1-9 检验条款

（8）索赔条款如图 1-10 所示。

CLAIM: Any claim by the buyer regarding the goods shipped should be filed within 30days after the arrivals of the goods at the port/place of destination specified in the relative bill of lading or transport document and supported by a survey report issued by a surveyor approved by the seller. Claims in respect of matters within responsibility of insurance company, shipping company/other transportation organization will not be considered or entertained by the seller.

图 1-10 索赔条款

（9）迟交货和罚金条款如图 1-11 所示。

LATE DELIVERY AND PENALTY: In case of late delivery, the buyer shall have the right to cancel this contract, reject the goods and lodge a claim against the seller. Except for Force Majeure, if late delivery occurs, the seller must pay a penalty, and the buyer shall have the right to lodge a claim against the seller. The rate of penalty is charged at 0.1% for every day. The total penalty amount will not exceed 5% of the shipment value. The penalty shall be deducted by the paying bank or the buyer from the payment.

图 1-11 迟交货和罚金条款

（10）不可抗力条款如图 1-12 所示。

FORCE MAJEURE: If the shipment of contracted goods is prevented or delayed in whole or in part by reason of war, earthquake, fire, flood, heavy snow, storm or other causes of Force Majeure, the Seller shall not be liable for nonshipment or late shipment of the goods of this contract. However, the Sellers shall notify the Buyers by cable or telex and furnish the letter within 15 days by registered airmail with a certificate issued by the China Council for the Promotion of International Trade attesting such event or events.

图 1-12 不可抗力条款

（11）仲裁条款如图 1-13 所示。

ARBITRATION: All disputes arising out of performance of, or relating to this contract, Shall be settled amicably through friendly negotiation. In case no settlement can be reached through negotiation, the case shall then be submitted for arbitration, the location of arbitration shall be in the country of the domicile of the defendant. If in China, the arbitration shall be conducted by the China International Economic and Trade Arbitration Commission, Beijing in accordance with its rules of arbitration. The arbitral award is final and binding upon both parties. The charges arising from the arbitration shall be undertaken by the losing party.

图 1-13　仲裁条款

3．约尾

约尾一般包括合同份数、使用文字及其效力，以及双方当事人的签字等内容。如果通过传真签约，则可不列明合同份数；如果合同使用两种或两种以上语言，要明确使用文字及其效力；如果合同生效受某个条件约束，则需注明生效时间。本业务中填写的约尾如图 1-14 所示。

THE SELLER: DALIAN SINIAN TEXTILES IMP.&EXP. Co., LTD.	
THE BUYER: POLISH PULICI TEXTILE GROUP Co., LTD.	
Signature: 王小明	*Ania Wilczak*

图 1-14　约尾

1.2.3　第三步：理解完整的外贸合同内容，并做好履行合同的准备

出口方单证员蔡平理解了完整的外贸合同内容，并做好履行合同的准备。本业务中外贸合同如表 1-1 所示。

表 1-1　外贸合同

外贸合同	
	合同编号　S/C No.：PG1061 合同日期　Date：JUN.9,2012
卖方：大连思念纺织品进出口公司 中国大连职工路 53 号 **THE SELLER**: DALIAN SINIAN TEXTILES IMP. &EXP. Co.,LTD 53 ZHIGONG STREET, DALIAN, P.R. CHINA	买方：波兰普利希纺织品公司 波兰欧司特街 57 号 **THE BUYER**: POLISH PULICI TEXTILE GROUP Co., LTD. UL. KILIŃSKIEGO 57, 27-400 OSTROWIEC ŚW. POLAND
Tel（电话）: +86 0411 54345659 **Fax（传真）: +86 0411 54345659**	**Tel（电话）: +48 41 2651326** **Fax（传真）: +48 41 2651326**

续表

双方同意按下列条款由卖方出售，买方购进下列货物：

THE SELLER AGREE TO SELL AND THE BUYER AGREES TO BUY THE UNDERMENTIONED GOODS ON THE TERMS AND CONDITIONS STATED BELOW.

品名及规格 COMMODITY&SPECIFICATION	数量 QUANTITY	单价 UNIT PRICE	总值 AMOUNT
LADIES'S KNITTED CARDIGAN ARTICLE No.		CIF GDANSK	
11574	2 400 PCS	EUR 6.50/PC	EUR 15 600.00
11575	3 000 PCS	EUR 5.50/PC	EUR 16 500.00
11576	2 400 PCS	EUR 8.50/PC	EUR 20 400.00
11577	1 600 PCS	EUR 8.00/PC	EUR 12 800.00
TOTAL	9 400 PCS		EUR 65 300.00

MORE OR LESS 5% OF THE QUANTITY AND THE AMOUT ARE ALLOWED.

TOTAL CONTRACT VALUE: SAY EURO SIXTY FIVE THOUSAND THREE HUNDRED ONLY.

尺码明细（SIZE ASSORTMENT）：

货号 ARTICLE No.	S(PCS)	M(PCS)	L(PCS)	XL(PCS)
11574	600	800	500	500
11575	500	1 000	1 000	500
11576	600	800	500	500
11577	200	800	400	200

唛头（SHIPPING MARKS）：

POLISH
PG1061
GDANSK
C/N：1-UP

包装（PACKING）：

EACH PIECE IN A POLYBAG, 40 POLYBAGS TO ONE EXPORT STANDARD CARTON.

装运港（PORT OF LOADING）：DALIAN

目的港（PORT OF DESTINATION）：GDANSK

转运（TRANSHIPMENT）：ALLOWED

分批装运（PARTIAL SHIPMENTS）：ALLOWED

续表

装运时间（TIME OF SHIPMENT）: BEFORE JULY 30, 2012

保险：由卖方按发票金额的 110%投保一切险，以中国人民保险公司 1981 年 1 月 1 日的有关海洋运输货物保险条款为准。

INSURANCE: To be effected by the seller for 110% of full invoice value covering all risks as per ocean marine cargo clauses of The People's Insurance Company of china dated 1/1, 1981.

付款条件：不可撤销的信用证 30 天远期汇票，于装运月前 30 天开立。

PAYMENT: By irrevocable L/C at 30 days after sight, reaching the seller 30 days before the shipment month.

检验：卖方应当在装船前仔细检查产品的外观和品质、规格、数量并出具相关的检验证书。

INSPECTION: The seller shall have the performance and qualities, specifications, quantities of the goods carefully inspected and issue inspection certificate before shipment.

索赔：买方对于装运货物的任何索赔，必须于货物到达提单或运输单据所订目的港（地）日起 30 天内提出，并提供卖方同意的公证机构出具的检验报告。属于保险公司、轮船公司或其他有关运输机构责任范围内的索赔，卖方不予受理。

CLAIM: Any claim by the buyer regarding the goods shipped should be filed within 30 days after the arrivals of the goods at the port/place of destination specified in the relative bill of lading or transport document and supported by a survey report issued by a surveyor approved by the seller. Claims in respect of matters within responsibility of insurance company, shipping company/other transportation organization will not be considered or entertained by the seller.

迟交货和罚金条款：在卖方不能按时交货的情况下，买方有权取消此合同，拒收货物并且向卖方提出索赔。除不可抗力原因外，如果延期交货，卖方必须支付罚金，并且买方有权向卖方提出索赔。罚金率按每天收取货值的 0.1%计算。罚金总额不超过货值的 5%。罚金在付款银行或买方的支付款项中扣除。

LATE DELIVERY AND PENALTY: In case of late delivery, the buyer shall have the right to cancel this contract, reject the goods and lodge a claim against the seller. Except for force majeure, if late delivery occurs, the seller must pay a penalty, and the buyer shall have the right to lodge a claim against the seller. The rate of penalty is charged at 0.1% for every day. The total penalty amount will not exceed 5% of the shipment value. The penalty shall be deducted by the paying bank or the buyer from the payment.

不可抗力：由于战争、地震、火灾、水灾、雪灾、暴风雨或其他不可抗力因素，致使卖方不能全部或部分装运或延迟装运合同货物时，卖方对这种不能装运或延迟装运本合同货物的情况不负有责任。但卖方须用电报或电传方式通知买方，并应在 15 天内通过航空挂号信件向买方提供由中国国际贸易促进委员会出具的证明此类事件的证明书。

续表

FORCE MAJEURE: If the shipment of contracted goods is prevented or delayed in whole or in part by reason of war, earthquake, fire, flood, heavy snow, storm or other causes of force majeure, the seller shall not be liable for nonshipment or late shipment of the goods of this contract. However, the seller shall notify the buyer by cable or telex and furnish the letter within 15 days by registered airmail with a certificate issued by the china council for the promotion of international trade attesting such evetn or events.

仲裁：凡因执行本合同所发生的或与本合同有关的一切争议，双方应通过友好协商办法解决，如果协商不能解决，应提交仲裁。仲裁在被申请一方所在国进行。如果在中国，则由中国国际经济贸易仲裁委员会根据其仲裁程序规则进行仲裁。仲裁裁决是终局的，对双方都具有约束力，仲裁费用由败诉方负担。

ARBITRATION: All disputes arising out of performance of, or relating to this contract, shall be settled amicably through friendly negotiation. In case no settlement can be reached through negotiation, the case shall then be submitted for arbitration, the location of arbitration shall be in the country of the domicile of the defendant. If in china, the arbitration shall be conducted by the china international economic and trade arbitration commission in accordance with its rules of arbitration. The arbitral award is final and binding upon both parties. The charges arising from the arbitration shall be undertaken by the losing party.

卖方（SELLER）:	买方（BUYER）:
DALIAN SINIAN TEXTILES IMP. &EXP. Co.,LTD.	POLISH PULICI TEXTILE GROUP Co.,LTD.
Signature:	Signature:
王小明	Ania Wilczak

1.3 知识扩展

1.3.1 外贸合同的种类

在国际贸易中，买卖双方就交易条件经磋商达成一致协议，交易即告达成，合同即告订立，买卖双方就构成了合同关系，双方必须分别履行其所承担的合同义务。合同是具有约束力的法律文件，任何一方违反合同规定都将承担法律责任。尽管双方在磋商过程中的往来函电是书面合同的证明，但根据国际贸易习惯，买卖双方还需签订书面合同，以进一步明确双方的权利和义务。

书面外贸合同的形式比较多样，买卖双方既可采用正式合同（Contract）、确认书（Confirmation）、协议（Agreement），也可采用备忘录（Memorandum）等形式。

除了上面常用的合同形式外，订单和委托订购单有时也被采用。订单（Order）是指由进口商或实际买主拟制的货物订购单；委托订购单（Indent）是指由代理商或佣金商拟制的代客购买货物的订购单。

1.3.2 外贸合同的主要条款

1．品名、品质、数量和包装条款

货物的品名、品质、数量和包装是货物描述的构成要素，是国际货物买卖合同的主要条件，是买卖双方交接货物的重要依据。

2．价格条款

价格条款是外贸合同的核心内容，制约着合同的其他条款。

3．装运条款

装运条款是对何时交货和如何交货等问题的规定，包括装运时间、装运港和目的港、分批装运和转运，有时还有滞期和速遣等条款。买卖双方应根据各自的实际情况，实事求是地做出安排。

4．保险条款

为了使货物可能遭到的意外损失得到补偿，合同的一方当事人需要按合同规定向保险公司办理保险手续。为了明确买卖双方在货运保险方面的责任，应在合同中订立保险条款，对投保人、保险人、险别、保险金额等事项加以规定。

5．支付条款

支付条款是合同的主要条款，它涉及双方相互提供信用的程度及要价的高低，不是单一和孤立的条款，必须结合各种交易条件进行综合考虑。它主要包括付款金额、付款方式、时间、地点及方式。

6．检验条款

检验条款的内容包括检验的时间、地点、机构、标准与方法、复检、检验内容及检验证书的种类。订立检验条款时要注意与其他合同条款的衔接，准确规定检验标准和方法，明确复检的期限、地点和机构。

7．索赔、不可抗力和仲裁条款

索赔、不可抗力和仲裁条款是买卖双方为了使争议或违约得到恰当解决而签订的条款。

1.4 能力实训

阅读下面的外贸合同（见素材 1-1），将合同主要条款翻译成中文。

素材 1-1 外贸合同

外贸合同

SALES CONTRACT

No.: NEO2001026

DATE: Feb. 28, 2010

SIGNED IN: TIANJIN, CHINA

SELLER:	**BUYER**:
GUANGDONG FOREIGN TRADE IMP. & EXP. CORP. 15-18/F., GUANGDONG FOREIGN ECONOMIC AND TRADE BUILDING 351 TIANHE ROAD GUANGZHOU, CHINA	NEO GENERAL TRADING Co. P.O. BOX 99552, RIYADH 22766, KSA TEL: 00966-1-4659220 FAX: 00966-1-4659213

This contract is made by and agreed between the BUYER and SELLER, in accordance with the terms and conditions stipulated below.

CFR DAMMAM PORT

Commodity & Specification	Quantity	Unit Price & Trade Terms	Amount
ABOUT 1700 CARTONS CANNED MUSHROOMS PIECES & STEMS 24 TINS × 425 GRAMS NET WEIGHT (D.W. 227 GRAMS) ROSE BRAND	1 700 CTNS	CFR DAMMAM USD 7.80	USD13 260.00
Total	1 700 CTNS		USD13 260.00

With more or less of shipment allowed at the sellers' option.

Total Value	USD THIRTEEN THOUSAND TWO HUNDRED AND SIXTY ONLY.
Packing	EXPORTED BROWN CARTON
Shipping Marks	ROSE BRAND 178/2001 RIYADH
Time of Shipment & Means	Not Later Than Apr.30, 2010 BY VESSEL

续表

Port of Loading & Destination	From: GUANGZHOU,CHINA To: DAMMAM PORT, SAUDI ARABIA
Insurance	TO BE COVERED BY THE BUYER
Terms of Payment	The Buyer shall open through a bank acceptable to the Seller an
Irrevocable Letter of Credit payable at sight of reaching the seller 30 days before the month of shipment, valid for negotiation in China until the 15th day after the date of shipment.	
Remarks	
THE BUYER	**THE SELLER**
NEO GENERAL TRADING Co. Y. Baker	GUANGDONG FOREIGN TRADE IMP. & EXP. CORP. 张立

1.5 能力扩展

读懂业务磋商的往来函电内容（见素材 1-2），并根据磋商函电内容拟订一份外贸合同。外贸合同框架如素材 1-3 所示。

素材 1-2　业务磋商函电

THE SELLER: HANGZHOU HAIWU LEATHER PRODUCTS Co.,LTD.
No.888 SHANGHAI ROAD, HANGZHOU CHINA
THE BUYER: PICHLER VERTRIEBS GMBH.NFG.KG
KINDERMANNGASSE9，A-8020 GRAZ, AUSTRIA.

B: Jan.7, 2011

THANKS FOR YOUR MAILED CATALOGUE AND PRICE LIST. WE ARE INTERESED IN STYLE No. FC96905 AND FC98465, PLEASE QUOTE US YOUR LOWEST CIF GRAZ, AUSTRIA WITH INDICATIONS OF PACKING, MARCH SHIPMENT. QTY: 10000 PIECES EACH.

S: Jan.9, 2011

THANKS FOR YOUR INQUIRY. WE WOULD LIKE TO QUOTE AS FOLLOWINGS: FC96905 12000 PIECES CIF GRAZ USD 4.60 PER PIECE AND FC98465 12000 PIECES CIF GRAZ USD 5.10 PER PIECE, 12 PIECE TO ONE POLYBAG AND 100 POLYBAGS TO ONE CARTON, MARCH SHIPMENT AND CONFIRMED IRREVOCABLE LETTER OF CREDIT TO BE AVAILABLE AT 45 DAYS AFTER SIGHT DRAFT FOR FULL INVOICE VALUE. THE INSURANCE IS FOR 110 PERCENT OF THE INVOICE VALUE AGAINST ALL RISKS, SUBJECT TO CIC DATED 1/1/1981.

续

B: Jan.12,2011

CAMPING CHAIRS FC96905 12000 PIECES CIF GRAZ USD 4.20 PER PIECE AND FC98465 12000 PIECES CIF GRAZ USD 4.80 PER PIECE, VALID 15TH, 2011.

S: Jan.15,2011

WE BELIEVE THAT OUR PRICE IS QUITE REALISTIC FOR THEIR GOOD QUALITY. WHILE TAKING YOUR QUALITY INTO FULL CONSIDERATION, WE DECIDED TO OFFER YOU AS FOLLOWS: FC96905 12000 PIECES CIF GRAZ USD 4.50 PER PIECE AND FC98465 12000 PIECES CIF GRAZ USD 5.00 PER PIECE PLEASE REPLY AS SOON AS POSSIBLE.

B: Jan.16,2011

AFTER DUE CONSIDERATION, WE DECIDE TO ACCEPT YOUR PRICE. PLEASE SEND US THE S/C.

素材 1-3　外贸合同框架

SALES CONTRACT

DATE: S/C No.:

TO:

DEAR SIRS:

WE HEREBY CONFIRM HAVING SOLD TO YOU THE FOLLOWING GOODS ON TERMS AND CONDITIONS AS SPECIFIED BELOW:

MARKS& No.	DESCRIPTION	QUANTITY	UNIT PRICE	AMOUNT

(1) PACKING:

(2) DELIVERY:

(3) TIME OF SHIPMENT:

(4) PARTIAL SHIPMENT:

TRANSSHIPMENT:

(5) INSURANCE:

(6) TERMS OF PAYMENT:

THE SELLER: THE BUYER:

项目 2

申请开立信用证

学习目标

知识目标：了解进口商申请开立信用证的流程，掌握开证申请书的主要内容。

能力目标：能够根据外贸合同缮制开证申请书。

2.1 工作任务

大连思念纺织品进出口公司与波兰普利希纺织品公司于 2012 年 6 月 10 日签订了外贸合同后，出口方开始着手准备货物，进口方应按合同要求在规定的时间内向有关银行办理申请开立信用证的手续。

在本业务中，进口方波兰普利希纺织品公司业务员在 6 月 25 日到其开户行 NATIONAL BANK OF POLAND 申请开立信用证。申请人账号为 14587982134564。

任务 以进口方业务员的身份，根据外贸合同模拟向银行申请开立信用证的过程。

2.2 操作步骤

2.2.1 第一步：进口方在规定期限内向银行申请开立信用证

进出口双方签订外贸合同确认以信用证为结算方式后，即由进口方波兰普利希纺织品公司按合同规定的时间或在规定的装船前一定时间内向有关银行申请开立信用证。

双方合同规定："BY IRREVOCABLE L/C AT 30 DAYS AFTER SIGHT, REACHING

THE SELLER 30 DAYS BEFORE THE SHIPEMENT MONTH.”因此，进口方应在装运月的前 30 日内尽早申请开立信用证。

在本业务中，进口方在 2012 年 6 月 25 日向银行申请开证。

2.2.2　第二步：递交有关合同副本及其他进口证明文件

进口方向银行申请开立信用证，递交有关合同副本及其他进口证明文件。

2.2.3　第三步：进口方业务员根据填写规范缮制开证申请书

1．开证申请书填写规范

开证申请书部分主要条款填写规范如下。

（1）开证行名称（To）。填写开证行名称。

（2）申请开证日期（Date）。必须符合日期格式且不迟于合同规定的最迟开证日期。

（3）信用证号码（L/C No.）。由开证行填写。

（4）合同号码（Contract No.）。填写有关合同号码。

（5）信用证的到期日期和地点（Date and Place of Expiry）。填写信用证的有效期及到期地点。到期日期一般规定在最迟装运日期后 10~15 天，到期地点一般规定在受益人所在国。

（6）传递方式（Establish by）。一般有信开（Airmail）、简电后随寄电报证实书（With Brief Advice by Teletransmission）、电开（Teletransmission）、快递（Courier/Express Delivery）方式。申请人只需在备选传递方式前方框中画“×”。

（7）信用证金额（Amount）。填写合同规定的总值，分别用数字和文字两种形式表示，并且表明币制。如果允许有一定比率的上下浮动，要在信用证中明确表示出来。

（8）受益人（Beneficiary）。填写受益人的全称及详细地址，并注明联系电话、电传等号码。

（9）分批装运（Partial Shipment）和转运（Transshipment）。合同中如规定不允许则应明确注明，且对应方框画“×”。

（10）装运条款（Shipment Terms）。根据合同规定填写装运地（港）（Loading on Board From）、目的地（港）（For Transport to）的名称，以及最迟装运日期（Latest Date Of Shipment），如允许有转运地（港）（Place/Port Of Transshipment），也应列明。

（11）商品描述（Description Of Goods）。包括商品名称（Name Of Commodity）、规格（Specification）、包装（Packing）、单价（Unit Price）、唛头（Shipping Marks）等。所有内容都必须与合同内容相一致，尤其是单价和数量条款。包装条款如有特殊要求，如规格、包装物等，应具体、明确地表示清楚。

（12）押汇方式（Credit Available With）。有四种选择：即期支付（Sight Payment）、承

兑支付（Acceptance）、议付（Negotiation）、延期支付（Deferred Payment）。申请人在对应方框中画“×”。

（13）汇票要求。主要有以下三个方面的内容。

1）汇票金额（Draft For...）。根据合同规定填写信用证项下应支付发票金额的百分之几。如合同规定所有货款都用信用证支付，则应填写信用证项下汇票金额是发票金额的100%；如合同规定货款由信用证和托收两种方式各付50%，则应填写信用证项下汇票金额是全部金额的50%。

2）支付期限（Draft at...）。主要有即期、远期两种，如果是远期汇票，则必须填写具体天数，如30日或60日等。

3）付款人（Draft on...）。根据《UCP 600》，汇票的付款人是开证行（Issuing Bank）或指定银行。

（14）价格术语（Price Terms）。信用证申请书上有FOB、CFR、CIF、OTHER TERMS，根据合同成交条件在对应方框中画“×”。

（15）单据条款。开证申请书中已印就单据条款共12项，第12项是“其他单据”，前面11条中没有的单据可全部填写在该处。填写单据条款时应注意以下几点。

1）在所需的单据前画“×”。

2）在该单据条款后填上具体要求，如一式几份，应包括什么内容等。如开证申请书上已印制的要求不完整，可在该条款后面填写清楚。

3）申请人必须根据合同规定填写单据条款，不能随意提出超出合同规定的要求，也不能降低或减少合同规定的要求。

（16）附加条款（Additional Instructions）。此栏一般印就以下五项条款。

1）所有单据加列合同号码。

2）所有开证行以外的费用由受益人承担。

3）每项数量与金额允许___%的浮动。

4）第三方作为托运人是不能接受的。

5）单据必须在提单后___天内送达银行并且在信用证有效期内。

如需要已印好的上述条款，可在条款前的括号里画“×”，或在该项条款后加补充内容。

（17）授权人（法人代表）签字及电话、传真等内容（Signature of Authorised Person, TEL No., FAX）。申请书最下面的一栏由有关授权人签字，并加注电话和传真号码。

2．进口方业务员开证申请书填写内容

本业务中进口方业务员开证申请书要填写的内容如表2-1所示。

表 2-1 开证申请书

<table>
<tr><td colspan="3">IRREVOCABLE DOCUMENTARY CREDIT APPLICATION
To: NATIONAL BANK OF POLAND   Date: 120625</td></tr>
<tr><td colspan="2" rowspan="3">Beneficiary
DALIAN SINIAN TEXTILES IMP.&EXP. Co.,LTD.
53 ZHIGONG STREET, DALIAN, P.R. CHINA
Tel: +86 0411 54345659
Fax: +86 0411 54345659</td><td>L/C No.:
Ex-Card No.:</td></tr>
<tr><td>Contract No.: PG1061</td></tr>
<tr><td>Date and place of expiry
OCT.13.2012 AT BNEFICIARY'S COUNTRY</td></tr>
<tr><td>Partial shipments
☒ allowed
☐ not allowed</td><td>Transshipment
☒ allowed
☐ not allowed</td><td>☐ Issue by airmail
☐ With brief advice by teletransmission
☐ Issue by express delivery
☒ Issue by teletransmission (which shall be the operative instrument)</td></tr>
<tr><td colspan="2">Loading on board / dispatch / taking in charge at / from
DALIAN,CHINA
Not later than JULY 30, 2012
To GDANSK,POLAND</td><td>Amount (both in figures and words)
EUR 65 300.00
SAY EURO SIXTY FIVE THOUSAND THREE HUNDRED ONLY.</td></tr>
<tr><td colspan="2" rowspan="2">Description of goods

LADIES'S KNITTED CARDIGAN
ARTICLE No. 11574
11575
11576
11577

PACKING: EACH PIECE IN A POLYBAG, 40 PIECES TO ONE EXPORT STANDARD CARTON.</td><td>Credit available with
☐ by sight payment ☐ by acceptance ☒ by negotiation
☐ by deferred payment at against the documents detailed herein
☐ and beneficiary's draft for % of the invoice value at 30 days after sight
on BANK OF CHINA LIAONING BRANCH
☐ FOB ☐ CFR ☒ CIF ☐ other terms</td></tr>
<tr><td></td></tr>
</table>

续表

Documents required: (marked with ×)
- (×) Signed Commercial Invoice in 3 copies indicating invoice no., contract no.
- (×) Full set of clean on board ocean Bills of Lading made out to order and blank endorsed, marked "freight ( ) to collect / (×)prepaid (×) showing freight amount" notifying ACCOUNT.
- ( ) Air Waybills showing "freight ( ) to collect / ( ) prepaid ( ) indicating freight amount" and consigned to____.
- ( ) Memorandum issued by ____consigned to ____.
- (×) Insurance Policy / Certificate in 2 copies for 110 % of the invoice value showing claims payable in China in currency of the draft, bank endorsed, covering ( ) Ocean Marine Transportation / ( ) Air Transportation / ( ) Over Land Transportation(×) All Risks, War Risks.
- (×) Packing List / Weight Memo in 3 copies indicating quantity / gross and net weights of each package and packing conditions as called for by the L/C.
- (×) Certificate of Quantity / Weight in 3 copies issued an independent surveyor at the loading port, indicating the actual surveyed quantity / weight of shipped goods as well as the packing condition.
- (×) Certificate of Quality in 3 copies issued by (×) manufacturer / ( ) public recognized surveyor / ( ).
- (×) Beneficiary's certified copy of FAX dispatched to the accountees with 2 days after shipment advising ( ) name of vessel / (×) date, quantity, weight and value of shipment.
- ( ) Beneficiary's Certificate certifying that extra copies of the documents have been dispatched according to the contract terms.
- ( ) Shipping Co.'s Certificate attesting that the carrying vessel is chartered or booked by accountee or their shipping agents.
- ( ) Other documents, if any:
  a) Certificate of Origin in 3 copies issued by authorized institution.
  b) Certificate of Health in 3 copies issued by authorized institution.

Additional instructions:

1. (×) All banking charges outside the opening bank are for beneficiary's account.
2. (×) Documents must be presented with 30 days after the date of issuance of the transport documents but within the validity of this credit.
3. ( ) Third party as shipper is not acceptable. Short Form / Blank Back B/L is not acceptable.
4. ( ) Both quantity and amount 10 % more or less are allowed.
5. ( ) Prepaid freight drawn in excess of L/C amount is acceptable against presentation of original charges voucher issued by Shipping Co. / Air line / or it's agent.
6. ( ) All documents to be forwarded in one cover, unless otherwise stated above.
7. (×) Other terms, if any:

Account No.: 14587982134564 with POLISH PULICI TEXTILE GROUP Co., LTD.

Signature:

2.3 知识扩展

进口是出口的反向操作，多数进口单据与出口单据的区别不大。在信用证付款方式下，准确填写开证申请书的相关内容是进口方（申请人）必须掌握的一种技能。开证申请书由银行提供，统一格式，一式三份。其中一份交银行，另两份留进口商业务部门和财务部门。开证申请书是申请人与开证行之间明确彼此权利义务关系的契约，也是银行开立信用证的依据，必须按合同的具体规定写明信用证的各项要求，内容要明确、完整，无词义不清的记载。

申请开立信用证的基本要求如下。

2.3.1 提供准确的开证路线

开证路线（L/C Guidance）由受益人在签订合同后向申请人提供，通常包括收款人名称、地址和账号（Payee's Name, Address and A/C No.），以及收款行名称、地址（Name and Address of Payee's Bank）等内容。

2.3.2 准备开证资料

首次到银行办理进口开证手续的企业应提交营业执照副本、企业有权从事外贸经营活动的文件原件、法人代表授权书、被授权人的签样、外汇局备案表等。

2.3.3 了解办理手续

开立信用证的申请办理手续包括递交有关合同的副本及附件、填写开证申请书（有的银行称开证承诺书）、缴纳保证金、支付手续费等。

2.3.4 按时开证

如合同规定了开证日期，进口方应在规定期限内开立信用证；如合同只规定了装运期的起止日，则应保证受益人在装运期开始前收到信用证；如合同只规定了最迟装运日期，则应在合理时间内开证，以使卖方有足够的时间备妥货物并予出运，通常在交货期前 1 个月至 1 个半月左右。

2.3.5 信用证的条件应单据化

进口方在申请开证时，应将合同的有关规定转化成单据。例如，合同以 CFR/CIF 条件成交，信用证应要求受益人在提交的清洁已装船提单上注明“运费已付”字样等。

银行单证中心的开证人员对开证申请人提交的有关文件进行审核，确认资料完整、符合规定后，通常按 SWIFT 规定的 MT700 格式将信用证开出。

各银行事先印制的固定格式开证申请书中凡涉及选择的项目，一律在有关项目前面“×” 表示选中。除非有特殊要求和规定，开证申请书原则上应是英文。

2.4 能力实训

阅读下面的开证申请书（见素材 2-1），将其翻译成中文。

素材 2-1 开证申请书

<table>
<tr><td colspan="2">IRREVOCABLE DOCUMENTARY CREDIT APPLICATION
TO:BANK OF CHINA GUANGZHOU BRANCH Date: Credit No.:</td></tr>
<tr><td>Description of goods
MEN'S DENIM UTILITY SHORT
COLOR: MEDDEST SANDBLAS
FABRIC CONTENT: 100% COTTON
QUANTITY: 2 000 CARTON</td><td>Date and place of expiry
JULY 30, 2010 IN CHINA
Beneficiary (Full name and address)
ROYAL TRADERS LTD.
333 BARRON BLVD. , INGLESIDE , ILLINOIS
(UNITED STATES)</td></tr>
<tr><td>☐ Issue by airmail
☐ With brief advice by teletransmission
☐ Issue by express delivery
☒Issue by teletransmission (which shall be the operative instrument)</td><td>Amount
USD 570 000.00
SAY U.S.DOLLARS FIVE HUNDRED AND SEVENTY THOUSAND ONLY</td></tr>
<tr><td>Partial shipments Transhipment
☐ allowed ☐ allowed
☒not allowed ☒not allowed</td><td>Credit available with
ANY BANK
By
☐ sight payment ☐ acceptance ☒negotiation</td></tr>
<tr><td>Loading on board/dispatch/taking in charge at/from
NEW YORK
not later than JULY 15, 2010
For Transportation to
GUANGZHOU, CHINA</td><td>☐ deferred payment at against the documents detailed herein
☒and beneficiary's draft(s) for 100 % of invoice value at****sight
drawn on
☒FOB ☐ CFR ☐ CIF ☐ or other terms</td></tr>
</table>

续

Documents required: (marked with ×)
1．(×) Signed commercial invoice in 3 copies indicating L/C No. and Contract No.
2．(×) Full set of clean on board Bills of Lading made out to order and blank endorsed, marked "freight [×] to collect / [ ]prepaid [ ] showing freight amount" notifying THE APPLICANT WITH FULL NAME AND ADDRESS .
3．( ) Airway bills/cargo receipt/copy of railway bills issued by______showing "freight [ ] to collect/[ ] prepaid [ ] indicating freight amount" and consigned to______.
4．( ) Insurance Policy/Certificate in_____copies for______% of the invoice value showing claims payable in______currency of the draft, blank endorsed, covering All Risks, War Risks and______.
5．( ) Packing List/Weight Memo in 3 copies indicating quantity, gross and weights of each package.
6．( ) Certificate of Quantity/Weight in______copies issued by______.
7．( ) Certificate of Quality in_____copies issued by [ ] manufacturer/[ ] public recognized surveyor______.
8．(×) Certificate of Origin in 2 copies.
9．(×) Beneficiary's certified copy of fax / telex dispatched to the applicant within 1 days after shipment advising L/C No., name of vessel, date of shipment, name, quantity, weight and value of goods.
10．( ) Other documents, if any
Additional instructions:
1．(×) All banking charges outside the opening bank are for beneficiary's account.
2．(×) Documents must be presented within 10 days after date of issuance of the transport documents but within the validity of this credit.
3．( ) Third party as shipper is not acceptable, Short Form/Blank back B/L is not acceptable.
4．( ) Both quantity and credit amount ______ % more or less are allowed.
5．(×) All documents must be sent to issuing bank by courier/speed post in one lot.
6．( ) Other terms, if any

2.5 能力扩展

根据外贸合同（见素材 2-2）和补充资料，模拟进口公司 PICHLER VERTRIEBS GMBH. NFG.KG 的业务员向开证行 BKAUATWW BANK 申请开立信用证的过程，账号为 165464101546。开证申请书框架如素材 2-3 所示。

补充资料：

1. INVOICE IN TRIPLICATE.
2. PACKING LIST IN TRIPLICATE.
3. FULL SET OF CLEAN ON BOARD BILLS OF LADING MADE OUT ORDER AND BLANK ENDORSED NOTIFYING THE APPLICANT WITH FULL NAME AND ADDRESS MARKED FREIGHT COLLECT.
4. CERTIFICATE OF ORIGIN IN DUPLICATE.
5. ALL DOCUMENTS MUST BE MAILED IN ONE LOT TO THE ISSUING BANK BY COURIER SERVICE.

素材 2-2　外贸合同

SALES CONTRACT

S/C No.: AB123

DATE: JAN.20,2011

TO: PICHLER VERTRIEBS GMBH. NFG.KG

KINDERMANNGASSE9, A-8020 GRAZ, AUSTRIA

DEAR SIRS:

WE HEREBY CONFIRM HAVING SOLD TO YOU THE FOLLOWING GOODS ON TERMS AND CONDITIONS AS SPECIFIED BELOW:

MARKS&No.	DESCRIPTION	QUANTITY	UNIT PRICE	AMOUNT
P.V.G.N	CAMPING CHAIRS		CIF GRAZ	
AB123	FC96905	12 000 PIECES	USD 4.50 PERPIECE	USD 54 000.00
GRAZ,AUSTRIA	FC98465	12 000 PIECES	USD 5.00 PERPIECE	USD 60 000.00
C/No.:1-200				
TOTAL		24 000 PIECES		USD 114 000.00

(1) PACKING: 12 PIECES TO ONE POLYBAG AND 100 POLYBAGS TO ONE CARTON.

(2) DELIVERY: FROM HANGZHOU, CHINA TO GRAZ, AUSTRIA

(3) TIME OF SHIPMENT: NOT LATER THAN FEB.20,2011

(4) PARTIAL SHIPMENT: NOT ALLOWED

TRANSSHIPMENT: NOT ALLOWED

(5) INSURANCE: TO BE EFFECTED BY THE SELLER FOR 110% OF INVOICE VALUE COVERING ALL RISKS AS PER CIC OF PICC DATED 01/01/1981.

(6) TERMS OF PAYMENT: BY IRREVOCABLE LETTER OF CREDIT TO BE AVAILABLE AT 45 DAYS AFTER SIGHT DRAFT FOR FULL INVOICE VALUE.

THE SELLER:
HANGZHOU HAIWU LEATHER PRODUCTS Co.,LTD.
No.888 SHANGHAI ROAD, HANGZHOU CHINA

THE BUYER:
PICHLER VERTRIEBS GMBH.NFG.KG
KINDERMANNGASSE9,A-8020 GRAZ,AUSTRIA.

素材 2-3　开证申请书框架

IRREVOCABLE DOCUMENTARY CREDIT APPLICATION

<table>
<tr><td>To:</td><td>Date:</td></tr>
<tr><td>☐ Issue by airmail ☐ With brief advice by teletransmission
☐ Issue by express delivery
☐ Issue by teletransmission (which shall be the operative instrument)</td><td>Credit No.

Date and place of expiry</td></tr>
<tr><td>Applicant</td><td>Beneficiary (Full name and address)</td></tr>
<tr><td>Advising Bank</td><td>Amount</td></tr>
<tr><td>Partial shipments ☐ allowed ☐ not allowed
Transshipment ☐ allowed ☐ not allowed</td><td>Credit available with</td></tr>
<tr><td>Loading on board/dispatch/taking in charge at/from

not later than
For transportation to:</td><td>By
☐ sight payment ☐ acceptance ☐negotiation
☐ deferred payment at against the documents detailed herein

☐ and beneficiary's draft(s) for___% of invoice value at___sight
drawn on
☐ FOB ☐ CFR ☐ CIF ☐ or other terms</td></tr>
</table>

Documents required: (marked with ×)

1. ( ) Signed commercial invoice in____copies indicating L/C No. and Contract No.
2. ( ) Full set of clean on board Bills of Lading made out to order and blank endorsed, marked "freight [ ] to collect / [ ]prepaid [ ] showing freight amount" notifying____.
3. ( ) Airway bills/cargo receipt/copy of railway bills issued by____showing “freight [ ] to collect/[ ] prepaid [ ] indicating freight amount" and consigned to____.
4. ( ) Insurance Policy/Certificate in ___copies for__% of the invoice value showing claims payable at ____ in currency of the draft, blank endorsed, covering All Risks, War Risks and____.

续

5. ( ) Packing List/Weight Memo in___copies indicating quantity, gross and weights of each package.
6. ( ) Certificate of Quantity/Weight in___copies issued by____.
7. ( ) Certificate of Quality in___copies issued by [ ] manufacturer/[ ] public recognized surveyor____.
8. ( ) Certificate of Origin in___copies .
9. ( ) Beneficiary's certified copy of fax / telex dispatched to the applicant within___days after shipment advising L/C No., name of vessel, date of shipment, name, quantity, weight and value of goods.
10. Other documents, if any

Description of goods:

Additional instructions:

1. ( ) All banking charges outside the opening bank are for beneficiary's account.
2. ( ) Documents must be presented within___days after date of issuance of the transport documents but within the validity of this credit.
3. ( ) Third party as shipper is not acceptable, Short Form/Blank back B/L is not acceptable.
4. ( ) Both quantity and credit amount___% more or less are allowed.
5. ( ) All documents must be sent to issuing bank by courier/speed post in one lot.
6. ( ) Other terms, if any

项目 3

审证和改证

学习目标

知识目标：掌握信用证的格式与主要条款内容，以及信用证审核的要点。

能力目标：能够分析信用证条款的内容和含义，能够根据合同找出信用证中存在的不符条款并对其进行修改。

3.1 工作任务

2012 年 6 月 28 日，大连思念纺织品进出口公司单证员蔡平收到了中国银行辽宁省分行国际业务部的信用证通知函，告知波兰普利希纺织品公司已经通过 NATIONAL BANK OF POLAND 开来信用证。信用证内容如表 3-1 所示。

表 3-1 波兰普利希纺织品公司开来的信用证

MESSAGE TYPE: MT700	ISSUE OF A DOCUMENTARY CREDIT
SEQUENCE OF TOTAL	*27: 1/1
FORM OF DOC. CREDIT	*40B: IRREVOCABLE
DOC. CREDIT NUMBER	*20: DCTBT123456
DATE OF ISSUE	31C: 120628
APPLICABLE RULES	*40E: UCP LATEST VERSION
EXPIRY	*31D: DATE 120913 POLISH
APPLICANT BANK	51D: NATIONAL BANK OF POLAND

续表

	P.O.BOX 586, GDANSK, POLAND
APPLICANT	*50: POLISH TEXTILE GROUP Co.,LTD. UL. KILIŃSKIEGO 57,OSTROWIEC ŚW.,POLAND
BENEFICIARY	*59: DALIAN SINIAN TEXTILES IMP.&EXP. Co.,LTD. 53 ZHIGONG STREET, DALIAN,P.R. CHINA
AMOUNT	*32B: CURRENCY USD AMOUNT 65300.00
AVAILABLE WITH/BY	*41D: ANY BANK BY NEGOTIATION
DRAFTS AT…	42C: AT SIGHT
DRAWEE	42D: POLISH PULICI TEXTILE GROUP Co.,LTD.
PARTIAL SHIPMENTS	43P: NOT ALLOWED
TRANSSHIPMENT	43T: ALLOWED
PORT OF LOADING	44E: SHANGHAI IN CHINA
PORT OF DISCHARGE	44F: GDANSK,POLAND
LATEST DATE OF SHIP.	44C: 120630
DESCRIPT OF GOODS	45A: FOB GDANSK LADIES'S KNITTED CARDIGAN AS PER PURCHASE CONTRACT No. PG1161 LADIES'S KNITTED CARDIGAN PACKED IN 50PCS/CTN ARTCLE No. 11 574 2 500 PCS AT USD 6.50/PC 11 575 2 000 PCS AT USD 6.00/PC 11 576 2 400 PCS AT USD 8.50/PC 11 577 1 600 PCS AT USD 8.00/PC
DOCUMENTS REQUIRED	46A: 1. COMMERCIAL INVOICE MANUALLY SIGNED IN 2 ORIGINALS PLUS 1 COPY. 2. PACKING LIST IN TRIPLICATE. 3. FULL SET (2/3) OF ORIGINAL CLEAN ON BOARD BILL OF LADING PLUSE 3/3 NON NEGOTIABLE COPIES,MADE OUT TO ORDER OF ISSUING BANK AND BLANK ENDORSED NOTIFY THE APPLICANT, MARKED FREGHT COLLECT. 4. INSURANCE POLICY/CERTIFICATE IN DUPLICATE BLANK ENDORSED FOR 130% INVOICE VALUE COVERING ALL RISKS & WAR RISKS SHOWING CLAIMS PAYABLE IN POLAND IN THE CURRENCY OF THE CREDIT.

续表

5．G.S.P. CERTIFICATE OF ORIGIN FORM AIN 1 DUPLICATE STATING THAT THE GOODS ARE OF CHINESE ORIGIN. 6．PRESHIPMENT INSPECTION CERTIFICATE ISSUED BY A REPRSENTATIVE OF GOOD TRADE LTD. WITH POSITIVE RESULT. 7. BENEFICIARY'S CERTIFICATE STATING THAT ONE SET OF NON-NEGOTIABLE SHIPPING DOCUMENTS TOGETHER WITH THE 1/3 ORIGINAL B/L AND ORIGINAL FORM A HAVE BEEN SENT TO THE APPLICANT BY DHL WITHIN 3 DAYS AFTER SHIPMENT DATE. 8．SHIPPING ADVICE SHOWING THE NAME OF THE CARRYING VESSEL, DATE OF SHIPMENT, MARKS, QUANTITY, NET WEIGHT AND GROSS WEIGHT OF THE SHIPMENT TO APPLICANT WITHIN 3 DAYS AFTER THE DATE OF BILL OF LADING. ADDITIONAL COND.　　47A: +ALL DOCS MUST BE ISSUED IN ENGLISH. +DOCUMENTS ISSUED PRIOR TO L/C ISSUING DATE ARE NOT ACCEPTABLE. +SHIPMENT MUST BE EFFECTED BY FCL. +B/L MUST SHOW SHIPPING MARKS: ABC ,S/C PG1061,GDAND, C/ No. + DOCUMENTS MUST BE PRESENTED WITHIN 14 DAYS AFTER SHIPMENT DATE BUT IN ANY EVENT NOT LATER THAN THE EXPIRY DATE OF THIS CREDIT. +FOR DOCS WHICH DO NOT COMPLY WITH L/C TERMS AND CONDITIONS, WE SHALL DEDUCT FROM PROCEEDS A CHARGE OF EUR50.00 PAYABLE IN USD EQUIVALENT PLUS ANY INCURRED SWIFT CHARGES IN CONNECTION WITH. DETAILS OF CHARGES　　71B: ALL CHARGES ARE TO BE BORN BY BENEFICIARY'S ACCOUNT. PRESENTATION PERIOD　　48: 5DAYS AFTER B/L DATE, BUT WITHIN L/C VALIDITY. CONFIRMATION　　*49: WITHOUT

在本业务中，出口方单证员蔡平需要完成以下工作任务。

任务 1　根据外贸合同 PG1061，仔细推敲信用证条款，审核信用证。

任务 2　信用证审核后如有不符之处，向业务部王经理汇报，提出修改意见。

任务 3　向进口方发送改证函，要求修改信用证。

3.2　操作步骤

3.2.1　第一步：仔细阅读信用证条款，理解信用证的内容

出口方单证员蔡平首先应熟悉信用证内容，特别是信用证开证日期、到期日、金额、

到期地点、交单期、装运期、单据要求等主要条款的含义。

3.2.2 第二步：对照外贸合同审核信用证，找出信用证中的问题条款

1. 对照合同条款逐项排查

蔡平审核后发现有如下不符点。

（1）信用证到期日“2012 年 9 月 13 日”与合同“2012 年 10 月 13 日”不符；到期地点为“波兰”，容易造成受益人延误交单，对受益人不利。

（2）信用证中开证申请人名称“POLISH TEXTILE GROUP Co., LTD.”与合同不符，应改为“POLISH PULICI TEXTILE GROUP Co.,LTD.”。

（3）信用证金额的币值“USD”与合同不符，应改为“EUR”。

（4）信用证中汇票的付款期限“AT SIGHT”与合同不符，应改为“AT 30 DAYS AFTER SIGHT”。

（5）信用证中汇票的付款人“POLISH PULICI TEXTILE GROUP Co., LTD.”错误，应改为“NATIONAL BANK OF POLAND”。

（6）信用证中分批装运“NOT ALLOWED”与合同不符，应改为“ALLOWED”。

（7）信用证中装运港“SHANGHAI”与合同不符，应改为“DALIAN”。

（8）信用证中最迟装运日“120630”与合同不符，应改为“120730”。

（9）信用证中有关货物描述的贸易术语“FOB GDANSK”应改为“CIF GDANSK”；合同号“PG1161”应改为“PG1061”；包装方式“PACKED IN 50PCS/CTN”应改为“PACKED IN 40PCS/CTN”；单价、数量应改为：

ARTICLE No.	11574	2 400 PCS AT EUR 6.50/PC
	11575	3 000 PCS AT EUR 5.50/PC
	11576	2 400 PCS AT EUR 8.50/PC
	11577	1 600 PCS AT EUR 8.00/PC

（10）信用证中提单只要求提交 2/3 正本提单，而另 1/3 直接寄给申请人，并出具寄单证明，风险很大。提单不应标注“FREIGHT COLLECT”，应改为“FREGHT PREPAID”。

（11）信用证的保险条款中投保金额比例“130% INVOICE VALUE”及投保险别“ ALL RISKS & WAR RISK”与合同不符，应改为“110% INVOICE VALUE COVERING ALL RISKS”。

（12）信用证的唛头与合同不符，应改为：

POLISH
PG1061
GDANSK
C/N：1-UP

(13) 信用证中费用条款“ALL CHARGES ARE TO BE BORN BY BENEFICIARY'S ACCOUNT”不合理，应改为“ALL CHARGES OUTSIDE POLAND ARE ON BENEFICIARY'S ACCOUNT”。

(14) 信用证中交单期“5 DAYS AFTER B/L DATE”错误，应改为“15 DAYS”。

2．对照合同审核有无信用证漏开条款

审核后发现，信用证中遗漏了合同条款“MORE OR LESS 5% OF THE QUANTITY AND THE AMOUT ARE ALLOWED”。

3.2.3 第三步：提出修改建议

出口方单证员蔡平向业务部王经理提出信用证修改建议，王经理采纳了蔡平合理的改证建议，并于 2012 年 6 月 29 日给波兰普利希纺织品公司发送如下改证函。

DEAR SIRS,

WE ARE PLEASED TO RECEIVE YOUR L/C No. DCTBT123456 ISSUED BY NATIONAL BANK OF POLAND. BUT WE FIND THAT IT CONTAINS SOME DISCREPANCIES WITH S/C No. PG1061.PLEASE INSTRUCT THE ISSUING BANK TO AMEND THE L/C A.S.A.P. THE L/C SHOULD BE AMENDED AS FOLLOWS:

1．THE L/C EXPIRE DATE SHOULD BE 121013, NOT 120913 AND THE EXPIRES PLACE SHOULD BE CHINA NOT POLISH.

2．THE NAME OF THE APPLICANT SHOULD BE POLISH PULICI TEXTILE GROUP Co.,LTD., NOT POLISH TEXTILE GROUP Co., LTD..

3．THE CURRENCY CODE OF AMOUNT SHOULD BE EUR NOT USD.

4．THE DRAFT SHOULD BE PAID AT 30 DAYS AFTER SIGHT INSTEAD OF AT SIGHT.

5．THE DRAWEE OF DRAFT SHOULD BE “NATIONAL BANK OF POLAND” NOT “POLISH PULICI TEXTILE GROUP Co., LTD.”.

6．THE L/C PROHIBITS PARTIAL SHIPMENTS, SHOULD BE “ALLOWED PARTIAL SHIPMENTS”.

7．THE L/C PORT OF LOADING SHOULD BE “DALIAN” INSTEAD OF “SHANGHAI”.

8．THE LATEST SHIPMENT OF L/C SHOULD BE “120730” INSTEAD OF “120630”.

9．THE TRADE TERMS SHOULD BE “CIF GDANSK” NOT “FOB GDANSK”.

10．THE CONTRACT No. SHOULD BE “PG1061” INSTEAD OF “PG1161”.

11．THE PACKING CLAUSE SHOULD BE “PACKED IN 40PCS/CTN” INSTEAD OF “PACKED IN 50PCS/CTN”.

12．AMEND THE “2/3 OF ORIGINAL CLEAN ON-BOARD MARINE BILL OF LADING” TO “FULL SET OF ORIGINAL CLEAN ON-BOARD MARINE BILL OF LADING”.

13．THE GOODS ARE INSURED FOR 110% OF THE INVOICE VALUE INSTEAD OF 130% THE INVOICE VALUE AGAINST ALL RISKS AS PER CIC OF PICC DATED 01/01/1981.

14．IN THE CLAUSE OF “DESCRIPTIONS OF GOODS”, THE QUANTITY AND UNIT PRICE ARE WRONG, SHOULD BE

ARTICLE No. 11574 2 400 PCS AT EUR 6.50/PC
11575 3 000 PCS AT EUR 5.50/PC
11576 2 400 PCS AT EUR 8.50/PC
11577 1 600 PCS AT EUR 8.00/PC

15．DOCUMENTS ARE TO BE PRESENTED ULTIMATELY NOT WITH IN 5 DAYS, BUT WITH IN 15 DAYS AFTER B/L DATE.

16．THE SHIPPING MARKS SHOULD BE:

POLISH
PG1061
GDANSK
C/N：1-UP

17．DELETE THE CLAUSE “BENEFICIARY'S CERTIFICATE STATING THAT ONE SET OF NON-NEGOTIABLE SHIPPING DOCUMENTS TOGETHER WITH THE 1/3 ORIGINAL B/L AND ORIGINAL FORM A HAVE BEEN SENT TO THE APPLICANT BY DHL WITHIN 3 DAYS AFTER SHIPMENT DATE.” AND THE WORDING “BENEFICIARY'S CERTIFICATE STATING THAT ONE SET OF NON-NEGOTIABLE SHIPPING DOCUMENTS HAS BEEN SENT TO THE APPLICANT BY DHL WITHIN 3 DAYS AFTER SHIPMENT DATE.”

18．PLEASE ADD THE CLAUSE “MORE OR LESS 5% OF THE QUANTITY AND THE AMOUT ARE ALLOWED.”

19．THE FEE CHARGES SHOULD BE“ALL CHARGES OUTSIDE POLAND ARE ON BENEFICIARY'S ACCOUNT.”INSTEAD OF “ALL CHARGES ARE TO BE BORN BY BENEFICIARY'S ACCOUNT.”

THANK YOU FOR YOUR KIND COOPERATION. PLEASE SEE TO IT THAT THE L/C AMENDMENT REACH US WITHIN 3 DAYS, OTHERWISE WE CANNOT EFFECT PUNCTUAL SHIPMENT.

3.2.4 第四步：提出改证申请

波兰普利希纺织品公司收到信用证改证函后，同意上述改证要求，向 NATIONAL BANK OF POLAND 提出改证申请。2012 年 7 月 3 日，中国银行辽宁省分行通知大连思念纺织品进出口公司业务员蔡平，国外开来的信用证修改书已到，蔡平拿到信用证修改书，信用证修改书成为原信用证的组成部分，并替代原信用证对应条款而使其失效。信用证修改书如表 3-2 所示。

表 3-2 信用证修改书

MESSAGE TYPE: MT707 AMENDMENT TO A DOCUMENTARY CREDIT
SENDER NATIONAL BANK OF POLAND
RECEIVER CHINA BANK YANTAI BRANCH
DOC. CREDIT NUMBER 20: DCTBT123456
DATE OF ISSUE 31C: 120702
NUMBER OF AMENDMENT 26E: 01
NEW DATE AND PLACE OF EXPIRY 31E: DATE 121013IN CHINA
APPLICANT (BEFORE THIS AMENDMENT) 50 :POLISH PULICI TEXTILE GROUP Co.,LTD.
NEW DOC. CREDIT AMOUNT AFTER AMENDMENT 34B: CURRENCY EUR AMOUNT 65 300.00
NARRATIVE 79:

① UNDER FIELD 45A, THE TRADE TERMS TO CIF GDANSK AND THE CONTRACT No. TO PG1061, PACKED IN 40PCS/CTN.

ARTICLE No.

11574 2 400 PCS AT EUR 6.50/PC
11575 3 000 PCS AT EUR 5.50/PC
11576 2 400 PCS AT EUR 8.50/PC
11577 1 600 PCS AT EUR 8.00/PC

② UNDER FIELD 42C AMENDED TO: AT 30 DAYS AFTER SIGHT
③ UNDER FIELD 42D AMENDED TO: NATIONAL BANK OF POLAND
④ UNDER FIELD 43P AMENDED TO: ALLOWED
⑤ UNDER FIELD 44E AMENDED TO: DALIAN
⑥ UNDER FIELD 44C AMENDED TO: 120730
⑦ UNDER FIELD 46A, B/L AMENDED TO: FULL SET OF ORIGINAL CLEAN ON-BOARD MARINE BILL OF LADING AND MARKED FREIGHT PREPAID.
⑧ UNDER FIELD 46A,THE AMOUNT INSURED AMENDED TO: 110% OF THE INVOICE VALUE COVERING ALL RISKS AS PER CIC OF PICC DATED 01/01/1981.

续表

⑨ UNDER FIELD 46A, DELETE THE CLAUSE "BENEFICIARY'S CERTIFICATE STATING THAT ONE SET OF NON-NEGOTIABLE SHIPPING DOCUMENTS TOGETHER WITH THE 1/3 ORIGINAL B/L AND ORIGINAL FORM A HAVE BEEN SENT TO THE APPLICANT BY DHL WITHIN 3 DAYS AFTER SHIPMENT DATE."
⑩ UNDER FIELD 47A, SHIPPING MARKS AMENDED TO: POLISH/PG1061/GDANSK/C/N: 1-UP.
⑪ UNDER FIELD 71B, CHARGES AMENDED TO: ALL CHARGES OUTSIDE POLAND ARE ON BENEFICIARY'S ACCOUNT.
⑫ UNDER FIELD 48, DOCUMENTS ARE TO BE PRESENTED ULTIMATELY NOT WITH IN 5 DAYS, BUT WITH IN 15 DAYS AFTER B/L DATE.

3.2.5 第五步：备货出运

经审核信用证修改书，大连思念纺织品进出口公司认为其符合改证要求，随即开始根据信用证的相关规定备货出运。

3.3 知识扩展

在履行出口合同的过程中，认真细致地对国外开来的信用证进行审核关系到出口商能否安全、及时地收取货款。出口商审核信用证的主要依据是国内的有关政策和规定、交易双方成交的合同、国际商会《UCP 600》及实际业务操作中出现的具体情况。审核信用证通常遵循的原则是：信用证条款的规定比合同条款严格时，应当作为信用证中存在的问题提出修改；信用证条款的规定比合同宽松时，往往不去修改。

3.3.1 审核信用证的基本要点

1．有关信用证本身的审核

（1）信用证性质。审核信用证是否不可撤销；信用证是否存在限制性生效及其他保留条款；电开信用证是否为简电信用证；信用证是否申明所运用的国际惯例规则；信用证是否按合同要求加保兑。

（2）核对开证申请人和受益人的名称及地址。对于开证申请人和受益人的名称及地址要加以仔细核对。另外，如果开证行所在国家或地区政局不稳，或者开证行本身资信较差，可要求进口商在申请开证时要求开证行在信用证中列明本证由通知行（或其他出口商接受的银行）保兑。

（3）审核信用证到期日和到期地点。信用证的到期日应该符合合同的规定，一般为货物装运后 21 天。到期地点一定要规定为出口商所在地，以便做到及时交单。

2．专项审核

（1）审核信用证金额、币种、付款期限规定是否与合同一致。

（2）审核货物项目是否与合同一致，如商品名称、货号、规格、数量、包装（含唛头）等是否与合同一致。

（3）审核装运项目是否与合同一致，如装运/卸货港、装运期限、分批转运的规定是否与合同一致。

（4）审核单据项目是否与合同一致。信用证项下要求受益人提交议付的单据通常包括商业发票、海运提单、保险单、装箱单、原产地证、检验证书及其他证明文件。要注意单据由谁出具、能否出具、信用证对单据是否有特殊要求、单据的规定是否与合同条款一致等。

（5）对信用证批注的审核。对信用证上用铅字印好的文句内容和规定，特别是信用证空白处、边缘处加注的打字、缮写或橡皮戳记加注字句应特别注意。这些词句往往是信用证内容的主要补充或修改，如不注意可能造成事故或损失。

3．信用证审核中的常见问题

（1）信用证性质的问题。例如，信用证未生效或有限制性生效的条款；信用证中没有保证付款的责任文句；信用证内漏列适用国际商会《UCP 600》规则条款；信用证未按合同要求加保兑；信用证密押不符。

（2）信用证期限的问题。例如，信用证中没有到期日（有效期）；到期地点在国外；信用证的到期日和装运期有矛盾；装运期、到期日或交单期规定与合同不符；装运期或有效期的规定与交单期矛盾；交单期过短。

（3）信用证当事人的问题。开证申请人公司名称或地址与合同不符；受益人公司名称或地址与合同不符。

（4）金额货币的问题。例如，信用证金额不够（不符合合同规定，未达到溢短装要求）；金额大小写不一致；信用证货币币种与合同规定不符。

（5）汇票的问题。例如，付款期限与合同规定不符；没有将开证行作为汇票的付款人。

（6）分批和转运的问题。例如，分批规定与合同规定不符；转运规定与合同规定不符；转运港口与合同规定或成交条件不符；目的地不符合合同或成交条件；转运期限与合同规定不符。

（7）货物的问题。例如，货物品名、规格不符；货物数量不符；货物包装有误；贸易术语错误；使用术语与条款有矛盾；货物单价数量与总金额不吻合；信用证中援引的合同号码与日期错误；漏列溢短装规定。

（8）单据的问题。例如，发票种类不当；商业发票要求领事签证；提单收货人一栏的填制要求不当；提单抬头和背书要求有矛盾；提单运费条款规定与成交条件矛盾；正本提单全部或部分直寄客户；产地证明出具机构有误（国外机构或无授权机构）；漏列必须提交的单据（如 CIF 成交条件下的保险单）；费用条款规定不合理；运输工具限制过严；要求提交的检验证书种类与实际不符；保险单种类不对；保险险别范围与合同规定不一致；投保金额不符合合同规定。

以上审核的内容要求与合同相符。如果不符，应要求开证申请人修改；如果信用证要求比合同条款宽松，可不要求修改。

4．常见的影响安全收汇的软条款

（1）信用证暂不生效条款。

（2）信用证规定必须由开证申请人或其指定的人签署有关单据的条款。

（3）信用证对银行的付款、承兑行为规定了若干前提条件，如货物清关后才付款等。

（4）信用证前后条款相互矛盾等。

3.3.2 改证要点

1．修改信用证时应注意的问题

对信用证做全面审核后，如发现问题，应分情况及时处理。对于影响安全收汇，或者难以接受或做到的信用证条款，必须要求开证申请人进行修改。修改信用证时应注意以下几点。

（1）信用证中非改不可的必须修改，可改可不改的则酌情处理。如果需要多处修改，应做到一次性向开证申请人提出，避免多次修改信用证的情况。

（2）对于不可撤销信用证中任何条款的修改，都必须取得各方当事人的同意后才能生效。

（3）对于收到的信用证修改书，要认真进行审核。如果发现修改的内容有误或我方不能同意的，我方有权拒绝修改，但应及时将拒绝修改的通知送交通知行，以免延误合同的履行。

（4）对于同一修改书中的内容，要么全部接受，要么全部拒绝，部分接受信用证的修改是无效的。

（5）受益人应发出接受或拒绝修改的通知。通知行有责任将受益人接受或拒绝修改的通知告知开证行。在受益人向通知行表示接受修改之前，原信用证条款对受益人仍然有效。

（6）有关信用证修改必须通过原信用证通知行转递才真实有效。通过开证申请人直接寄送的修改书或修改书复印件不是有效的修改。

（7）对于需经修改方能使用的信用证，应该在收到修改书并经审核认可后方可发运货物。

信用证的修改一般通过向开证申请人发送改证函来实现，改证函中要明确列出需修改的和正确的条款。

2．改证函的撰写要点

当合同约定买卖双方以信用证结算时，卖方在收到买方的信用证后需要审证。如果卖方在审证过程中发现信用证里有己方难以接受的要求，则需要向买方递交改证函。改证函的撰写要点如下。

（1）感谢对方开来信用证。

（2）列明不符点并说明如何修改。

（3）感谢对方合作，并希望信用证修改书早日开到。

3.4 能力实训

实训 1

根据外贸合同（见素材 3-1）审核相关的信用证（见素材 3-2），找出不符点并修改。

素材 3-1 外贸合同

SALES CONTRACT

Contract No.: GW2008X06

Date: 2008.4.22

Seller: GREAT WALL TRADING Co.,LTD. Signed at: NINGBO

Address: No.36, FURONG ROAD, NINGBO, P.R.CHINA. Fax: 0574-25763368

Buyer: F.T.C CORP.

Address: AKEDSANTERINK 5. HELSINKI, FINLAND Fax:

This Sales Contract is made by and between the Seller and the Buyer, whereby the seller agrees to sell and buyer agrees to buy the under-mentioned goods according to the terms and conditions stipulated below:

（1）货号、品名及规格 Name of Commodity and Specifications	（2）数量 Quantity	（3）单位 Unit	（4）单价 Unit Price	（5）金额 Amount
PLASTIC TOY Art No.88	9 600 PCS	PC	CIF HELSINKI USD 3.80/PC	USD 36 480.00
	Total Amount			USD 36 480.00

(6) Packing: CARTON

(7) Delivery: from NINGBO to HELSINKI

(8) Shipping Marks: N/M

(9) Time of Shipment: Within 30 days after receipt of L/C. allowing transshipment and partial shipment.

续

(10) Terms of Payment: By 100% Irrevocable Letter of Credit in favor of the Sellers to be available by sight draft to be opened and to reach China before MAY 1, 2004 and to remain valid for negotiation in China until the 15th days after the foresaid Time of Shipment. L/C must mention this contract number L/C advised by BANK OF CHINA NINGBO BRANCH. All banking Charges outside China (the mainland of China) are for account of the Drawee.

(11) Insurance: To be effected by Sellers for 110% of full invoice value covering F.P.A up to HELSINKI.

(12) Arbitration: All disputes arising from the execution of or in connection with this contract shall be settled amicable by negotiation. In case no settlement can be reached through negotiation the case shall then be submitted to Economic Trade Arbitration Commission. In Shenzhen (or in Beijing) for arbitration in act with its sure of procedures. The arbitral award is final and binding upon both parties for setting the Dispute. The fee, for arbitration shall be borne by the losing party unless otherwise awarded.

The Seller: GREAT WALL TRADING Co.,LTD. The Buyer: F.T.C.CORP.

素材 3-2 信用证

SEQUENCE OF TOTAL	*27: 1/1
FORM OF DOC. CREDIT	*40A: REVOCABLE
DOC. CREDIT NUMBER	*20: LRT9802457
DATE OF ISSUE	31C: 080428
DATE AND PLACE OF EXPIRY	*31D: DATE 080612 PLACE FINLAND
APPLICANT	*50: F. T. C. CORP. AKEDSANTERINK 5 HELSINKI, FINLAND
ISSUING BANK:	52A: NORDEA BANK LTD., FINLAND
ADVISING BANK:	BANK OF CHINA, NINGBO BRANCH
BENEFICIARY	*59: GREAT WALL Co., LTD. No.36, FURONG ROAD, NINGBO, P.R. CHINA
AMOUNT	*32B: USD 3648.00 (SAY U.S. DOLLARS THIRTY SIX THOUSAND FOUR HUNDERD AND EIGHT ONLY)
AVAILABLE WITH/BY	*41D: ANY BANK BY NEGOTIATION
DRAFT AT …	42C: AT DRAFTS AT 20 DAYS' SIGHT FOR FULL INVOICE VALUE
PARTIAL SHIPMENT	43P: NOT ALLOWED
TRANSSHIPMENT	43T: ALLOWED
LOADING IN CHARGE	44A: NINGBO

续

FOR TRANSPORT TO	44B: HELSINKI
LATEST DATE OF SHIP.	44C: MAY 28, 2008
DESCRIPT. OF GOODS	45A: 960 PCS OF PLASTIC TOY ART No.88, USD 3.80 PER PC AS PER S/C No. GW2005M06 CIF HELSINKI
DOCUMENTS REQUIRED	46A：
+COMMERCIAL INVOICE 1 SIGNED ORIGINAL AND 5 COPIES +PACKING LIST IN 2 COPIES +FULL SET OF CLEAN ON BOARD MARINE BILLS OF LADING, MADE OUT TO ORDER OF SHIPPER AND BLANK ENDORSED, MARKED "FREIGHT PREPAID" AND NOTIFY APPLICANT (AS INDICATE ABOVE) +GSP CERTIFICATE OF ORIGIN FORM A, CERTIFYING GOODS OF ORIGIN IN CHINA,ISSUED BY COMPETENT AUTHORITIES +INSURANCE POLICY/CERTIFICATE COVERING ALL RISKS AND WAR RISKS OF PICC. INCLUDING WAREHOUSE TO WAREHOUSE CLAUSE UP TO FINAL DESTINATION AT HELSINKI, FOR AT LEAST 120 PCT OF CIF VALUE +SHIPPING ADVICES MUST BE SENT TO APPLICANT WITH 2 DAYS AFTER SHIPMENT ADVISING NUMBER OF PACKAGES, GROSS & NET WEIGHT, VESSEL NAME, BILL OF LADING No. AND DATE, CONTRACT No. AND VALUE	
PRESENTATION PERIOD	48: 6 DAYS AFTER ISSUANCE DATE OF SHIPPING DOCUMENT
CONFIRMATION	*49: WITHOUT
INSTRUCTIONS:	
THE NEGOTIATION BANK MUST FORWARD THE DRAFTS AND ALL DOCUMENTS BY REGISTERED AIRMAIL DIRECT TO US IN TWO CONSECUTIVE LOTS, UPON RECEIPT OF THE DRAFTS AND DOCUMENTS IN ORDER. WE WILL REMIT THE PROCEEDS AS INSTRUCTED BY THE NEGOTIATING BANK.	

实训 2

根据外贸合同（见素材 3-3）审核相关的信用证（见素材 3-4），找出不符点并修改。

素材 3-3　外贸合同

SALES CONTRACT

Contract No.: TC101-16HB024

Seller: SHANGHAI KNITWEAR AND MANUFACTURED GOODS IMP. AND EXP. CORP.

Date: 2011.3.22

Signed at: SHANGHAI

Address: 1321, ZHONGSHAN ROAD SHANGHAI, P.R.CHINA　　Fax: 021-25763368

Buyer: TKAMLA CORPORATION, LTD.

Address: 6 - 7, KAWARAMACHI, OSAKA, JAPAN　　Fax: ________

This Sales Contract is made by and between the Seller and the Buyer, whereby the seller agrees to sell and buyer agrees to buy the under-mentioned goods according to the terms and conditions stipulated below:

（1）货号、品名及规格 Name of Commodity and Specifications	（2）数量 Quantity	（3）单位 Unit	（4）单价 Unit Price	（5）金额 Amount
MEN'S SHIRT SIZE 44	9 000 PCS	PC	CIF HELSINKI USD 22.00/PC	USD 198 000.00
	Total Amount			USD 198 000.00

(6) Packing: CARTON

(7) Delivery: from SHANGHAI to OSAKA

(8) Shipping Marks: N/M

(9) Time of Shipment: Within 30 days after receipt of L/C, partial shipment allowed transshipment not allowed.

(10) Terms of Payment: By 100% Documentary Letter of Credit in favor of the Sellers to be available by sight draft to be opened and to reach China before MAY 1, 2011 and to remain valid for negotiation in China until the 15th days after the foresaid Time of Shipment. L/C must mention this contract number L/C advised by BANK OF CHINA SHANGHAI BRANCH. ALL banking Charges outside China (the mainland of China) are for account of the Drawee.

(11) Insurance: To be effected by Sellers for 110% of full invoice value covering A.R. and War Risks up to OSAKA.

(12) Arbitration: All disputes arising from the execution of or in connection with this contract shall be settled amicable by negotiation. In case no settlement can be reached through negotiation the case shall then be submitted to Economic Trade Arbitration Commission. In Shenzhen (or in Beijing) for arbitration in act with its sure of procedures. The arbitral award is final and binding upon both parties for setting the Dispute. The fee, for arbitration shall be borne by the losing party unless otherwise awarded.

The Seller SHANGHAI KNITWEAR AND MANUFACTURED GOODS IMP. AND EXP. CORP.

The Buyer TKAMLA CORPORATION, LTD.

素材 3-4 信用证

SEQUENCE OF TOTAL	*27: 1/1
FORM OF CREDIT	*40A: CLEAN
DOC. CREDIT NUMBER	*20: 0071LC123756
DATE OF ISSUE	31C: 110427
DATE AND PLACE OF EXPIRY	*31D: DATE 110527 PLACE JAPAN
APPLICANT	*50: TKAMLA CORPORATION, LTD 6 - 7, KAWARAMACHI, OSAKA, JAPAN
ISSUING BANK:	52A: BANK OF JAPAN SNIKI BUILDING, 1412 BEKA STREET,JAPAN
ADVISING BANK:	BANK OF CHINA, SHANGHAI BRANCH
BENEFICIARY	*59: SHANGHAI KNITWEAR AND MANUFACTURED GOODS CORP. 1321, ZHONGSHAN ROAD SHANGHAI
AMOUNT	*32B: USD AMOUNT 19 800 (SAY U.S. DOLLARS ONE HUNDRED AND NINTY EIGHT THOUSAND ONLY)
AVAILABLE WITH/BY	*41D: ANY BANK BY NEGOTIATION
DRAFT AT…	42C: AT DRAFTS AT 20 DAYS' SIGHT FOR FULL INVOICE VALUE
PARTIAL SHIPMENT	43P: ALLOWED
TRANSSHIPMENT	43T: ALLOWED
LOADING IN CHARGE	44A: SHANGHAI
FOR TRANSPORT TO	44B: OSAKA
LATEST DATE OF SHIP.	44C: MAY 28, 2011
DESCRIPT. OF GOODS	45A: 9 000 PCS OF MEN'S SHIRT SIZE 44, USD22.00 PER PC AS PER S/C No. TC101-16HD024 CIF OSAKA
DOCUMENTS REQUIRED	46A:

+ COMMERCIAL INVOICE 1 SIGNED ORIGINAL AND 5 COPIES

+ PACKING LIST IN 2 COPIES

+ FULL SET OF CLEAN ON BOARD MARINE BILLS OF LADING, MADE OUT TO ORDER OF SHIPPER AND BLANK ENDORSED, MARKED "FREIGHT PREPAID" AND NOTIFY APPLICANT (AS INDICATE ABOVE)

续

+ GSP CERTIFICATE OF ORIGIN FORM A, CERTIFYING GOODS OF ORIGIN IN CHINA, ISSUED BY COMPETENT AUTHORITIES + INSURANCE POLICY/CERTIFICATE COVERING F.P.A. OF PICC. INCLUDING WAREHOUSE TO WAREHOUSE CLAUSE UP TO FINAL DESTINATION AT OSAKA, FOR AT LEAST 120 PCT OF CIF VALUE + SHIPPING ADVICES MUST BE SENT TO APPLICANT WITH 2 DAYS AFTER SHIPMENT ADVISING NUMBER OF PACKAGES, GROSS & NET WEIGHT, VESSEL NAME, BILL OF LADING No. AND DATE, CONTRACT No. AND VALUE PRESENTATION PERIOD 48: 6 DAYS AFTER ISSUANCE DATE OF SHIPPING DOCUMENT CONFIRMATION *49: WITHOUT INSTRUCTIONS: THE NEGOTIATION BANK MUST FORWARD THE DRAFTS AND ALL DOCUMENTS BY REGISTERED AIRMAIL DIRECT TO US IN TWO CONSECUTIVE LOTS, UPON RECEIPT OF THE DRAFTS AND DOCUMENTS IN ORDER. WE WILL REMIT THE PROCEEDS AS INSTRUCTED BY THE NEGOTIATING BANK.

3.5 能力扩展

根据 2.5 节能力扩展中拟订好的外贸合同的内容，审核信用证（见素材 3-5），找出不符点并修改。

素材 3-5 信用证

RECEIVED FORM: BKAUATWW BANK AUSTRIA AG VIENNA 1011 VIENNA AUSTRIA DESTINATION: ABOCCNBJA110 AGRICULTURAL BANK OF CHINA，THE HANGZHOU（ZHEJIANG BRANCH） MESSAGE TYPE: 700 ISSUE OF DOCUMENTARY CREDIT DATE: FEB.11，2011 SEQUENCE OF TOTAL *27: 1/1 FORM OF DOC. CREDIT *40B: IRREVOCABLE

续

DOC. CREDIT NUMBER	*20: AKB1102454
DATE OF ISSUE	31C: 110211
APPLICABLE RULES	*40E: UCP LATEST VERSION
EXPIRY	*31D: DATE 110421 CHINA
APPLICANT BANK	51D: BANK AUSTRIA AG VIENNA
APPLICANT	*50: PICHLER VERTRIEBS GMBH.KFG.KG KINDERMANNGASSE9,A-8020 GRAZ, AUSTRIA
BENEFICIARY	*59: HANGZHOU HAIWU LEATHER PRODUCTS Co.,LTD. No.555 SHANGHAI ROAD, HANGZHOU CHINA
AMOUNT	*32B: CURRENCY USD AMOUNT85 000.00
AVAILABLE WITH/BY	*41D: ANY BANK BY NEGOTIATION
DRAFTS AT…	42C: AT SIGHT
DRAWEE	42D: PICHLER VERTRIEBS GMBH.KFG.KG
PARTIAL SHIPMENTS	43P: ALLOWED
TRANSSHIPMENT	43T: NOT ALLOWED
PORT OF LOADING	44E: SHANGHAI IN CHINA
PORT OF DISCHARGE	44F: GRAZ
LATEST DATE OF SHIP.	44C: 110421
DESCRIPT. OF GOODS	45A:

20 000 PCS COMPING CHAIRS CFR GRAZ CAMPING CHAIRS

AS PER PURCHASE CONTRACT No. PIC01-1330

DOCUMENTS REQUIRED 46A:

+ SIGNED COMMERCIAL INVOICE IN 1 ORIGINALS PLUS 3 COPIES，ISSUED TO PICHLER VERTRIEBS GMBH.KFG.KG KINDERMANNGASSE9，A-8020 GRAZ, AUSTRIA.

+PACKING LIST IN TRIPLICATE.

+FULL SET (3/3) OF ORIGINAL CLEAN ON BOARD BILL OF LADING MADE OUT TO ORDER AND BLANK ENDORSED NOTIFY THE APPLICANT, MARKED FREIGHT COLLECT

+INSURANCE POLICY/CERTIFICATE IN DUPLICATE BLANK ENDORSED FOR150% INVOICE VALUE COVERING ALL RISKS & WAR RISKS SHOWING THE CLAIMING CURRENCY IS THE CURRENCY OF THE CREDIT.

续

+G.S.P. CERTIFICATE OF ORIGIN FORM A IN 1 DUPLICATE STATING THAT THE GOODS ARE OF CHINESE ORIGIN.
ADDITIONAL COND. 47A:
IN CASE DOCUMENTS PRESENTED NOT IN CONFORMITY WITH CREDIT TERMS, DISCREPANCY FEE USD 50.00 WILL BE CHARGED. DOCUMENTS ARE TO BE SENT TO BANK AUSTRIA AG VIENNA.
DETALLS OF CHARGES 71B:
ALL CHARGES ARE TO BE BORNE BY BENEFICIARY'S ACCOUNT.
PRESENTATION PERIOD 48:
DOCUMENTS MUST BE PRESENTED WITHIN 21 DAYS AFTER THE DATE OF SHIPMENT BUT WITHIN L/C VALIDITY.
CONFIRMATION *49: WITHOUT

项目 4

缮制商业发票与装箱单

学习目标

知识目标：了解商业发票、装箱单的作用，掌握商业发票、装箱单的内容与缮制要求。
能力目标：能够根据交易相关资料缮制商业发票和装箱单。

4.1 工作任务

大连思念纺织品进出口公司与波兰普利希纺织品公司签订了一份服装出口的外贸合同，经过单证员蔡平前期认真的审证和改证，信用证已经完全符合公司要求，于是他开始了单据的缮制工作。

在本业务中，单证员蔡平要根据信用证的要求和实际出运信息，完成以下工作任务。

任务 1 分析信用证中关于发票和装箱单的条款。

任务 2 制作商业发票。

任务 3 制作装箱单。

4.2 操作步骤

4.2.1 第一步：分析信用证中关于发票和装箱单的条款

本任务中的信用证如表 4-1 所示。

表 4-1　信用证

MESSAGE TYPE: MT700	ISSUE OF A DOCUMENTARY CREDIT
SEQUENCE OF TOTAL	*27:1/1
FORM OF DOC. CREDIT	*40B : IRREVOCABLE
DOC. CREDIT NUMBER	*20: DCTBT123456
DATE OF ISSUE	31C: 120628
APPLICABLE RELUES	*40E : UCP LATEST VERSION
EXPIRY	*31D: DATE 121013 IN CHINA
APPLICANT BANK	51D: NATIONAL BANK OF POLAND P.O.BOX 586, GDANSK, POLAND
APPLICANT	*50: POLISH PULICI TEXTILE GROUP Co. LTD. UL. KILIŃSKIEGO 57,OSTROWIEC ŚW. POLAND
BENEFICIARY	*59: DALIAN SINIAN TEXTILES IMP.&EXP. Co., LTD. 53 ZHIGONG STREET, DALIAN, P.R. CHINA
AMOUNT	*32B: CURRENCY EUR AMOUNT 65300.00
AVAILABLE WITH/BY	*41D: ANY BANK BY NEGOTIATION
DRAFTS AT…	42C: AT 30 DAYS AFTER SIGHT
DRAWEE	42D: NATIONAL BANK OF POLAND
PARTIAL SHIPMENTS	43P: ALLOWED
TRANSSHIPMENT	43T: ALLOWED
PORT OF LOADING	44E: DALIAN IN CHINA
PORT OF DISCHARGE	44F: GDANSK,POLAND
LATEST DATE OF SHIP.	44C: 120730
DESCRIPT. OF GOODS	45A: CIF GDANSK LADIES'S KNITTED CARDIGAN AS PER PURCHASE CONTRACT No. PG1061 LADIES'S KNITTED CARDIGA PACKED IN 40PCS/CTN ARTICLE No. 11574 2 400PCS AT EUR6.50/PC 11575 3 000PCS AT EUR 5.50/PC 11576 2 400PCS AT EUR 8.50/PC 11577 1 600PCS AT EUR 8.00/PC
DOCUMENTS REQUIRED	46A:

续表

1. COMMERCIAL INVOICE MANUALLY SIGNED IN 2 ORIGINALS PLUS 1 COPY 2. PACKING LIST IN TRIPLICATE. 3. FULL SET OF ORIGINAL CLEAN ON BOARD BILL OF LADING PLUS 3/3 NON NEGOTIABLE COPIES, MADE OUT TO ORDER OF ISSUING BANK AND BLANK ENDORSED NOTIFY THE APPLICANT, MARKED FREIGHT PREPAID. 4. INSURANCE POLICY/CERTIFICATE IN DUPLICATE BLANK ENDORSED FOR 110% INVOICE VALUE COVERING ALL RISKS SHOWING CLAIMS PAYABLE IN POLAND IN THE CURRENCY OF THE CREDIT. 5. G.S.P. CERTIFICATE OF ORIGIN FORM A IN 1 DUPLICATE STATING THAT THE GOODS ARE OF CHINESE ORIGIN. 6. PRESHIPMENT INSPECTION CERTIFICATE ISSUED BY A REPRSENTATIVE OF GOOD TRADE LTD WITH POSITIVE RESULT. 7. SHIPPING ADVICE SHOWING THE NAME OF THE CARRYING VESSEL, DATE OF SHIPMENT, MARKS, QUANTITY, NET WEIGHT AND GROSS WEIGHT OF THE SHIPMENT TO APPLICANT WITHIN 3 DAYS AFTER THE DATE OF BILL OF LADING. ADDITIONAL COND. 47A: +ALL DOCS MUST BE ISSUED IN ENGLISH. +DOCUMENTS ISSUED PRIOR TO L/C ISSUING DATE ARE NOT ACCEPTABLE. +SHIPMENT MUST BE EFFECTED BY FCL. +B/L MUST SHOW SHIPPING MARKS: POLISH/PG1061/GDANSK/C/N: 1-UP. + DOCUMENTS MUST BE PRESENTED WITHIN 14 DAYS AFTER SHIPMENT DATE BUT IN ANY EVENT NOT LATER THAN THE EXPIRY DATE OF THIS CREDIT. +FOR DOCS WHICH DO NOT COMPLY WITH L/C TERMS AND CONDITIONS, WE SHALL DEDUCT FROM PROCEEDS A CHARGE OF EUR 50.00 PAYABLE IN USD EQUIVALENT PLUS ANY INCURRED SWIFT CHARGES IN CONNECTION WITH. DETALLS OF CHARGES 71B: ALL CHARGES OUTSIDE POLAND ARE ON BENEFICIARY'S ACCOUNT. PRESENTATION PERIOD 48: 15 DAYS AFTER B/L DATE, BUT WITHIN L/C VALIDITY. CONFIRMATION *49: WITHOUT

大连思念纺织品进出口公司出口货物实际装运信息如下：① 生产单位为辽宁海城创新制衣厂（海城市西柳镇工业园区118号）；② 装箱号为MANU200454。

4.2.2 第二步：根据信用证和其他信息，制作商业发票

蔡平首先根据信用证中的发票条款“COMMERCIAL INVOICE MANUALLY SIGNED IN 2 ORIGINALS PLUS 1 COPY”和实际出运信息，根据商业发票填写规范制作符合信用证要求的商业发票。

1．商业发票填写规范

(1) 发票名称。发票上应用粗体字明确标明“INVOICE”或“COMMERCIAL INVOICE”字样。如果信用证规定的是“CERTIFIED INVOICE”或“DETAILED INVOICE”，则发票名称也应这样显示。为防止单证不符，发票名称应与信用证的规定一致。另外在发票的名称中不能有“PROVISIONAL INVOICE”或“PROFORMA INVOICE”等字样。

(2) 出单人（出口商）名称和地址（SELLER/EXPORTER）。一般出口企业都使用本企业专用的固定格式的发票，因此都会预先印好本公司的名称、地址，有时还包括电话号码等。在信用证支付方式下，出单人的名称应与信用证中的受益人一致。

(3) 受单人（进口商）名称和地址（BUYER/IMPORTER/TO…）。受单人即发票的抬头人，可以写成 FOR ACCOUNT OF ×××、TO ×××、TO MESSERS ×××等。发票上必须明确发票抬头人名称及地址、联系方式等内容。通常情况下进口商作为抬头人，信用证方式下为开证申请人。如信用证要求做成第三方，应照办。

(4) 发票号码和发票日期（INVOICE No.& INVOICE DATE）。发票号码通常由出口公司自行编制。发票日期通常指发票签发时的日期。一般而言，在全套单据中，发票是签发日最早的单据。它只要不早于合同的签订日期、不迟于提单的签发日期即可。通常在信用证开证日期之后、信用证有效期之前。《UCP 600》规定，如果信用证没有特殊规定，银行可以接受签发日期早于开证日期的发票。

(5) 合同号和合同日期（S/C No.& S/C DATE）。发票中应反映进出口双方贸易合同的号码，应与信用证上列明的一致。若信用证上规定“AS PER S/C No.×××”，即使是错误的，也要按信用证缮制；若信用证无具体规定，则按实际合同号码填制。发票的出具都有买卖合同作为依据，但买卖合同不都以“S/C”为名称，有时出现“Order”、“P.O.”、“Contract”等。因此，当合同的名称不是“S/C”时，应将本项的名称修改后，再填写该合同的号码。

(6) 信用证号码、开证日、开证行（L/C No., L/C DATE & ISSUED BY）。信用证号码、开证日、开证行只有在采用信用证付款时才填写。

(7) 装运地和目的地（FROM…TO…）。按信用证填写，如果货物需要转运，应该把转运港的名称表示出来。例如，FROM SHANGHAI TO DUBAI, U.A.E. w/t at HONGKONG by vessel.

(8) 唛头（MARKS）。信用证中有指定唛头的，必须按规定制作唛头。如无规定，出口商可自行设计唛头，其内容包括进口商名称的缩写、合同号（或发票号）、目的港、件号。如货物运送到目的港后还要转运到内陆城市，可在目的港下面加打“IN TRANSIT TO

×××”或“IN TRANSIT”字样。如信用证中没有规定唛头，则发票上打“N/M”。如信用证规定唛头用英文表示图形，如“IN DIAMOND”或“IN TRIANGLE”，则发票上应将菱形或三角形等具体图形表示出来。

(9) 货物描述 (DESCRIPTION OF GOODS/MERCHANDISE/SHIPMENT OF GOODS)。货物描述部分是发票的中心内容，在信用证方式下，商业发票中对货物的描述必须逐字符合信用证中的描述。在实务中通常有以下几种情况。

1）信用证只规定了货物的总称，这时，发票除照样显示外，还可加上详细的货名，但不得与总称矛盾；信用证未规定货物的总称，但列举货名很详细，则发票应照信用证规定列明；信用证规定的货名并非英文，发票也应照原文显示；信用证规定了多种货名，应根据实际发货情况注明是其中的一种或几种，不得盲目照抄；除了信用证规定的货物外，发票不能再显示其他货物或免费样品等。

2）信用证中的商品名称有错误或漏字等，未来得及修改。这时，发票上的商品名称也应将错就错，以保证发票与信用证规定的完全一致。不过，可在错误的名称后面加注正确的名称。信用证规定的一些证明文句可打在该栏下方。

(10) 数量（QUANTITIES)。发票中货物的数量是指货物实际装运数量而非包装件数，若有不同品种、不同价格，应分别列明。按重量计的货物在制单时应排除不合理的计量方法，按信用证规定的计量单位填写。商品数量单位应与单价中的数量单位保持一致。值得注意的是，信用证中的金额、数量或单价，如果用了“约（About)”、“大约（Circa)”、“近似（Approximately)”等字样，则允许有不超过 10%的增减幅度。但需要注意的是，“约”放在哪一项，就适用哪一项，不能以此类推。例如，信用证中货物的单价与数量条款中有“约”等词语，但金额中没有此类词语，金额就不允许有上述幅度的增减。如果信用证规定的货物以重量、长度、面积或体积等作为数量单位，而不按商品包装单位或个数计数，则在信用证对货物数量没有不得增减要求，以及所支取的金额未超过信用证金额的前提下，允许货物数量有 5%的增减幅度。

(11) 单价（UNIT PRICE)。单价的构成包括计价货币、单位金额、计量单位和价格术语。此栏的填写应完全符合信用证的规定，若无规定则按合同填写。对不同货物标明相应单价时，要注意货币单位、数量单位与信用证一致。

(12) 金额（AMOUNT)。金额是根据实际装货数量和单价正确计算的货物总价。应注意，发票的金额总值一般不应超过信用证规定的最高金额。按照《UCP 600》规则，开证银行可以拒绝接受超过信用证许可金额的商业发票。但如果采取部分金额用信用证支付、部分金额用其他方式支付的支付方式，开具的发票金额就可能超过信用证规定金额。

实际制单时，若来证要求在发票中扣除佣金，则必须扣除。折扣与佣金的处理方法相同。有时证内无扣除佣金规定，但金额正好是扣除佣金后的金额，发票应显示扣除佣金，否则会造成发票金额超证。有时合同规定了佣金，但来证金额内未扣除，而且证内也未提及佣金事宜，则发票不宜显示，待货款收回后另行汇给买方。另外，在 CFR 和 CIF 价格条件下，佣金一般应按扣除运费和保险费之后的 FOB 价格计算。如合同规定有溢短装条款，可在允许浮动限额内增减金额和数量。有时还需列明佣金、折扣、运费、保费等。

（13）总计（TOTAL）。总计栏应分别填入所有货物累计的总数量和总金额（包括相应的计量单位与币种）。若一笔合同中同时交易了同一类型的多种商品，如果这些商品的销售单位不同，总计中单位栏应填“Packages”。

（14）金额大写（SAY TOTAL/ TOTAL AMOUNT IN WORDS）。此栏填写货款金额的英文大写，应与（13）栏小写一致。

（15）签署（SIGNATURE）。除非信用证规定签署，否则按《UCP 600》规定，商业发票不需要签署。若信用证规定“SIGNED INVOICE”，这时需要签署。若信用证规定“MANUALLY SIGNED”或“HAND SIGNED”，则必须是手签。

（16）发票份数。发票份数应与信用证规定相一致。如果信用证没有特殊要求，则至少其中一份必须是正本，通常的做法是在其中一张发票上加注“ORIGINAL”字样。

有时，由于各国法令或习惯不同，有的国家或地区开来的信用证要求在发票上加注一些声明文句或特定号码，对此，应根据情况办理，只要不伤害卖方利益，一般照办。例如，在发票下方空白处加注“WE HEREBY CERTIFY THAT THE CONTENTS OF INVOICE HEREIN ARE TRUE AND CORRECT”。此时，应将发票下端印好的“有错当查”（E.&O.E.）字样删去。

2．本业务中单证员缮制的商业发票

本业务中单证员缮制的商业发票如表 4-2 所示。

表 4-2　商业发票

(16) TWO ORIGINAL ONE COPY

(1) COMMERCIAL INVOICE

(2) SELLER	(4) INVOICE No: 12GEP3298
DALIAN SINIAN TEXTILES IMP.& EXP. Co.,LTD.	INVOICE DATE: JULY.10,2012
53 ZHIGONG STREET, DALIAN,P.R. CHINA	(5) S/C No: PG1061
Tel: +86 0411 54345659	S/C DATE: JUN.9,2012
Fax: +86 0411 54345659	(6) L/C No. : DCTBT123456
(3) BUYER	L/C DATE: JUNE 28,2012
POLISH PULICI TEXTILE GROUP Co., LTD.	ISSUED BY: NATIONAL BANK OF POLAND
UL. KILIŃSKIEGO 57,OSTROWIEC ŚW.	
POLAND	
Tel: +48 41 2651326	

续表

(7) FROM: DALIAN TO: GDANSK BY SEA				
(8) MARKS	(9) DESCRIPTION	(10) QUANTITIES	(11) UNIT PRICE	(12) AMOUNT
POLISH PG1061 GDANSK C/N：1-235	LADIES'S KNITTED CARDIGAN ARTICLE No. 11574 11575 11576 11577 PACKED IN 40PCS/CTN, TOTALLY TWO HUNDRED AND FOURTY-FIVE CARTONS ONLY	CIF GDANSK POLAND 2 400 PCS 3 000 PCS 2 400 PCS 1 600 PCS	 EUR 6.50/PC EUR 5.50/PC EUR 8.50/PC EUR 8.00/PC	 EUR 15 600.00 EUR 16 500.00 EUR 20 400.00 EUR 12 800.00
(13) TOTAL		9 400 PCS		EUR 65 300.00
(14) TOTAL AMOUNT IN WORDS		SAY EURO SIXTY FIVE THOUSAND THREE HUNDRED ONLY.		
(15) DALIAN SINIAN TEXTILES IMP.& EXP. Co.,LTD 蔡平				

4.2.3 第三步：制作符合信用证要求的装箱单

根据信用证、货物实际出运信息和已制作的商业发票，根据装箱单填写规范，可以制作符合信用证要求的装箱单。

1．装箱单填写规范

（1）单据名称。单据名称应与信用证规定的一致。信用证规定的是“PACKING LIST IN TRIPLICATE”，则单据名称也应这样显示（PACKINGLIST）。包装单据的名称还可能是“WEIGHT MEMO”、“ASSORTMENT LIST”、“MEASUREMENT LIST”等。

（2）出单人（出口商）名称和地址（SELLER/EXPORTER）。出单人的地址、联系方式等内容，应与信用证中的受益人一致。

（3）受单人（进口商）名称和地址（BUYER/IMPORTER/TO…）。填写受单人的地址、联系方式等内容。

（4）发票号码和出单日期（INVOICE No.& DATE）。装箱单可以有自己的编号，但因为商业发票是核心单据，所以一般用商业发票的编号作为装箱单号。出单日期可按发票日期填写。

（5）唛头及件数编号（MARKS AND NUMBERS）。唛头应与发票、提单等单据的唛头一致，有的注实际唛头，有时也可以只注“AS PER INVOICE No.×××”。

在单位包装数量或品种不固定的情况下，需注明每个包装件内的包装情况，因此包装件应编号。在每个包装件内，一般要尽可能详细地列出包装细节，如规格、型号、色泽、内装量等。

（6）包装种类和件数，以及货物描述（NUMBER AND KIND OF PACKAGES, DESCRIPTION OF GOODS）。必须与发票和信用证一致。货物如有总称，应先注总称，然后逐项列明每一包装件的货名、规格、品种等内容。

（7）外包装件数（PACKAGE）。分别填写每种货物的包装件数。

（8）重量（WEIGHT）。重量包括毛重（GROSS WEIGHT, G.W.）和净重（NET WEIGHT, N.W.）。要注明每个包装件的毛重或净重，以及此包装件内不同规格、品种、花色的货物各自的总毛重和总净重，最后在总计栏处分别注明总毛重和总净重。

（9）箱外尺寸（MEAS.）。注明每个包装件的体积，最后在总计栏处注总体积。

（10）货物总计（TOTAL）。分别填写所有货物累计的总包装数、总毛重、总净重和总体积（包括相应的计量单位）。若一笔合同中同时交易了同一类型的多种商品，如果这些商品的销售单位不同，总计中单位栏应填“PACKAGES”。

（11）包装件数大写（SAY TOTAL）。用大写文字写明总包装数量，必须与数字表示的包装数量一致。

（12）出口公司盖章和签字（SIGNATURE）。由出具本单据的单位和负责人签字盖章，应与发票的签章一致。若信用证要求中性包装（NEUTRAL PACKING）或规定中性包装单（IN WHITE PAPER/IN PLAIN），则本栏空白不签章。

若信用证对装箱单有其他特殊条款要求，则需要打印在其后。

2．单证员缮制装箱单

本业务中单证员缮制的装箱单如表 4-3 所示。

表 4-3 装箱单

（2）DALIAN SINIAN TEXTILES IMP.& EXP. Co., LTD. 53 ZHIGONG STREET, DALIAN, P.R. CHINA Tel: +86 0411 54345659 Fax: +86 0411 54345659 **（1）PACKING LIST**	
（3）**TO**: POLISH PULICI TEXTILE GROUP Co., LTD.	（4）INVOICE No.: 12GEP3298
UL. KILIŃSKIEGO 57, OSTROWIEC ŚW. POLAND	DATE: JULY.10,2012
Tel: +48 41 2651326	

续表

(5) MARKS & No.	(6) NUMBER AND KIND OF PACKAGES, DESCRIPTION OF GOODS	(7) PACKAGE (CARTON)	(8) WEIGHTS(KGS)		(9) MEAs. M^3
			N.W.	G.W.	
POLISH PG1061 GDANSK C/N：1-235	LADIES'SKNITTED CARDIGAN				
	ARTICLE No.				
1～60	11574	60 CTNS	756.0KGS	918.0KGS	5.670 M^3
61～135	11575	75 CTNS	945.0KGS	1 147.5KGS	7.088 M^3
136～195	11576	60 CTNS	756.0KGS	918.0KGS	5.670 M^3
196～235	11577	40 CTNS	504.0KGS	612.0KGS	3.780 M^3
	EACH PIECE IN A POLYBAG, 40 POLYBAG S TO ONE EXPORT STANDARD CARTON.				
	(10) TOTAL	235 CTNS	2 961.00 KGS	3 595.50KGS	22.208 M^3
(11) SAY TOTAL: TWO HUNDRED AND THIRTY-FIVE CARTONS ONLY.					
(12) DALIAN SINIAN TEXTILES IMP.& EXP. Co.,LTD. 蔡平					

4.3　知识扩展

4.3.1　商业发票

商业发票是由出口商填制并开给进口商的一种商业单据，是进出口交易中最重要的单据之一。商业发票标明了所交易商品的品质、数量、价格、包装等条款。有时，商业发票还记载着卖方所做的证明、声明等内容。同时，商业发票还是进口国海关审查进口商品以确定相应进口关税税率的重要文件。

一般来说，商业发票无正副本之分。信用证要求几份，制单时要在此基础上多制一份供议付行使用。如需正本，加打“ORIGIN”。

不同商业发票的名称表示不同用途，要严格根据信用证的规定制作发票名称。一般发票都印有“INVOICE”字样，前面不加修饰语。若信用证规定用“COMMERCIAL INVOICE”、“SHIPPING INVOICE”、“TRADE INVOICE”或“INVOICE”，均可作为商业发票理解。

信用证若规定“DETAILED INVOICE”（详细发票），则应加打“DETAILED INVOICE”字样，而且发票内容中的货物名称、规格、数量、单价、价格条件、总值等应一一详细列出。信用证若要求“CERTIFIED INVOICE”（证实发票），则发票名称为“CERTIFIED INVOICE”，同时，在发票内注明“We hereby certify that the contents of invoice herein are true & correct”，发票下端通常印就的“E. &. O. E.”（有错当查）就应去掉。信用证若要求“MANUFACTURE'S INVOICE”（厂商发票），则可在发票内加注“We hereby certify that we are actual manufacturer of the goods invoice”，同时要用人民币表示国内市场价，此价应低于出口 FOB 价。此外，商业发票还有“RECEIPT INVOICE”（钱货两讫发票）、“SAMPLE INVOICE”（样品发票）、“CONSIGNMENT INVOICE”（寄售发票）等。

4.3.2 装箱单

装箱单是商业发票的一种补充单据，主要显示货物的包装、毛重、净重及尺码等。其主要栏目可以参考商业发票。需要特别注意的是第（5）项“MARKS AND NUMBERS”中的“C/NOS.”应填写不同货号商品的包装序列号；第（9）项“MEAS.”中的计量单位是立方米，且数值保留三位小数。装箱单一般不显示货物的单价和总金额，因为进口商把商品转售给第三者时，只愿意交付装箱单和货物，不愿意泄露其购买成本。

4.4 能力实训

实训 1

根据信用证（见素材 4-1）及补充资料（见素材 4-2），制作商业发票和装箱单，要求格式清楚、内容完整。

素材 4-1 信用证

FROM: BRITISH BANK OF THE MIDDLE EAST,JEBEL HUSSEIN, AMMAN, JORDAN

TO: THE HONG KONG AND SHANGHAI BANKING CORPORATION LIMITED
SHANGHAI OFFICE: 6/F FU TAIANSION 104 HUQIU ROAD,SHANGHAI, CHINA

BENEFICIARY: GOOD FRIEND ARTS AND CRAFTS IMP.& EXP. Co.
301 SAN TIAO XIANG , CHAOZHOU, GUANGDONG, CHINA

APPLICANT: INTERNATIONAL TRADING AND RE-EXPORT Co. (ZERKA FREE ZONE),P.O.BOX 1147.AMMAN-JORDAN.,FAX:623267,TEL:630353

DC No.: DCFJOM970603

FORM OF DC: IRREVOCABLE

DATE OF ISSUE: 20 MAY,2004

续

EXPIRY DATE AND PLACE: 30 JULY, 2004 CHINA

DC AMOUNT: USD26 160.00, CFR AQABA, JORDAN

MAX CR AMT: NOT EXCEEDING…

AVAILABLE WITH/BY: ANY BANK BY NEGOTIATION

DRAFTS AT: AT SIGHT FOR FULL INVOICE VALUE, MENTIONING THIS DC No.

DRAWEE: ISSUING BANK

LATEST DATE OF SHIPMENT: 15 JULY, 2004

GOODS: 24 000 PAIRS "EVA" SLIPPER MODEL DO27 SIZE 36～40
24 000 PAIRS "EVA" SLIPPER MODEL DO02 SIZE 30～35
ALL IN 4 ASSORTED COLORS, LIGHT BLUE, RED, PINK AND VIOLET
AS PER S/C 97 ACX417 DATED 17.4,2004

DOUMENTS REQUIRED:

SIGNED INVOICES IN SIX COPIES SHOWING THAT THE GOODS EXPORTED ARE OF CHINESE ORIGIN, THE ORIGINAL INVOICE IS TO BE DULY CERTIFIED BY THE CHINA COUNCIL FOR THE PROMOTION OF INTERNATIONAL TRADE.

ADDITIONAL CONDITIONS:

1）"MADE IN CHINA" MUST BE STICKED ON EACH PAIR AND THE RELATIVE INVOICES MUST CERTIFY TO THIS EFFECT.

2）INVOICES MUST CERTIFY THAT THE CARTON SIZE ASSORTMENT IS AS FOLLOWS:
FOR SIZE 36-40:36/6,37/12,38/15,39/15,40/12,EQUAL 60 PAIRS.
FOR SIZE 30-35:30/8,31/8,32/10,33/10,34/12,35/12,EQUAL 60 PAIRS.

3）ALL DOCUMENTS REQUIRED UNDER THIS DOCUMENTARY CREDIT SHOULD BE ISSUED IN ARABIC AND/OR ENGLISH.

4）ALL DOCUMENTS REQUIRED UNDER THIS DOCUMENTARY CREDIT MUST MENTION THIS DC NUMBER AND THE ISSUING BANK NAME.

素材4-2 补充资料

装箱单上需表明总箱数（数字、文字两种表示方法）、总毛重、总净重、总数量及总体积，并且要有唛头，还须表明每箱毛重、净重、体积。设每箱毛重、净重、体积的资料如下：

ART No.	SIZE	QTY.(PAIR)	CTNS.	G.W.(KG)	N.W.(KG)	MEAS.(CM)
DO27	36～40	24 000	400	25/10 000	23/9 200	60×55×40
DO02	30～35	24 000	400	22/8 800	20/8 000	60×50×40

实训 2

根据外贸合同（见素材 4-3）制作商业发票和装箱单，要求格式清楚、内容完整。

素材 4-3 外贸合同

SALES CONTRACT

No.: 03CAN-1109

DATE: NOV.08,2004

SELLER: JIANGSU INTERNATIONAL IMP.&EXP. CORP., LTD.
80 ZHONGSHAN ROAD, NANJING, CHINA
FAX: 86-025-23456789 TEL: 86-025-23456789

BUYER: SHEMSY NEGOCE ID CORP.
75 ROUTE 96570 DARDILLY, FRANCE
FAX: 33-56-12345678 TEL: 33-56-12345678
BUYER'S ORDER No.:FE021G

THIS SALES CONFIRMATION IS HEREBY MUTUALLY CONFIRMED, TERMS AND CONDITIONS ARE AS FOLLOWS:

NAME OF GOODS AND SPECIFICATIONS	QUANTITY	UNIT PRICE	AMOUNT
LUGGAGE SET OF 8PCS	400 SETS	USD20.00/SET	FOB SHANGHAI USD 8 000.00
TOTAL	400 SETS		USD 8 000.00

SAY US DOLLARS EIGHT THOUSAND ONLY

PACKING: ONE SET IN ONE SEAWORTHY CARTON

GROSS WEIGHT: 22.00KGS EACH CARTON

NET WEIGHT: 20.00KGS EACH CARTON

MEASUREMENT (L×W×H): 82.5CM×25.5CM×61CM PER CARTON

SHIPPING MARKS: AS PER BUYER'S DEMANDS

SHIPMENT:_×_TO BE MADE (45 DAYS BY SEA AFTER RECEIVED 30% T/TPAYMENT) FROM CHINA PORT TO (AS BUYER'S DEMANDS) PARTIAL SHIPMENTS AND TRANSSHIPMENT ARE ALLOWED

PAYMENT: _×_ 30% T/T IN DEPOSIT, 70% AGAINST FAXED B/L

INSURANCE:____TO BE EFFECTED BY THE SELLER FOR (___) % OF INVOICE VALUE TO COVER (___) RISK AND WAR RISK UPTP (___) AS PER THE OCEAN MARINE CARGO CLAUSE AND WAR RISK CLAUSE OF THE PEOPLE'S INSURANCE COMPANY OF CHINA_×_TO BE EFFECTED BY THE BUYER

SELLER: JIANGSU INTERNATIONAL IMP. & EXP. CORP.,LTD.

BUYER: SHEMSY NEGOCE ID CORP.

4.5 能力扩展

根据信用证及补充信息（见素材 4-4），缮制商业发票（见素材 4-5）和装箱单（见素材 4-6）。

素材 4-4　信用证及补充信息

RECEIVED FROM: BKAUATWW BANK
AUSTRIA AG VIENNA 1011 VIENNA AUSTRIA
DESTINATION: ABOCCNBJA110
AGRICULTURAL BANK OF CHINA, THE HANGZHOU (ZHEJIANG BRANCH)
MESSAGE TYPE: 700 ISSUE OF DOCUMENTARY CREDIT
DATE: FEB.11, 2011

SEQUENCE OF TOTAL	*27: 1/1
FORM OF DOC. CREDIT	*40B: IRREVOCABLE
DOC. CREDIT NUMBER	*20: AKB1102454
DATE OF ISSUE	31C: 110211
APPLICABLE RELUES	*40E: UCP LATEST VERSION
EXPIRY	*31D: DATE 110421 CHINA
APPLICANT BANK	51D: BANK AUSTRIA AG VIENNA
APPLICANT	*50: PICHLER VERTRIEBS GMBH. NFGKG KINDERMANNGASSE9,A-8020 GRAZ, AUSTRIA
BENEFICIARY	*59: HANGZHOU HAIWU LEATHER PRODUCTS Co.,LTD. No.888 SHANGHAI ROAD, HANGZHOU CHINA
AMOUNT	*32B: CURRENCY USD AMOUNT 114 000.00
AVAILABLE WITH/BY	*41D: ANY BANK BY NEGOTIATION
DRAFTS AT…	42C: AT 45 DAYS AFTER SIGHT
DRAWEE	42D: BKAUATWW BANK
PARTIAL SHIPMENTS	43P: NOT ALLOWED
TRANSSHIPMENT	43T: NOT ALLOWED
PORT OF LOADING	44E: SHANGHAI IN CHINA
PORT OF DISCHARGE	44F: GRAZ

续

LATEST DATE OF SHIP.	44C: FEB.20，2011
DESCRIPT. OF GOODS	45A: 24 000 PCS CAMPING CHAIRS CIF GRAZ CAMPING CHAIRS AS PER PURCHASE CONTRACT No. AB123
DOCUMENTS REQUIRED	46A:
+ SIGNED COMMERCIAL INVOICE IN 1 ORIGINAL PLUS 3 COPIES，ISSUED TO PICHLER VERTRIEBS GMBH. NFGKG KINDERMANNGASSE9，A-8020 GRAZ, AUSTRIA. +PACKING LIST IN TRIPLICATE. +FULL SET (3/3) OF ORIGINAL CLEAN ON BOARD BILL OF LADING MADE OUT TO ORDER AND BLANK ENDORSED NOTIFY THE APPLICANT, MARKED FREIGHT PREPAID. +INSURANCE POLICY/CERTIFICATE IN DUPLICATE BLANK ENDORSED FOR 110% INVOICE VALUE COVERING ALL RISKS & WAR RISKS SHOWING THE CLAIMING CURRENCY IS THE CURRENCY OF THE CREDIT. +G.S.P. CERTIFICATE OF ORIGIN FORM A IN 1 DUPLICATE STATING THAT THE GOODS ARE OF CHINESE ORIGIN.	
ADDITIONAL COND.	47A:
IN CASE DOCUMENTS PRESENTED NOT IN CONFORMITY WITH CREDIT TERMS，DISCREPANCY FEE USD50.00 WILL BE CHARGED.DOCUMENTS ARE TO BE SENT TO BANK AUSTRIA AG VIENNA.	
DETALLS OF CHARGES	71 B:
ALL CHARGES OUTSIDE OF AUSTRIA ARE TO BE BORN BY BENEFICIARY'S ACCOUNT.	
PRESENTATION PERIOD	48:
DOCUMENTS MUST BE PRESENTED WITHIN 21 DAYS AFTER THE DATE OF SHIPPMENT BUT WITHIN L/C VALIDITY.	
CONFIRMATION	*49: WITHOUT

补充信息：

INVOICE No.: HW001

DATE: FEB.06,2011

MEAS: 35×45×50 CM/CTN

G.W.: 45 KGS/CTN

N.W.: 40 KGS/CTN

唛头自行设计。

素材 4-5　商业发票框架

COMMERCIAL INVOICE

TEL: 　　　　INV No.:______

FAX: 　　　　DATE:______

S / C No.:______

TO: 　　　　L / C No.: ______

FROM ______ TO ______

MARKS & No.	DESCRIPTION OF GOODS	QUANTITY	U / PRICE	AMOUNT

TOTAL AMOUNT:

WE HEREBY CERTIFY THAT THE CONTENTS OF INVOICE HEREIN ARE TRUE AND CORRECT.

SIGNED:______

素材 4-6　装箱单框架

PACKING LIST

TEL: 021-65788877 　　　　INV No.: ______

FAX: 021-65788877 　　　　DATE:______

S / C No.: ______

TO: 　　　　L / C No.: ______

GOODS DESCRIPTION & PACKING	QTY（PCS）	CTNS	G.W.（KGS）	N.W.（KGS）	MEAS（M^3）
TOTAL					

SIGNED:______

项目 5

缮制订舱委托书和办理运输手续

学习目标

知识目标：熟悉托运操作流程及主要海运航线、主要港口名称和主要船公司。

能力目标：能根据信用证和或合同条款，正确填制订舱委托书，并办理订舱。

5.1 工作任务

2012 年 7 月 13 日，大连思念纺织品进出口公司单证员蔡平得知生产企业已经备妥货，他首先需要上网查找船期、比较运价，选择一家资信好的国际货运代理公司（大连万翔国际货运代理有限公司），准备出运货物。然后根据辽宁海城创新制衣厂提供的货物出货信息、商业发票、装箱单和 NATIONAL BANK OF POLAND 银行开给大连思念纺织品进出口公司的 DCTBT123456 号信用证 46A 条款要求，制作订舱委托书和办理相关运输手续。

在本业务中，出口方单证员蔡平需要完成以下工作任务。

任务 1　选择国际货运代理公司。

任务 2　制作出口货物明细单。

任务 3　缮制订舱委托书。

任务 4　办理订舱等运输手续。

5.2　操作步骤

5.2.1　第一步：选择国际货运代理公司

大连思念纺织品进出口公司单证员蔡平登录中国国际海运网（http://port.shippingchina.com/），通过船期、装运港、目的港信息的查询，查到若干家国际货运代理公司的信息。他通过点击各大国际货运代理公司的网站，进行电话联系，获得了大连港至格丹斯克港的运价表。最终通过比较，确定大连万翔国际货运代理有限公司代理中国远洋运输（集团）总公司 2012 年 7 月 30 日的船期进行运输。

于是蔡平与大连万翔国际货运代理有限公司小陈联系，交流订舱和确认运输事宜。最后确认 2012 年 7 月 30 日的船期，船名为 JINGBI，航次为 HV300W，报价为 USD1500/20'。

5.2.2　第二步：制作出口货物明细单

当日，大连思念纺织品进出口公司业务部王经理要求蔡平制作出口货物明细单，为后续工作做准备。本业务中制作的出口货物明细单如表 5-1 所示。

表 5-1　出口货物明细单

<table>
<tr><td colspan="3" rowspan="3">出口货物明细单
(1) 2012 年 7 月 13 日</td><td>(6) 信用证号</td><td colspan="2">DCTBT123456</td></tr>
<tr><td>银行编号</td><td>外运公司编号</td><td>XXXXXXX</td></tr>
<tr><td>(7) 合同号</td><td>PG1061</td><td></td></tr>
<tr><td>开证银行</td><td>NATIONAL BANK OF POLAND</td><td>开证日期</td><td>JUN.28, 2012</td><td>收到日期</td><td>JUN.28, 2012</td></tr>
<tr><td colspan="2" rowspan="2">(2) 经营单位/ (3) 托运人
大连思念纺织品进出口公司
DALIAN SINIAN TEXTILESIMP.& EXP. Co., LTD.
53 ZHIGONG STREET, DALIAN, P.R. CHINA</td><td>(8) 金额</td><td>EUR65 300.00</td><td>(9) 收汇方式</td><td>L/C</td></tr>
<tr><td>(10) 货物性质</td><td>(×)贸易
( )补偿
( )退运</td><td>(11) 贸易国别（地区）</td><td>POLAND</td></tr>
<tr><td>(4) 收货人</td><td>POLISH PULICI TEXTILE GROUP Co.,LTD.UL. KILIŃ SKIEGO57,OSTROWIEC ŚW. POLAND</td><td>汇票付款人</td><td colspan="3">NATIONAL BANK OF POLAND</td></tr>
<tr><td>提单或承运收据</td><td>抬头人</td><td>TO ORDER OF NATIONAL BANK OF POLAND</td><td>汇票期限</td><td colspan="2">AT 30 DAY'S AFTER SIGHT</td></tr>
</table>

续表

<table>
<tr><td rowspan="3"></td><td rowspan="2">（4）通知人</td><td rowspan="2">POLISH PULICI TEXTILE GROUP Co.,LTD.
UL. KILIŃSKIEGO 57,
OSTROWIEC ŚW.
POLAND</td><td>（11）出口口岸</td><td colspan="2">DALIAN</td><td>（11）目的港</td><td>GDANSK</td></tr>
<tr><td>可否转运</td><td colspan="2">YES</td><td>可否分批</td><td>YES</td></tr>
<tr><td>（5）运费</td><td>FREIGHT PREPAID</td><td>（12）装运期限</td><td colspan="2">JUL.30,2012</td><td>有效期限</td><td>AUG.15,2012</td></tr>
<tr><td rowspan="2">（13）标记唛码</td><td rowspan="2">货名规格及货号</td><td rowspan="2">件数及包装式样</td><td rowspan="2">数量或尺码</td><td rowspan="2">毛重（KGS）</td><td rowspan="2">净重（KGS）</td><td colspan="2">价格(成交条件)</td></tr>
<tr><td>单　价</td><td>总　价</td></tr>
<tr><td rowspan="2">POLISH
PG1061
GDANSK
C/N:1-235</td><td rowspan="2">LADIES'S
KNITTED
CARDIGAN
ART. No. 11574
11575
11576
11577</td><td rowspan="2">60 CTNS
75 CTNS
60 CTNS
40 CTNS</td><td rowspan="2">2 400 PCS
3 000 PCS
2 400 PCS
1 600 PCS</td><td rowspan="2">918.0 KGS
1 147.5 KGS
918.0 KGS
612.0 KGS</td><td rowspan="2">756.0 KGS
945.0 KGS
756.0 KGS
504.0 KGS</td><td colspan="2">CIF GDANSK</td></tr>
<tr><td>EUR 6.50/PC
EUR 5.50/PC
EUR 8.50/PC
EUR 8.00/PC</td><td>EUR 15 600.00
EUR 16 500.00
EUR 20 400.00
EUR 12 800.00</td></tr>
<tr><td colspan="2" rowspan="4">本公司注意事项</td><td colspan="2" rowspan="4"></td><td>总体积</td><td colspan="3">22.208CBM</td></tr>
<tr><td rowspan="3">保险单</td><td>险别</td><td colspan="2"></td></tr>
<tr><td>保额</td><td colspan="2">按发票金额加　　%</td></tr>
<tr><td>赔款地</td><td colspan="2"></td></tr>
<tr><td colspan="2" rowspan="5">外运外轮注意事项</td><td colspan="2" rowspan="5"></td><td>船　　名</td><td colspan="3"></td></tr>
<tr><td>海关编号</td><td colspan="3"></td></tr>
<tr><td>放行日期</td><td colspan="3"></td></tr>
<tr><td>制 单 员</td><td colspan="3"></td></tr>
<tr><td>存储地点</td><td colspan="3"></td></tr>
</table>

出口货物明细单中以下几点是必填项。

（1）日期。填写填单日期。

（2）经营单位。按实际情况填写。

（3）托运人。与提单中的发货人保持一致，如果有明确规定不接受第三方提单，将另行通知。

（4）收货人、通知人。根据提单上的收货人和通知人填写。

（5）运费。根据实际情况在“预付”或“到付”处打钩。

（6）信用证号。

（7）合同号。据实填写。

（8）金额。按报关金额填写。

（9）收汇方式。按实际收汇方式填写（T/T、L/C、D/P）。

（10）货物性质。按实际情况在对应小括号内打钩。

（11）贸易国别（地区）、出口口岸、目的港。按报关单和提单填写，与报关单和提单保持一致。

（12）装运期限。按实际填写，不早于提单出运日期。

（13）标记唛码、货名规格及货号、件数及包装式样、数量或尺码、毛重、净重、价格（成立条件）。按提单、报关发票、装箱单、报关单上的内容填写。

其他几点按实际填写，也可以不填，根据具体情况由代理公司自行决定。

5.2.3 第三步：缮制订舱委托书

单证员蔡平根据信用证条款，特别是信用证中的装运条款（见表 5-2），如装运期、结汇期、装运港、目的港等，缮制了订舱委托书。本业务中缮制的订舱委托书如表 5-3 所示。

表 5-2 信用证中的装运条款

DOCUMENTS REQUIRED 46A:

+FULL SET (3/3) OF ORIGINAL CLEAN ON BOARD BILL OF LADING PLUSE 3/3 NON NEGOTIABLE COPIES, MADE OUT TO ORDER OF ISSUING BANK AND BLANK ENDORSED NOTIFY THE APPLICANT, MARKED FREIGHT PREPAID.

ADDITIONAL COND. 47A:

+ALL DOCS MUST BE ISSUED IN ENGLISH.

+DOCUMENTS ISSUED PRIOR TO L/C ISSUING DATE ARE NOT ACCEPTABLE.

+SHIPMENT MUST BE EFFECTED BY FCL.

+B/L MUST SHOW SHIPPING MARKS:

POLISH
PG1061
GDANSK
C/N：1-UP

表 5-3　订舱委托书

<table>
<tr><td colspan="5">订舱委托书
2012 年 7 月 13 日</td></tr>
<tr><td rowspan="4">托运人</td><td rowspan="4">DALIAN SINIAN TEXTILES IMP. &EXP. Co.
53 ZHIGONG STREET,
DALIAN, P.R. CHINA</td><td colspan="2">合同号</td><td>PG1061</td></tr>
<tr><td colspan="2">发票号</td><td>12GEP3298</td></tr>
<tr><td colspan="2">信用证号</td><td>DCTBT123456</td></tr>
<tr><td colspan="2">运输方式</td><td>BY SEA</td></tr>
<tr><td rowspan="3">收货人</td><td rowspan="3">TO ORDER OF ISSUING BANK</td><td colspan="2">起运港</td><td>DALIAN IN CHINA</td></tr>
<tr><td colspan="2">目的港</td><td>GDANSK,POLAND</td></tr>
<tr><td colspan="2">装运期</td><td>JUL.30,2012</td></tr>
<tr><td rowspan="4">通知人</td><td rowspan="4">POLISH PULICI TEXTILE GROUP Co., LTD.
UL. KILIŃSKIEGO 57, 27-400
OSTROWIEC ŚW. POLAND</td><td colspan="2">可否转运</td><td>ALLOWED</td></tr>
<tr><td colspan="2">可否分批</td><td>ALLOWED</td></tr>
<tr><td colspan="2">运费支付方式</td><td>FREIGHT PREPAID</td></tr>
<tr><td colspan="2">正本提单份数</td><td>3</td></tr>
<tr><td>标记唛码</td><td>货号规格</td><td>包装件数</td><td>总毛重</td><td>总体积</td></tr>
<tr><td>LISHPG1061GD
ANSKC/N：1-235</td><td>LADIES'S KNITTED CARDIGAN</td><td>235CTNS</td><td>3595.50KGS</td><td>22.208CBM</td></tr>
<tr><td>注意事项</td><td colspan="4">1．请订 2012 年 7 月的船期，1 个 20 英尺柜 FCL/FCL，门到门
2．仓库地址：海城市西柳镇工业园区 118 号。联系人：朱欣怡
3．提单上要显示以下内容：
SHIPPING MARKS: POLISH
PG1061
GDANSK
C/N：1-235</td></tr>
<tr><td colspan="2">受托人：</td><td colspan="3">委托人：DALIAN SINIAN TEXTILES IMP. &EXP. Co.</td></tr>
<tr><td colspan="2">电话：</td><td colspan="3">电话：86 0411 54345659</td></tr>
<tr><td colspan="2">传真：</td><td colspan="3">传真：86 0411 54345659</td></tr>
<tr><td colspan="2">联系人:</td><td colspan="3">联系人：蔡平</td></tr>
</table>

订舱委托书一般无统一格式，填写时大体上应注意以下内容。

（1）托运人。订舱委托书中的托运人是货主。如信用证无特殊规定，通常填出口人，即信用证的受益人。

（2）收货人。填写运输单据的抬头人（提单收货人），要严格按信用证中提单条款的具体规定填写。

1）记名抬头。直接填写收货人名称。

2）指示抬头。完全按照来证提单条款填写，如“To Order of Shipper/To Order of (Issuing Bank)”等。

(3) 通知人。填写船公司在货物到达目的港时发送到货通知的收件人。通知人接到承运人的到货通知后，通知收货人去办理换单提货。

1）如信用证有规定，严格按照信用证填，且注明详细地址。

2）如信用证无规定，留空不填，填买方亦可。

一般在订舱委托书上会注明托运人、收货人和通知人这三栏为海运提单项目要求，即将来船公司签发的海运提单上相应栏目的填写也会参照订舱委托书的写法。因此，这三栏的填写应该按照信用证提单条款的相应规定来填写（具体可参照海运提单的填制方法）。

(4) 运输方式。根据具体情况填写海洋运输、航空运输、铁路运输等运输方式。

(5) 起运港和目的港。根据合同或信用证规定填写。

(6) 可否转运和可否分批。填写可否转船运输和分批装运。若合同或信用证规定了转运港，则需要标出转运港，否则只要标注是否允许转运即可；若信用证没有规定转运港，则根据《UCP 600》规定，允许转运。关于分批装运，只要标注是否允许分批装运即可，若信用证没有规定是否允许分批装运，则根据《UCP 600》规定，允许分批装运。

(7) 运费支付方式。在CFR、CIF、CPT、CIP贸易术语下，填写“运费预付”(FREIGHT PREPAID)；在FOB 和FCA贸易术语下，填写“运费到付”(FREIGHT COLLECT/FREIGHT PAYABLE AT DESTINATION)。

(8) 正本提单份数。若信用证没有规定，一般要求2～3份正本。

(9) 标记唛码。填写货物的装运标志，即通常所说的“唛头”。每个字母、数字、图形、排列位置等均应与信用证规定完全一致，如信用证规定有数个唛头， 应按要求一一列明；如来证中的运输标记上的件号为No.1-Up（1/Up），则按实际托运的总件数填写件号。若信用证与成交合同中对运输标记均无具体规定，则出口人可自己编制，要求至少包括主标记（合同号码/信用证号码/发票号码/客户订单号码/收货人简称均可）、目的港标记及件号。若无唛头，可填写“NO MARK”或“N/M”。

(10) 货号规格。可以填写商品的统称。

(11) 包装件数。指所有货号即该批货物的总包装件数。

(12) 总毛重。指托运货物的总毛重。

(13) 总体积。填写货物的总尺码，以立方米为单位，保留至小数点后第三位。

(14) 装运期。填写信用证规定的最迟装运期，同时要结合实际备货情况在“注意事项”中写明预订船期。

（15）预配箱量。根据货物的性质、总毛重、总体积填写合理的箱数。本业务中已在表 5-3“注意事项”中写明预配箱量。

（16）集装箱交接方式。集装箱货运的交接方式主要有以下几种。

1）整箱交，整箱接（FCL/FCL）。货主在工厂或仓库把装满货后的整箱交给承运人，收货人在目的地同样整箱接货。换言之，承运人以整箱为单位负责交接。货物的装箱和拆箱均由货方负责。

2）拼箱交，拆箱接（LCL/LCL）。货主将不足整箱的小票托运货物在集装箱货运站或内陆转运站交给承运人，由承运人负责拼箱和装箱（Stuffing，Vanning）运到目的地货站或内陆转运站，由承运人负责拆箱（Unstuffing，Devanning），拆箱后，收货人凭单接货。货物的装箱和拆箱均由承运人负责。

3）整箱交，拆箱接（FCL/LCL）。货主在工厂或仓库把装满货后的整箱交给承运人，在目的地的集装箱货运站或内陆转运站由承运人负责拆箱后，各收货人凭单接货。

4）拼箱交，整箱接（LCL / FCL）。货主将不足整箱的小票托运货物在集装箱货运站或内陆转运站交给承运人，由承运人分类调整，把同一收货人的货集中拼装成整箱，运到目的地后，承运人以整箱交，收货人以整箱接。

上述各种交接方式中，以整箱交、整箱接效果最好，也最能发挥集装箱的优越性。

本业务中已在表 5-3“注意事项”中写明集装箱交接方式。

（17）集装箱货物交接地点。根据贸易条件规定的交接地点不同，一般分为以下几种。

1）门到门（Door to Door）。从发货人工厂或仓库至收货人工厂或仓库。

2）门到场（Door to CY）。从发货人工厂或仓库至目的地或卸箱港的集装箱堆场。

3）门到站（Door to CFS）。从发货人工厂或仓库至目的地或卸箱港的集装箱货运站。

4）场到门（CY to Door）。从起运地或装箱港的集装箱堆场至收货人工厂或仓库。

5）场到场（CY to CY）。从起运地或装箱港的堆场至目的地或卸箱港的集装箱堆场。

6）场到站（CY to CFS）。从起运地或装箱港的集装箱堆场至目的地或卸箱港的集装箱货运站。

7）站到门（CFS to Door）。从起运地或装箱港的集装箱货运站至收货人工厂或仓库。

8）站到场（CFS to CY）。从起运地或装箱港的集装箱货运站至目的地或卸箱港的集装箱堆场。

9）站到站（CFS to CFS）。从起运地或装箱港的集装箱货运站至目的地或卸箱港的集装箱货运站。

本业务中已在表 5-3“注意事项”中写明集装箱货物交接地点。

（18）特殊条款。指出口人对订舱、进库、运输、装船和提单条款等的特殊规定。可以写在“注意事项”中。

（19）委托人。委托人进行盖章签名，写上联系人的名称、电话和传真号码。

5.2.4　第四步：缮制货物托运单

单证员蔡平向货运代理公司传真出口货物订舱委托书和出口货物明细单，随附商业发票、装箱单及其他必要单证，被告知 2012 年 7 月 20 日拉柜。货运代理公司在接受出口方的订舱委托后，需缮制货物托运单，这是货运代理公司机构向船公司配载的依据。本业务中缮制的货物托运单如表 5-4 所示。

表 5-4　货物托运单（货主留底）

<table>
<tr><td colspan="4">Shipper（托运人）
DALIAN SINIAN TEXTILES IMP. &EXP. Co.
53 ZHIGONG STREET, DALIAN,P.R. CHINA</td><td colspan="2" rowspan="5">D/R No.（编号）：12GEP3298
集装箱货物托运单
货主留底</td></tr>
<tr><td colspan="4">Consignee（收货人）
TO ORDER OF ISSUING BANK</td></tr>
<tr><td colspan="4">Notify Party（通知人）
POLISH PULICI TEXTILE GROUP Co.,LTD.
UL. KILIŃSKIEGO 57, 27-400 OSTROWIEC ŚW. POLAND</td></tr>
<tr><td colspan="2">Pre-carriaged by（前程运输）</td><td colspan="2">Place of Receipt（收货地点）</td></tr>
<tr><td>Ocean Vessel （船名）
JINGBI</td><td>Voy No.（航次）
V.036</td><td colspan="2">Port of Loading（装货港）
DALIAN,CHINA</td></tr>
<tr><td colspan="2">Port of Discharge（卸货港）
GDANSK,POLAND</td><td colspan="2">Place of Delivery（交货地点）</td><td colspan="2">Final Destination（目的地）
GDANSK,POLAND</td></tr>
<tr><td>Container No.（集装箱号）
MANU200454（20'）</td><td>Seal No.（封志号）
Marks & Nos.（标记与号码）
POLISH
PG1061
GDANSK
C/N：1-235</td><td>No.of Containers or P`kgs.（箱数或件数）
235 CTNS</td><td>Kind of Packages; Description of Goods（包装种类与货名）
235 CARTONS
(9 400.00 PCS)OF
LADIES'S KNITTED CARDIGAN</td><td>Gross Weight（毛重/kg）
3 595.5 KGS</td><td>Measurement（尺码/立方米）
22.208 M^3</td></tr>
<tr><td colspan="2">Total Number of Containers or Packages（in words）
集装箱数或件数合计（大写）</td><td colspan="4">SAY TWO HUNDRED AND THIRTY FIVE CARTONS ONLY</td></tr>
</table>

续表

Freight & Charges （运费与附加费） “FREIGHT PREPAID”	Revenue Tons （运费吨）	Rate （运费率）	Per （每）	Prepaid （运费预付）	Collect （到付）
Ex Rate（兑换率）	Prepaid at（预付地点） DALIAN, CHINA	Payable at （到付地点）		Place of Issue（签发地点） DALIAN, CHINA	
	Total Prepaid（预付总额）	No. of Original B(S)/L （正本提单份数） THREE			
Service Type On Receiving -CY　-CFS　-DOOR	Service Type On Delivery □ -CY □-CFS □-DOOR	Payable at No.of Original B（S）/L （冷藏温度）		F	C
Type of Goods （货物种类）	■ Ordinary（普通）　□ Reefer（冷藏） □ Dangerous（危险品）　□ Auto.（裸装车辆） □ Liquid（液体）　□ Live animal（活动物）　□ Bulk（散货）	危险品		Class: Property: IMDG Code Page: UN No.	
Partial Shipment（可否转船） ALLOWED	Transshipment（可否分批） ALLOWED	其他：			
Date of Shipment（装运期） JUL 30, 2012	Date of Expiry（有效期） OCT 30, 2012				
金　额　EUR 65 300.00				签字：蔡平	
制单日期　JUN 25, 2012					

集装箱货物托运单部分主要项目填制方法如下。

（1）托运人（Shipper）。此处一般填写出口合同的卖方，信用证支付方式下应与信用证受益人的名称、地址一致。若由外贸运输公司代理货主租船订舱，则填该外贸运输公司名称。

（2）收货人（Consignee）。根据信用证要求填写收货人。

（3）通知人（Notify Party）。填写接受船方发出货到通知的人的名称与地址。

（4）编号（D/R No.）。一般填写商业发票号。

（5）前程运输（Pre-carriaged by）。若是港至港提单，此栏不填。若是多式联运，则填运输工具统称，如“Train，Truck”。

（6）收货地点（Place of Receipt）。此栏仅供多式联运使用，填写多式联运经营人前程运输的收货地点。

（7）船名和航次（Ocean Vessel，Voy No.）。船名可留给船方安排船只舱位后填写。

（8）装货港和卸货港（Port of Loading，Port of Discharge）。按合同/信用证规定填写装货港和目的港具体名称，遇世界重名港口时，应在港口名称后面加注国名。

（9）交货地点（Place of Delivery）。此栏仅供多式联运使用，填写多式联运经营人在目的国或地区的内陆交货地。

（10）目的地（Final Destination）。填写货物实际到达的目的地，供货主参考。

（11）集装箱号（Container No.）。填写具体的集装箱号。

（12）封志号、标记与号码（Seal No.，Marks & Nos. ）。填写具体的封志号、标记与号码。

（13）箱数或件数（No. of Containers or P`kgs.）。按最大包装实际件数填写，应与唛头中的件数一致。

（14）包装种类与货名（Kind of Packages, Description of Goods）。填写货物大类名称或统称，与发票（信用证）中的货名一致。

（15）毛重（Gross Weight）。填写整批货物的毛重，以千克（KG）为单位。

（16）尺码（Measurement）。填写整批货物的体积实数，以立方米（M^3）为单位，是计算运费的主要依据之一，计算应务求准确。

（17）集装箱数或件数合计（大写）[Total Number of Containers or Packages（in words）]。据实填写。

（18）运费与附加费（Freight & Charges）、预付地点（Prepaid at）、签发地点（Place of Issue）、正本提单份数 [No. of Original B(S)/L]。与海运提单填写一致，后面将具体阐述。

（19）货物种类（Type of Goods）。根据货物实际情况填写。

（20）货物交接方式（Service Type On Receiving，Service Type On delivery）。根据货物装运实际情况选择。

（21）可否转船（Partial Shipment）、可否分批（Transshipment）。应严格按合同或信用证填写“允许”（ALLOWED）或“不允许”（NOT ALLOWED）。

（22）装运期（Date of Shipment）、有效期（Date of Expiry）。根据信用证规定的最迟装运期和有效期填写。

（23）制单日期。与发票日期一致。

（24）其他。由船方填写。

（25）签字。由出口企业盖章，经办人签字。

5.2.5 第五步：船公司装货，并缮制海运提单

货运代理公司将集装箱货物托运单中的“装货单”和“大副联”交给船公司，凭此装货。船公司装妥货物，在“大副联”上签字后返还。货运代理公司凭经船方签署的“大副联”向船公司换取正本已装船海运提单。本业务中的海运提单如表 5-5 所示。

表 5-5 海运提单

<table>
<tr><td colspan="2">1．Shipper （托运人）
DALIAN SINIAN TEXTILES IMP. &EXP. Co.
53 ZHIGONG STREET, DALIAN,P.R. CHINA</td><td rowspan="6">10．B/L No. CPNE12789
COSCO
中国远洋运输（集团）总公司
CHINA OCEAN SHIPPING (GROUP) Co.

ORIGINAL
Combined Transport Bill of Lading</td></tr>
<tr><td colspan="2">2．Consignee（收货人）
TO ORDER OF ISSUING BANK</td></tr>
<tr><td colspan="2">3．Notify Party（通知人）
POLISH PULICI TEXTILE GROUP Co.,LTD
UL. KILIŃSKIEGO 57, 27-400 OSTROWIECŚW. POLAND</td></tr>
<tr><td>4．Place of Receipt
（收货地点）</td><td>5．Ocean Vessel
（船名）
JINGBI</td></tr>
<tr><td>6．Voy. No.（航次）
V.036</td><td>7．Port of Loading
（装运港）
DALIAN,CHINA</td></tr>
<tr><td>8．Port of Discharge
（卸货港）
GDANSK,POLAND</td><td>9．Place of Delivery
（交货地点）</td></tr>
</table>

11．Marks and Nos., Container /Seal No.（标记和号码集装箱号码与封号）	12．Nos. & Kinds of Pkgs（包装种类和数量）	13．Description of Goods（货物名称）	14．G.W.(KG)（毛重）	15．MEAS(M^3)（尺码）
POLISH PG1061 GDANSK C/N：1-235	235CTNS	LADIES' KNITTED CARDIGAN	3 595.50KGS	22.208M^3

续表

<table>
<tr><td colspan="6">16. Total Number of Containers or Packages(in Words) （总件数）
SAY TWO HUNDRED AND THIRTY FIVE CARTONS ONLY</td></tr>
<tr><td>17. Freight and
Charges（运费）
FREIGHT PREPAID</td><td>Revenue Tons
（运费吨）</td><td>Rate
（运费率）</td><td>PER
（计费单位）</td><td>Prepaid
（运费预付）</td><td>Collect
（运费到付）</td></tr>
<tr><td>Prepaid at
（预付地点）</td><td>Payable at
（到付地点）</td><td colspan="4">18. Place and Date of Issue
（出单地点及签发日期）
DALIAN,JUL 30, 2012</td></tr>
<tr><td>Total Prepaid
（预付总金额）</td><td>19. Number of
Original B(S)L
（正本提单的份数）
THREE(3)</td><td colspan="4" rowspan="3">22. Signed for The Carrier
（承运人签章）

中国远洋运输（集团）总公司
CHINA OCEAN SHIPPING (GROUP) Co.
×××</td></tr>
<tr><td colspan="2">Loading on Board the Vessel
（船名）</td></tr>
<tr><td colspan="2">20. Date
（装船日期）
JUL 30,2012
21. On Board（装运日期）
JUL.30，2012
ON BOARD
23. Endorsement（背书）
POLISH PULICI TEXTILE GROUP Co.,LTD..
蔡平
JUL 30,2012</td></tr>
</table>

海运提单缮制方法如下。

（1）托运人(Shipper)。托运人即委托运输的人，在进出口贸易中通常就是出口人。一般为信用证的受益人、合同的卖方，也可以是第三方。本栏填写出口人的名称和地址。

（2）收货人（Consignee）。收货人即提单的抬头人，应按信用证规定填写。

1）记名抬头。直接填写收货人名称和地址，如“To ABC Co.”。

2）不记名抬头。填“To Bearer”（谁拿到这种提单都可以提货，很危险，我国不用）。

3）指示抬头。按信用证规定填写，如“To Order （空白抬头)”、“To Order of ×××”。

填写“To Order ”、“To Order of Shipper”两种情况都是托运人指示提单。如果填写“To order of ××× （凭谁指定）”，则称为记名指示提单，记名指示人可以是银行，也可以是贸易商。

4）提单的抬头决定了海运提单的性质和货权的归属。在进出口贸易中多使用指示式抬头，以便单据可以通过背书转让。

（3）通知人（Notify Party）。信用证方式下，按信用证规定填写，须注明被通知人的详细名称和地址。

若来证规定“Full set of B/L…notify applicant”，应在本栏中将开证申请人的全称及地址填上。

若信用证无规定，正本提单可留空不填，但随船的副本提单须填列开证申请人的详细名称和地址（正本提单是交给银行议付的，所以可以不填，但是船公司应该知道货到后通知谁来取货）。

注意：不可以直接在 Notify Party 栏目中填写 APPLICANT，要写具体名称和联系方式，否则货物到达目的港后船公司无法通知。

（4）收货地点（Place of Receipt）。填写实际接收货物的地点。在一般海运提单中没有此栏，但在多式联运提单中有此栏。

（5）船名（Ocean Vessel）。填写实际载货船舶的名称。

（6）航次（Voyage No.）。填写本次航行的航次。

（7）装运港（Port of Loading）。装运港即起运港，应按信用证规定填写。

若信用证只笼统规定“CHINA MAIN PORTS”,则应填写实际装运港口的名称，如“DALIAN”。

若来证同时列明几个装货港，如“QINGDAO/QINHUANGDAO/DALIAN”，提单只能填写其中一个实际装运的港口名称。

根据《UCP 600》的规定，如果提单没有表明信用证规定的装货港为装运港，则需以已装船批注表明信用证规定的装运港、发运日期及实际船名。

（8）卸货港（Port of Discharge）。卸货港即目的港，应按信用证规定填写。

除 FOB 价格条件外，卸货港不能填写笼统的名称，如“EUROPEAN MAIN PORT”，必须列出具体的港口名称。遇到国际上重名港口的，还应加注国别名称。

在转船情况下可以在卸货港名称之后加注转船港名称，如“Rotterdam W/T at HongKong”，或者在货名栏下方的空白处加注转船的说明。若有印就的转船港栏目，则直接填入转船港名称即可。

（9）交货地点（Place of Delivery）。写最终目的地名称。如果货物的目的地就是目的港，此栏可以留白，也可以填写目的港名称。

（10）提单号码（B/L No.）。提单上必须注明承运人及其代理人规定的提单编号，以便核查，否则提单无效。

（11）标记和号码、集装箱号码与封号（Marks and Nos.,Container /Seal No.）。

1）提单上的标记、号码应与信用证和其他单据中的唛头一致。若没有唛头，用“N/M”，不能空白。

2）据实填写集装箱号码。封号是海关查验货物后作为封箱的铅制关封号，应如实注明。

（12）包装种类和数量（NOS.&Kinds of PKGS）。

1）按货物实际装运情况填写外包装的件数，如“100 bales”、“250 drums”。在栏目下面的空白处或大写栏内加注大写件数，如“SAY ONE HUNDRED BALES ONLY”。

2）散装货可注明“In bulk”字样，无须列明大写件数。

3）若有多种货物采用多种包装，则应分别列明各种货物的件数和包装种类并加列合计总件数。例如：

100 cartons

50 bales

30 cases

TOTAL: 180 Packages

SAY ONE HUNDRED AND EIGHTY PACKAGES ONLY.（大写）

（13）货物名称（Description of Goods）。按信用证和发票货名填写，若发票名称过多或过细，提单可打货物总称，但不能和发票货名相矛盾。

（14）毛重（Gross Weight,G.W.）。以公斤（KG）为单位填写装运货物的毛重，公斤以下四舍五入处理。

（15）尺码（Measurement，MEAS）。以立方米（M^3）为单位填写货物的尺码，保留至小数点后第三位数。

（16）总件数[Total Number of Containers or Packages(in Words)]。本栏由大写英文数字、包装单位和“ONLY”组成，如“SAY ONE HUNDRED CARTONS ONLY”。

（17）运费（Freight and Charges）。除非有特别规定，否则本栏只填列运费的付费情况，如“Freight Prepaid”或“Freight to Collect”,不填具体金额。

CIF、CIP 价或 CFR、CPT 价应列明“FREIGHT PREPAID”（运费预付）；FOB、FCA 价可列为“FREIGHT COLLECT”（运费到付）或“FREIGHT PAYABLE AT DESTINATION”（运费在目的港付）。

注意：在信用证中若规定“FREIGHT TO BE PREPAID”，提单上不能照打，而应该写成“Freight Prepaid”。

（18）出单地点及签发日期（Place and Date of Issue）。出单地点通常为装运地点。签发日期即为装运日期。

注意：出单地点一般是装运港，如不一致，也可以接受。每张提单必须有签发日期。

（19）正本提单的份数[Number Of Original B(S)L]。收货人凭正本提单提货。正本提单的份数应按信用证的要求，在本栏目内用大写注明。每份正本提单的效力相同，凭其中一份提货后，其余各份失效。根据信用证规定填写，用英文大写注明，如“TWO”或“THREE”等。

1）信用证规定的每种单据须至少提交一份正本。

2）如果信用证要求提交单据的副本，提交正本或副本均可。

3）提单为唯一的正本提单，或者如果以多份正本出具，提单中须表明全套正本的份数。

一般从货运代理公司处会得到三正三副的提单，根据信用证的要求交给银行。

本业务中信用证条款如下：

（20）～（21）装船日期、装运日期。注意：海运提单必须是已装船提单，即使信用证没有规定，提单也有“已装船”的表示。提单要显示装船日期，且此日期不能迟于信用证规定的最迟装运日。

1）提单上预先印就“已装船”字样或相同意思的其他字样，这种提单通常被称为已装船提单，不必另行加注“已装船”批注，提单的签发日期就是装船日期和装运日期。

2）如果提单加有“预期船只”或类似的关于船名的限定语，则需以已装船批注明确发运日期及实际船名。通常这种提单被称为收妥备运提单。

对于收妥备运提单，需在提单上加注“已装船”的批注，并在旁边显示装船日期，该装船日期即为装运日期，而提单的签发日期不能视为装船日期和装运日期。

（22）承运人签章（Signed for The Carrier）。以下是几种常见的签署形式。

1）可以是承运人或其具名代理或代表签章。

① 承运人签章。

例：XYZ SHIPPING COMPANY

张三

AS THE CARRIER

② 具名代理或代表签章。

例：ABC LOGISTICS COMPANY

MARK TWIN

AS AGENT FOR THE CARRIER: XYZ SHIPPING COMPANY

2）可以是船长或其具名代理或代表签章。

例：JOHN DOE AS THE MASTER

CARRIER: XYZ SHIPPING COMPANY

3）承运人、船长或代理人的任何签字或证实，必须表明“承运人”或“船长”的身份；

代理人的任何签字必须标明其代理承运人还是船长。

(23) 背书 (Endorsement)。背书分为以下三种类型。

1) 记名背书。记名背书是在提单背面写明被背书人的名称，并由背书人签名的背书形式。经过记名背书的提单成为记名提单性质的指示提单。

2) 不记名背书。不记名背书也称空白背书，是指背书人在提单背面签上自己的名字，但不记载任何受让人的背书形式。经过空白背书的提单成为不记名提单性质的指示提单。

3) 指示背书。指示背书是背书人在提单背面写明“凭×××指示”的字样，同时由背书人签名的背书形式。经过指示背书的指示提单还可以继续背书，但背书必须连续。

5.3 知识扩展

5.3.1 订舱委托书

订舱委托书 (Shipping Note) 是出口企业委托对外贸易运输公司或其他有权进行对外货运业务的货运代理公司，向承运人或其代理办理出口货物运输时提供的书面文件，用以委托货运代理公司代为租船订舱。订舱委托书是出口企业与货运代理公司之间委托代理关系的证明文件。

订舱委托书没有固定格式，不同进出口公司缮制的委托书不尽相同，但主要内容都要包含在内，包括托运人、收货人、起运港、目的港、唛头、货物描述、货物毛重、货物体积、运费支付方式等。

5.3.2 海运提单

1. 海运提单的定义和作用

(1) 海运提单的定义。海运提单一般简称提单，是指承运人或其代理人在收到货物后签发给托运人的一种证件，是用以证明海上货物运输合同和货物已由承运人接收或装船，以及承运人保证据以交付货物的单证。它体现了承运人与托运人之间的相互关系。

(2) 海运提单的作用。

1) 从法律规定角度看。

① 海运提单是承运人或其代理人出具的货物收据，证明已按海运提单的记载收到托运人的货物。

② 海运提单是代表货物所有权的凭证 (物权凭证)。

③ 海运提单是承运人和托运人双方订立的运输契约的证明。

2) 从外贸业务和运输业务角度看。

① 海运提单是承运人有条件地为托运人运输货物的书面确认。

② 海运提单是银行结汇文件中最重要的文件。

③ 海运提单是货主和货运代理公司之间、货运代理公司和承运人之间支付和收取运费、互相制约的有效文件。

2．海运提单的种类

海运提单的种类如表 5-6 所示。

表 5-6 海运提单的种类

分类方法	种　类	英文名称
根据货物是否已经装船	已装船提单	On Board B/L
	备运提单	Received for Shipment B/L
根据提单上有无对货物外表状况的不良批注	清洁提单	Clean B/L
	不清洁提单	Unclean B/L
根据提单收货人抬头的不同	记名提单	Straight B/L
	不记名提单	Bearer B/L
	指示提单	Order B/L
根据提单签发时间的不同	预借提单	Advanced B/L
	过期提单	Stale B/L
	倒签提单	Anti-dated B/L
根据运输方式的不同	直达提单	Direct B/L
	转船提单	Transshipment B/L
	联运提单	Through B/L

下面具体介绍不同种类提单的含义。

(1) 根据货物是否已经装船，将提单分为已装船提单和备运提单。

1）已装船提单（On Board B/L）。已装船提单是指船公司已经将货物装上指定船舶后才签发的提单，其特点是提单上必须以文字表明货物已经装到某船上，并载有装船日期，同时还应由船长或其代理人签字。

2）备运提单（Received for Shipment B/L）。备运提单又称收货待运提单，是指船公司已收到托运货物，在等待装运期间所签发的提单。

(2) 根据提单上有无对货物外表状况的不良批注，将提单分为清洁提单和不清洁提单。

1）清洁提单（Clean B/L）。清洁提单是指承运人对货物表面状况未加“货物残缺或包装破损”等不良批注的提单，在货物装船时，“表面状况良好”。如果信用证没有特别规定，所提交的提单必须是清洁的。

2）不清洁提单（Unclean B/L）。不清洁提单是指船公司在提单上对货物表面状况有包装不良或存在缺陷等批注的提单。不清洁提单不能拿到银行结汇。

(3) 根据提单收货人抬头的不同，将提单分为记名提单、不记名提单和指示提单。

1) 记名提单（Straight B/L）。记名提单是指在提单上的收货人栏内填明特定收货人名称的提单。这种提单不能转让。

2) 不记名提单（Bearer B/L）。不记名提单是指在提单上的收货人栏没有指明任何收货人的提单。这种提单不用背书就能转让，很危险。

3) 指示提单（Order B/L）。指示提单是指在提单的收货人栏填写“凭指定”(To Order) 或“凭某人指定”(To Order Of) 字样的提单。这种提单经过背书可以转让。

(4) 根据提单签发时间的不同，将提单分为预借提单、过期提单和倒签提单。

1) 预借提单（Advanced B/L）。因信用证装运日期和交单期都已到，而货物因故尚未装船或开始装船但尚未完毕，在这种情况下，托运人为了交单结汇，向承运人或其代理人提出预先签发已装船提单，这种行为称为预借，借得的提单称为预借提单。这一般是违法的，有欺骗性质。

2) 过期提单（Stale B/L）。出口商取得提单后未能及时到银行办理结汇，过了银行规定的结汇期限而形成过期提单。按照《UCP 600》的规定，凡超过装运日期21天后提交的单据即为过期提单，一般银行不予接受。

3) 倒签提单（Anti-dated B/L）。倒签提单是指在货物装船完毕后，承运人或其代理人应托运人的要求，由承运人或其代理人签发提单，但提单上的签发日期早于该批货物实际装船完毕的日期，以符合信用证装运期的规定。这种倒填日期签发的提单为倒签提单。这一般是违法的，有欺骗性质。

(5) 根据运输方式的不同，将提单分为直达提单、转船提单和联运提单。

1) 直达提单（Direct B/L）。直达提单是指轮船中途不经过换船而直接驶往目的港卸货所签发的提单，凡信用证规定不准转船者，必须使用这种提单。

2) 转船提单（Transshipment B/L）。转船提单是指从装运港装货的轮船，不直接驶往目的港，而需要在中途换装另外船舶所签发的提单。

3) 联运提单（Through B/L）。联运提单是指经过海运和其他运输方式组成联合运输时由第一程承运人所签发的包括全程运输的提单。联运提单虽包括全程运输，但签发联运提单的承运人一般只承担他负责运输的一段航程内的责任。

3．海运提单的内容

海运提单一般有正反两面内容。在海运提单的正面和背面还分别印有承运人条款。通常这些条款是根据国际公约、各国法律和承运人规则印制的，对托运人和承运人双方都有约束力。

不同的提单印制不同的条款，但基本条款相似，主要有以下几条。

（1）提单正面的确认条款。其大致内容是，承运人在货物和集装箱外表状况良好的条件下接受货物，并同意按照提单条款将货物或集装箱从起运地运往交货地，把货物交付给收货人。

（2）提单正面的不知条款。其大致内容是，承运人没有适当的方法对接受的货物进行检查，所装货物的重量、尺码、标志、数量、品质和价值等都由托运人提供，承运人并不明确知道（这是承运人为了免责的条款）。

（3）提单正面的承诺条款。其大致内容是，承运人签发的提单是有效的，承运人按条款承担义务和享受权利，也公平地要求货主承诺接受提单条款规定，承担义务和享受权利。

（4）提单正面的签署条款。其大致内容是，承运人签发的正本提单份数，具有相同法律效力，提取货物时必须交出经背书的一份正本提单，其中一份完成提货后，其余各份自行失效。

（5）提单背面的承运人赔偿责任条款。承运人赔偿责任条款是用以明确承运人对货物的灭失和损坏负有赔偿责任应支付赔偿金时，承运人对每件货物或每单位货物支付最高赔偿金额的条款。

4．海运提单中抬头与背书的填写方法

海运提单中抬头与背书的填写方法归纳如表 5-7 所示。

表 5-7　海运提单中抬头与背书的填写方法

信用证或合同对提单的要求	抬头填写	背　书
1．Full set of B/L consigned to Bearer	To Bearer （不记名抬头）	不需要背书就可以转让，很危险
2．Full set of B/L made out to XYZ Co.	XYZ Co. （记名抬头）	不可背书转让。不灵活，但很安全
3．Full set of B/L made out to order	To Order （指示抬头）	由 Shipper（托运人）背书
4．Full set of B/L made out to order of shipper	To Order of Shipper （指示抬头）	由 Shipper（托运人）背书
5．Full set of B/L made out to order of applicant	To Order of XYZ Co. （指示抬头）	由 XYZ Co.背书
6．Full set of B/L made out to our（指开证行）order	To Order of ABC Bank （指示抬头）	由 ABC Bank 背书

5.3.3　海运出口货物出口订舱托运流程

出口商办理出口订舱手续的前提是“货妥、证符”，又称“货证齐备”。所谓“货妥”

指的是出口货物已经备妥待运，出口商向供货厂商付清货款并收妥增值税发票；而“证符”是指出口商审核信用证（及其修改书）并确信无误，符合要求。在“货证齐备”的基础上，出口商开始进入出口合同履行的出口订舱环节。出口订舱托运流程如图 5-1 所示。

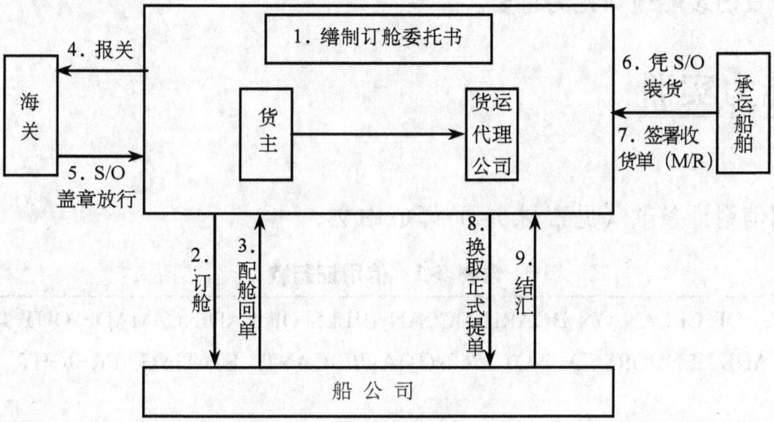

图 5-1　出口订舱托运流程

具体步骤如下。

（1）缮制订舱委托书。出口商作为货主缮制出口货物订舱委托书，并随附商业发票和装箱单及其他必要单证，一并交给货运代理公司，委托其向船公司订舱。有时还委托其进行代理报关、货物储运业务，及向拖车公司订拖车。

（2）订舱。货运代理公司收到出口商的订舱委托后，缮制集装箱货物托运单（Booking Note, 又称十联单），随同商业发票、装箱单及其他必要单证向船公司订舱。

（3）配舱回单。船公司根据货物托运单的内容，并结合船舶航线挂靠港、船期和舱位等条件考虑，如果接受订舱，则在货物托运单上注明和提单一致的编号（B/L No.）并填上拟装货物的船名（Vessel）、航次（Voy.）。确认订舱后，将与托运人有关的装货单（俗称下货纸）（Shipping Order, S/O）、收货单、配舱回单等退还给托运人。

（4）报关。托运人持船公司签署的 S/O，填制出口报关单、商业发票、装箱单及海关要求的其他单证报关。

（5）S/O 盖章放行。海关根据有关程序进行查验，如同意出口，则在 S/O 上加盖放行章，并将 S/O 退还给托运人。

（6）凭 S/O 装货。托运人持海关盖章的 S/O 要求船长装货。

（7）签署收货单（M/R）。装货后，由船长或大副签署收货单（又称大副收据）（Mate's Receipt，M/R）。收货单是船公司签发给托运人的表明货物已装妥的临时收据。

（8）换取正式提单。托运人凭收货单向货运代理公司交付运费并换取正式提单。

(9) 结汇。托运人凭正式海运提单（B/L）和其他货运单据去议付行结汇。

除上述程序外，在货物装船后，托运人应及时向国外收货人发出装船通知（Shipping Advice），以便对方准备付款赎单，办理进口报关和接货手续。CFR 和 FOB 合同由买方办理保险，及时发出装船通知尤为重要。

5.4 能力实训

实训 1

试将下列信用证条款（见素材 5-1）译成中文。

素材 5-1 信用证条款

FULL SET (3/3) OF CLEAN ON BOARD OCEAN BILLS OF LADING, MADE OUT TO ORDER OF SHIPPER, BLANK ENDORSED NOTIFYING APPLICANT, STATING FREIGHT PREPAID OR COLLECT.

实训 2

某提单显示内容如下：

Shipper:ABC Co.,LTD.

Consignee:To Order

Notify Party:XYZ Co.,Ltd.

请问，该提单属于哪种类型的提单？该提单由谁首先背书？

5.5 能力扩展

根据 2.5 节、3.5 节能力扩展中签订的外贸合同和修改后的信用证，制作海运提单，提单框架和补充信息如素材 5-2 所示。

素材 5-2 海运提单框架及补充信息

1．SHIPPER		10．B/L No. COSCO 中国远洋运输（集团）总公司 CHINA OCEAN SHIPPING (GROUP) Co.
2．CONSIGNEE		
3．NOTIFY PARTY		
4．PLACE OF RECEIPT	5．OCEAN VESSEL	
6．VOY. No.	7．PORT OF LOADING	*ORIGINAL* Combined Transport Bill of Lading

续

<table>
<tr><td colspan="2">8. PORT OF DISCHARGE</td><td colspan="2">9. PLACE OF DELIVERY</td><td colspan="2"></td></tr>
<tr><td>11. MARKS</td><td>12. NOS. & KINDS OF PKGS</td><td colspan="2">13. DESCRIPTION OF GOODS</td><td>14. G.W.(KG)</td><td>15.MEAS(M^3)</td></tr>
<tr><td colspan="6">16. TOTAL NUMBER OF CONTAINERS OR PACKAGES(IN WORDS)</td></tr>
<tr><td>17. FREIGHT & CHARGES</td><td>REVENUE TONS</td><td>RATE</td><td>PER</td><td>PREPAID</td><td>COLLECT</td></tr>
<tr><td>PREPAID AT</td><td>PAYABLE AT</td><td colspan="4">18. PLACE AND DATE OF ISSUE</td></tr>
<tr><td>TOTAL PREPAID</td><td>19. NUMBER OF ORIGINAL B(S)/L</td><td colspan="4" rowspan="3">22. SIGNED FOR THE CARRIER</td></tr>
<tr><td colspan="2">LOADING ON BOARD THE VESSEL</td></tr>
<tr><td>20. DATE</td><td>21. BY</td></tr>
</table>

补充信息：

提单号：BL3213314354

拟出运日期：2011.2.16

船名：SHENGLI

航次：V.945

每箱规格：MEAS: 35×45×50CM/CTN ；G.W.: 45KGS/CTN；N.W.: 40KGS/CTN

项目 6

缮制出境货物报检单和办理报检手续

学习目标

知识目标：了解出境货物报检业务流程与报检所需要的单据；掌握出境货物报检单的内容与缮制要求。

能力目标：能够根据相关资料缮制出境货物报检单。

6.1 工作任务

大连思念纺织品进出口公司单证员蔡平缮制好用于报检和报关的商业发票、装箱单后，了解到该批出口货物商品编码（6110120029）的监管证件代码是 B，即出境货物通关单，属于法定检验商品。于是蔡平在制作报检委托书和出境货物报检单后，于 2012 年 7 月 11 日将其连同商业发票和装箱单，以附件的形式发给辽宁海城创新制衣厂跟单员小朱，并电话协商该批货物的法定检验事宜，请小朱安排商检，尽快回复电子传单。

在本业务中，出口方单证员蔡平需要根据信用证的要求和实际出运信息，完成以下工作任务。

任务 1　制作报检委托书。

任务 2　缮制出境货物报检单。

任务 3　办理报检手续。

6.2 操作步骤

6.2.1 第一步：制作报检委托书

由于出口货物生产地点在辽宁省海城市，因此大连思念纺织品进出口公司单证员蔡平需要委托辽宁海城创新制衣厂向鞍山出入境检验检疫局办理代理报检，特制作报检委托书（见表 6-1）。

表 6-1　报检委托书

报检委托书

鞍山出入境检验检疫局：

本委托人郑重承诺保证遵守《中华人民共和国国境卫生检疫法》及其实施条例、《中华人民共和国进出境动植物检疫法》及其实施条例、《中华人民共和国食品卫生法》等有关法律、法规的规定和出入境检验检疫机构制定的各项规章制度。如有违法行为，自愿接受出入境检验检疫机构的处罚并负法律责任。

本委托人委托受委托人向出入境检验检疫机构提交的“报检申请单”和随附各种单据所列内容是真实无讹的。具体委托情况如下。

本单位将于 2012 年 7 月间出口如下货物：

品　　名：女士针织开衫

数（重）量：9400 件

合 同 号：PG1061

信 用 证 号：DCTBT123456

特委托 辽宁海城创新制衣厂（地址：海城市西柳镇工业园区 118 号）代表本公司办理所有检验检疫事宜，其间产生的一切相关法律责任由本公司承担。请贵局按有关法律规定予以办理。

委托方名称（公章）：大连思念纺织品进出口公司	受托方名称（公章）：辽宁海城创新制衣厂
单位地址：大连市职工路 53 号	单位地址：海城市西柳镇工业园区 118 号
邮政编码：116000	邮政编码：116008
法人代表：汪　明	法人代表：李　力
联系电话：0411-87803852	联系电话：0412-3837966
企业性质：国有控股公司	企业性质：私营有限责任公司
日　　期：2012 年 7 月 11 日	日　　期：2012 年 7 月 11 日

本委托书有效期至 2012 年 9 月 11 日

6.2.2 第二步：缮制出境货物报检单

单证员蔡平通过软件，根据出境货物报检单填写规范，缮制出境货物报检单（见表 6-2）。

表 6-2 出境货物报检单

<table>
<tr><td colspan="12">中华人民共和国出入境检验检疫
出境货物报检单
报检单位（加盖公章）：大连思念纺织品进出口公司　　编号：546554131000545
报检单位登记号：546546416315　　联系人：蔡平
电话：0411-54345659　　报检日期：2012 年 7 月 11 日</td></tr>
<tr><td rowspan="2">发货人</td><td colspan="11">（中文）大连思念纺织品进出口公司</td></tr>
<tr><td colspan="11">（外文）DALIAN SINIAN TEXTILES IMP. &EXP. Co,LTD</td></tr>
<tr><td rowspan="2">收货人</td><td colspan="11">（中文）波兰普利希纺织品公司</td></tr>
<tr><td colspan="11">（外文）POLISH PULICI TEXTILE GROUP Co., LTD.</td></tr>
<tr><td colspan="2">货物名称（中/外文）</td><td colspan="2">H.S. 编码</td><td>产 地</td><td colspan="2">数/重量</td><td colspan="2">货物总值</td><td colspan="3">包装种类及数量</td></tr>
<tr><td colspan="2">女士针织开衫
LADIES'S KNITTED
CARDIGAN</td><td colspan="2">6110120029</td><td>海城</td><td colspan="2">9 400 件</td><td colspan="2">60 730.00 欧元</td><td colspan="3">235 个纸箱</td></tr>
<tr><td colspan="2">运输工具名称及号码</td><td colspan="2">JINGBI
V.036/HV300W</td><td>贸易方式</td><td colspan="2">一般贸易</td><td colspan="3">货物存放地点</td><td colspan="2">海城</td></tr>
<tr><td>合同号</td><td colspan="3">PG1061</td><td>信用证号</td><td colspan="4">DCTBT123456</td><td colspan="2">用途</td><td>其他</td></tr>
<tr><td>发货日期</td><td colspan="2">2012 年 7 月 26 日</td><td>输往国家（地区）</td><td colspan="2">波兰</td><td colspan="3">许可证/审批单号</td><td colspan="3">无</td></tr>
<tr><td>起运地</td><td colspan="2">大连</td><td>到达口岸</td><td colspan="2">格丹斯克</td><td colspan="3">生产单位注册号</td><td colspan="3">210354021</td></tr>
<tr><td colspan="3">集装箱规格、数量及号码</td><td colspan="9">MANU200454/20/2275</td></tr>
<tr><td colspan="3">合同、信用证订立的检验检疫条款或特殊要求</td><td colspan="3">标记及号码</td><td colspan="6">随附单据（画“✓”或补填）</td></tr>
<tr><td colspan="3" rowspan="6"></td><td colspan="3" rowspan="6">POLISH
PG1061
GDANSK
C/N: 1-235</td><td colspan="3">☑ 合同</td><td colspan="3">☑包装性能结果单</td></tr>
<tr><td colspan="3">☑ 信用证</td><td colspan="3">☐ 许可/审批文件</td></tr>
<tr><td colspan="3">☑ 发票</td><td colspan="3">☐</td></tr>
<tr><td colspan="3">☐ 换证凭单</td><td colspan="3">☐</td></tr>
<tr><td colspan="3">☑ 装箱单</td><td colspan="3">☐</td></tr>
<tr><td colspan="3">☑ 厂检单</td><td colspan="3">☐</td></tr>
</table>

续表

<table>
<tr><td colspan="2">需要证单名称（画"✓"或补填）</td><td colspan="2">* 检验检疫费</td></tr>
<tr><td rowspan="3">□ 品质证书 _正_副
□ 重量证书 _正_副
□ 数量证书 _正_副
□ 兽医卫生证书 _正_副
□ 健康证书 _正_副
□ 卫生证书 _正_副
□ 动物卫生证书 _正_副</td><td rowspan="3">□ 植物检疫证书 _正_副
□ 熏蒸/消毒证书 _正_副
☑出境货物换证凭单
□ 出境货物通关单
□
□</td><td>总金额
（人民币元）</td><td></td></tr>
<tr><td>计费人</td><td></td></tr>
<tr><td>收费人</td><td></td></tr>
<tr><td colspan="2" rowspan="3">报检人郑重声明：
1．本人被授权报检。
2．上列填写内容正确属实，货物无伪造或冒用他人的厂名、标志、认证标志，并承担货物质量责任。
签名：蔡平</td><td colspan="2">领取证单</td></tr>
<tr><td>日期</td><td></td></tr>
<tr><td>签名</td><td></td></tr>
</table>

注：有"*"的栏目由出入境检验检疫机关填写。

出境货物报检单主要项目填写规范如下。

（1）报检单位。报检单位是指向出入境检验检疫机构申报检验、检疫、鉴定业务的单位。报检单应加盖报检单位公章。

（2）报检单位登记号。报检单位登记号是指报检单位在出入境检验检疫机构的报检注册登记号。

（3）发货人。发货人是指本批货物的贸易合同中的卖方名称或信用证中的受益人名称，需要出具英文证书的，填写中英文。

（4）收货人。收货人是指本批货物的贸易合同中或信用证中的买方名称，需要出具英文证书的，填写中英文。

（5）货物名称。按贸易合同或商业发票所列货物名称所对应的国家检验检疫机构制定公布的《出入境检验检疫机构实施检验检疫的进出境商品目录》所列的货物名称填写。

（6）H.S.编码。填写货物对应的海关《商品分类及编码协调制度》中的代码。

（7）产地。产地是指货物的生产或加工的省（自治区、直辖市）及地区（市）名称。

（8）数/重量。填写报检货物的数/重量，重量一般以净重填写，如填写毛重，或以毛重作净重，则需注明。

（9）货物总值。按本批货物贸易合同或商业发票上所列的总值填写（以美元计），如同一报检单报检多批货物，则需列明每批货物的总值（如申报货物总值与国内、国际市场价格有较大差异，出入境检验检疫机构保留核价权力）。

(10) 包装种类及数量。包装种类及数量是指本批货物运输包装的件数及种类。

(11) 运输工具名称及号码。填写货物实际装载的运输工具类别名称（如船、飞机、货柜车、火车等）及运输工具编号（船名、飞机航班号、车牌号码、火车车次）。报检时，未能确定运输工具编号的，可只填写运输工具类别名称。

(12) 贸易方式。贸易方式包括一般贸易、三来一补、边境贸易、进料加工和其他贸易。

(13) 货物存放地点。填写本批货物存放的地点。

(14) 合同号。填写贸易双方就本批货物出境而签订的贸易合同编号。

(15) 信用证号。填写本批货物所对应的信用证编号。

(16) 用途。用途是指本批货物出境用途，如种用、食用、奶用、观赏或演艺、伴侣、实验、药用、饲用、加工等。

(17) 发货日期。按本批货物信用证或贸易合同所列的出境日期填写。

(18) 输往国家（地区）。填写贸易合同中买方（进口方）所在国家或地区。

(19) 许可证/审批单号。对于《实施出口商品质量许可证制度的产品目录》下的出口货物和其他已实行许可制度、审批制度管理的货物，报检时填写安全质量许可证编号或审批单编号。

(20) 起运地。填写装运本批货物离境的交通工具的起运口岸或地区城市名称。

(21) 到达口岸。填写装运本批货物的交通工具最终抵达目的地停靠的口岸名称。

(22) 生产单位注册号。填写生产或加工本批货物的单位在出入境检验检疫机构的注册登记编号。

(23) 集装箱规格、数量及号码。填写装载本批货物的集装箱规格（如 40 英尺、20 英尺等）及分别对应的数量和集装箱号码全称。若集装箱太多，可用附单形式填报。

(24) 合同、信用证订立的检验检疫条款或特殊要求。填写贸易合同或信用证中贸易双方对本批货物特别约定而订立的质量、卫生等条款和报检单位对本批货物的检验检疫的其他特别要求。如没有则不填。

(25) 标记及号码。按出境货物实际运输包装标记填写，如没有标记，则填写“N/M”，标记填写不下时可用附页填报。

(26) 随附单据。按实际提供的单据，在对应的方框画“√”。

(27) 需要证单名称。按需要出入境检验检疫机构出具的证单，在对应的方框画“√”，并应注明所需证单的正副本的数量。

(28) 报检人郑重声明。必须有报检人的亲笔签名。

(29) 检验检疫费。检验检疫费由检验检疫机构计费人员核定费用后填写，如熏蒸费和消毒费等。

(30) 领取证单。报检人在领取证单时填写领证日期和领证人签名。

6.2.3　第三步：办理货物出口报检手续

大连思念纺织品进出口公司单证员蔡平把缮制好的出境货物报检单、报检委托书、商业发票、装箱单等单据寄给辽宁海城创新制衣厂小朱，委托其代为报检。小朱凭这些单据和厂检单、包装性能结果单，向鞍山出入境检验检疫局报检。2012 年 7 月 16 日，商品检验通过后，鞍山出入境检验检疫局发给大连思念纺织品进出口公司一张出境货物换证凭条。蔡平保存好这张换证凭条待用。出境货物换证凭条如表 6-3 所示。

表 6-3　出境货物换证凭条

转单号	5465541315768T		报检号	546554131000545	
报检单位	大连思念纺织品进出口公司				
品名	女士针织开衫				
合同号	PG1061	H.S.编码	6110120029		
数（重）量	9 400 件	包装件数	235 个纸箱	金额	60 730.00 欧元
评定意见： 贵单位报检的该批货物，经我局检验检疫已合格。请持此单到大连局本部办理出境验证业务。本单有效期截至 2012 年 9 月 16 日。 鞍山局本部　2012 年 7 月 16 日					

6.2.4　第四步：换取出境货物通关单

2012 年 7 月 21 日，大连思念纺织品进出口公司单证员蔡平将出境货物换证凭条和出口货物报关单、报关委托书、出口收汇单、商业发票、装箱单寄给大连万翔国际货运代理有限公司，委托其向商检局大连分局换出境货物通关单和代理报关。

2012 年 7 月 24 日，大连万翔国际货运代理有限公司从商检局大连分局换取出境货物通关单。官方出具的出境货物通关单如表 6-4 所示。

表 6-4　出境货物通关单

中华人民共和国出入境检验检疫 出境货物通关单 编号：×××××××	
1．发货人 大连思念纺织品进出口公司	5．标记及号码 POLISH PG1061 GDANSK C/N：1-235
2．收货人 波兰普利希纺织品公司	

续表

<table>
<tr><td>3. 合同/信用证号
FRJ-016/ DCTBT123456</td><td colspan="2">4. 输往国家或地区
波兰</td><td></td></tr>
<tr><td>6. 运输工具名称及号码
JINGBI V.036/HV300W</td><td colspan="2">7. 发货日期
2012 年 7 月 26 日</td><td>8. 集装箱规格、数量及号码
MANU200454/20/2275</td></tr>
<tr><td>9. 货物名称
女士针织开衫
LADIES'S KNITTED CARDIGAN</td><td>10. H.S.编码
6110120029</td><td>11. 申报总值
EUR 60 730.00</td><td>12. 数/重量、包装数量及种类
9 400 件/12.6 千克，
235 个纸箱</td></tr>
<tr><td colspan="4">13. 证明
上述货物业经检验检疫，请海关予以放行。
本通关单有效期至 2012 年 09 月 30 日。
2012 年 7 月 24 日</td></tr>
<tr><td colspan="4">14. 备注</td></tr>
</table>

出境货物通关单填制规范如下。

（1）发货人。填写本批货物的贸易合同中的卖方名称或信用证中的受益人名称，如需要出具英文证书，则填写中英文。

（2）收货人。填写本批货物的贸易合同中或信用证中的买方名称，如需要出具英文证书，则填写中英文。

（3）合同/信用证号。合同号指贸易双方就本批货物出境而签订的贸易合同编号。信用证号指本批货物所对应的信用证编号。

（4）输往国家或地区。填写贸易合同中买方（进口方）所在国家或地区。

（5）标记及号码。按出境货物实际运输包装标记填写，如没有标记，则填写“N/M”，标记填写不下时可用附页填报。

（6）运输工具名称及号码。填写货物实际装载的运输工具类别名称（如船、飞机、货柜车、火车等）及运输工具编号（船名、飞机航班号、车牌号码、火车车次）。报检时，未能确定运输工具编号的，可只填写运输工具类别名称。

（7）发货日期。按本批货物信用证或贸易合同所列的出境日期填写。

（8）集装箱规格、数量及号码。填写装载本批货物的集装箱规格（如 40 英尺、20 英尺等）及分别对应的数量和集装箱号码全称。若集装箱太多，可用附单形式填报。

（9）货物名称。按贸易合同或商业发票所列货物名称所对应的国家检验检疫机构制定公布的《出入境检验检疫机构实施检验检疫的进出境商品目录》所列的货物名称填写。

（10）H.S.编码。H.S.编码指货物对应的海关《商品分类及编码协调制度》中的代码，填写8位数或10位数。

(11) 申报总值。按本批货物贸易合同或商业发票上所列的总值填写（以美元计），如同一报检单报检多批货物，则需列明每批货物的总值（如申报货物总值与国内、国际市场价格有较大差异，出入境检验检疫机构保留核价权力）。

(12) 数/重量、包装数量及种类。填写报检货物的数/重量，重量一般以净重填写，如填写毛重，或以毛重作净重则需注明。包装数量及种类指本批货物运输包装的件数及种类。

(13) 证明。填写关于报检的进出口货物经过检验检疫，请海关予以放行的证明文字。需要写明出境货物通关单的有效期，并加盖出入境检验检疫局的检验检疫专用章。

(14) 备注。填写需要说明的其他事项。

6.3　知识扩展

6.3.1　检验检疫机构

国际贸易中的商检工作一般由专业的检验机构办理。在国际贸易中，可供买卖双方选用的商检机构很多，按组织性质大致分为以下几类。① 官方检验机构，即由国家设立的检验机构，如美国食品药品监督管理局（U.S. Food and Drug Administration，FDA）、法国国家实验室检测中心、日本通商产业检查所等。② 半官方检验机构，即有一定权威、由国家政府授权、代表政府行使某项商品检验或某一方面检验管理工作的民间机构，如美国担保人实验室等。③ 非官方检验机构，即由私人创办，具有专业检验及鉴定技术能力的公证行或检验公司，如英国劳埃氏公证行、瑞士日内瓦通用鉴定公司等。

在我国，原主管全国出入境商品检验检疫和鉴定管理工作的机构是中华人民共和国出入境检验检疫局及其设立在全国各地的分支机构，通常称为国家商检部门。后来，为进一步发挥质量监督和检验检疫作用以适应我国加入WTO及同国际接轨的需要，国务院在2001年4月10日将原国家质量技术监督局与之合并，成立了中华人民共和国质量监督检验检疫总局（以下简称国家质检总局），它是我国负责质量监督检验检疫工作的最高机构。合并以后，原通关模式不变，检验检疫职能不变，垂直管理体制不变。

6.3.2　办理出境货物报检手续

1. 出境货物报检方式

出境货物的报检方式通常分为三类：出境一般报检、出境换证报检、出境预检报检。申请出境一般报检和出境换证报检的货物，其特点是已生产完毕、包装完好、堆码整齐、相关单据齐全，已具备出口条件；申请出境预检报检的货物，其特点是暂不具备出口条件。

2．报检时限和地点

（1）出境货物最迟应在出口报关或装运前 7 日报检，对于个别检验检疫周期较长的货物，应留有相应的检验检疫时间。

（2）需隔离检疫的出境动物在出境前 60 日预报，隔离前 7 日报检。

（3）法定检验检疫货物，除活动物需由口岸检验检疫机构检验检疫外，原则上实施产地检验检疫。

3．报检需要提交的单证

出境报检时，应填写出境货物报检单，并提供外贸合同（销售确认书或函电）、信用证、发票、装箱单等必要的单证。下列情况还应按要求提供有关文件。

（1）凡实施出口质量许可、卫生注册登记或需审批审核的货物，应提供有关证明。

（2）凭样成交的货物，应提供经买卖双方确认的样品。

（3）实施品质检验的，须由生产经营部门出具厂检单原件；如有运输包装，还应提供出入境检验检疫机构签发的《出境货物运输包装性能检验结果单》（正本）。

（4）报检出境危险货物的，必须提供危险货物包装容器性能鉴定结果单和使用鉴定结果单。

（5）出境特殊物品的，应提供国家出口批文和有关证明、检验证书等，以及深圳出入境检验检疫局卫生检疫处签发的《入/出境特殊物品卫生检疫审批单》。

（6）出境废旧物品的，应提供深圳出入境检验检疫局各分支机构签发的《入/出境废旧物品检验检疫预申报证》。

（7）用于展览、工程、科研等的临时出境货物报检时，须提供政府批文或其他有效证明文件。

4．出境货物产地检验检疫原则

出入境检验检疫机构对出口货物实行产地检验检疫原则，出口企业必须到货物产地所属的出入境检验检疫机构办理报检手续。如货物需要异地报关，可由产地出入境检验检疫机构实施电子转单或出具《出境货物换证凭单》，然后持电子转单凭条或换证凭单到口岸检验检疫机构换发《出境货物通关单》，办理通关手续。

5．出境货物报检流程

目前，出口企业大多实行电子报检。电子报检是指报检人使用电子报检软件，通过检验检疫电子业务服务平台将报检数据以电子方式传输给出入境检验检疫机构，经检验检疫业务管理系统和检验检疫工作人员处理后，将受理报检信息反馈报检人，实现远程办理出入境检验检疫报检业务的过程。

（1）报检。

1）电子报检。对报检数据的审核以“先机审，后人审”的程序进行。

2）出境货物受理电子报检后，报检人应按受理报检信息的要求，在检验检疫机构施检时，提交报检单和随附单据。

3）入境货物受理电子报检后，报检人应按受理报检信息的要求，在领取《入境货物通关单》时，提交报检单和随附单据。

4）电子报检人已发送报检申请，又需更改或撤销报检时，应发送更改或撤销报检申请。

（2）施检。在现场检验检疫时，报检人持电子报检软件打印的报检单和全套随附单据交施检人员审核，不符合要求的，施检人员通知报检人立即更改，并将不符合情况反馈受理报检部门。

（3）计费和收费。计费由电子审单系统自动完成。

（4）签证放行。

6.3.3　办理入境货物报检手续

法定检验检疫的入境货物，在报关时必须提供报关地出入境检验检疫机构签发的《入境货物通关单》，海关凭《入境货物通关单》验放。

入境货物检验检疫的工作程序如下。① 法定检验检疫入境货物的货主或其他代理人首先向卸货口岸或到达站的出入境检验检疫机构报检。② 出入境检验检疫机构受理报检，转施检部门签署意见，并计收费；对来自疫区的，可能传播传染病、动植物疫情及可能夹带有害物质的入境货物的交通工具或运输包装实施必要的检疫、消毒、卫生除害处理后，签发《入境货物通关单》（入境废物、活动物等除外）供报检人办理海关通关手续。③ 货物通关后，入境货物的货主或其代理人需在出入境检验检疫机构规定的时间和地点到指定的检验检疫机构联系对货物实施检验检疫。经检验检疫合格的入境货物签发《入境货物检验检疫证明》放行，经检验检疫不合格的入境货物签发处理通知书，需要索赔的签发检验检疫证书。

6.3.4　检验检疫证书

根据出入境不同的检验检疫要求、鉴定项目和不同作用，我国检验检疫机构签发不同的检验检疫证书、凭单、监管类证单、报告单和记录报告，种类超过 85 种。常见的检验检疫证书如下。

（1）品质检验证书（Quality Certificate）。品质检验证书是出口商品交货结汇和进口商品结算索赔的有效凭证。法定检验商品的品质检验证书，是进出口商品报关、输出输入的合法凭证。

（2）数量检验证书（Quantity Certificate）。数量检验证书是进出口商品数量的证明文件。

（3）植物检疫证书（Phytosanitary Certificate）。植物检疫证书是植物不带有植物检疫对象的证明文件。

（4）兽医检验证书（Animal Health Certificate）。兽医检验证书是证明出口动物产品或食品经过检疫且合格的证件，也是对外交货、银行结汇和进口国通关输入的重要证件。该证书适用于冻畜肉、冻禽、禽畜罐头、冻兔、肠衣等出口商品。

（5）卫生/健康检验证书（Sanitary Certificate）。卫生/健康检验证书是证明可供人类食用的出口动物产品、食品等经过卫生检验或检疫合格的证件，也是对外交货、银行结汇和通关验放的有效证件。该证书适用于肠衣、罐头、冻鱼、蛋品、乳制品、蜂蜜等。

（6）消毒检验证书（Disinfection Certificate）。消毒检验证书是证明出口动物产品经过消毒处理，保证安全卫生的证件，也是对外交货、银行结汇和通关验放的有效凭证。该证书适用于猪鬃、马尾、羽毛、人发等商品。

（7）熏蒸证书（Fumigation Certificate）。熏蒸证书是用于证明出口粮谷、油籽、皮张等商品，以及包装用木材与植物性填充物等已经过熏蒸灭虫的证书。

（8）残损检验证书（Inspection Certificate on Damaged Cargo）。残损检验证书是证明进口商品残损情况的证件，适用于进口商品发生残、短、毁等情况，可作为收货人向发货人、承运人或保险人等有关责任方索赔的有效证件。

（9）货载衡量检验证书（Inspection Certificate on Cargo Weight and Measurement）。货载衡量检验证书是进出口商品的重量和体积吨位的证明书，可作为计算运费和制定配载计划的依据。

6.4 能力实训

根据信用证（见素材 6-1）和补充信息（见素材 6-2）缮制出境货物报检单。出境货物报检单框架如素材 6-3 所示。

素材 6-1 信用证

MESSAGE TYPE: MT700　　ISSUE OF A DOCUMENTARY CREDIT
RECEIVED FROM: BANK OF TOKYO_MITSUBISHI, LTD.,THE OSAKA JAPAN
DESTINATION: BANK OF CHINA,NINGBO BRANCH

SEQUENCE OF TOTAL	*27: 1/1
FORM OF DOC. CREDIT	*40B: IRREVOCABLE
DOC. CREDIT NUMBER	*20: H456-201254
DATE OF ISSUE	31: 120628
APPLICABLE RELUES	*40E: UCP LATEST VERSION
EXPIRY	*31D: DATE 120913 CHINA
APPLICANT	*50: TOKO TRADE CORPORATION. OSAKA 2-5-8,KAWA RAMACHI. 14-CHOME,OSAKA,JAPAN.

续

BENEFICIARY	*59: NINGBO HUADONG FOOD Co.,LTD. No.19 DONGSHAN ROAD,NINGBO,CHINA
AMOUNT	*32B: CURRENCY USD AMOUNT 30 600.00
AVAILABLE WITH/BY	*41D: ANY BANK ON SIGHT BASIS BY NEGOTIATION DRAFTS AT SIGHT FOR FULL INVOICE VALUE.
DRAWEE	42D: BANK OF TOKYO-MITSUBISHI,LTD., THE NEW YORK,NY.
PARTIAL SHIPMENTS	43P: NOT ALLOWED
TRANSSHIPMENT	43T: NOT ALLOWED
PORT OF LOADING	44E: SHANGHAI IN CHINA
PORT OF DISCHARGE	44F: OSAKA,JAPAN
LATEST DATE OF SHIP.	44C: 120730
DESCRIPT. OF GOODS	45A: CIF OSAKA 30M/T FROZEN PEAPODS AS PER PURCHASE CONTRACT No.JP1254
DOCUMENTS REQUIRED	46A: 14. COMMERCIAL INVOICE MANNUALLY SIGNED IN 3 ORIGINALS PLUS 3 COPY. 15. PACKING LIST IN TRIPLICATE. 16. FULL SET OF ORIGINAL CLEAN ON BOARD BILL OF LADING MADE OUT TO ORDER AND BLANK ENDORSED NOTIFY THE APPLICANT, MARKED FREGHT PREPAID. 17. INSURANCE POLICY/CERTIFICATE IN DUPLICATE BLANK ENDORSED FOR 110% INVOICE VALUE COVERING ALL RISKS & WAR RISKS SHOWING CLAIMS PAYALBLE AT OSAKA, JAPAN IN THE CURRENCY OF THE CREDIT. 18. BENEFIFIARY'S CERTIFICATE STATING THAT 1 ORIGINAL INSPECTION CERTIFICATE OF QUALITY AND 1 ORIGINAL B/L ONE ORIGINAL INSURANCE POLICY HAVE BEEN SENT TO APPLICANT BY COURIER. 19. INSPCTION CERTIFICATED ISSUED BY MANUFACTURERS.
ADDITIONAL COND.	47A: +ALL DOCS MUST BE ISSUED IN ENGLISH. + DOCUMENTS MUST BE PRESENTED WITHIN 10 DAYS AFTER SHIPMENT DATE BUT IN ANY EVENT NOT LATER THAN THE EXPIRY DATE OF THIS CREDIT.
DETALLS OF CHARGES	71B: ALL BANKING CHARGES OUTSIDE JAPAN ARE FOR ACCOUNT OF BENEFICIARY.
CONFIRMATION	*49 :WITHOUT

素材 6-2 补充信息

发票号码：12GESP879	发票日期：2012 年 7 月 5 日
提单号码：CAND7999	提单日期：2012 年 7 月 20 日
船名：PRESIDENT V.008	运费：USD1 600.00
保单号码：984646497	保险费：USD150.00
货物装箱情况：20KGS/CTN	商品编码：8 712.1000
毛重：21KGS/CTN	净重：20KGS/CTN
尺码：（50×40×60）CM/CTN	
唛头：TOKO MADE IN CHINA No.1-UP	
生产单位：宁波华东食品有限公司（221089763214）	
报检单位登记号：44789564647	
集装箱号码：CGHU85463/40`	
封号：HD20071221	

素材 6-3 出境货物报检单框架

中华人民共和国出入境检验检疫

出境货物报检单

编号：×××××××

<table>
<tr><td rowspan="2">发货人</td><td colspan="7">（中文）</td></tr>
<tr><td colspan="7">（外文）</td></tr>
<tr><td rowspan="2">收货人</td><td colspan="7">（中文）</td></tr>
<tr><td colspan="7">（外文）</td></tr>
<tr><td colspan="2">货物名称（中/外文）</td><td>H.S.编码</td><td>产地</td><td>数/重量</td><td>货物总值</td><td colspan="2">包装种类及数量</td></tr>
<tr><td colspan="2"></td><td></td><td></td><td></td><td></td><td colspan="2"></td></tr>
<tr><td colspan="2">运输工具名称及号码</td><td></td><td>贸易方式</td><td></td><td>货物存放地点</td><td colspan="2"></td></tr>
<tr><td>合同号</td><td colspan="2"></td><td>信用证号</td><td colspan="2"></td><td>用途</td><td></td></tr>
<tr><td>发货日期</td><td></td><td>输往国家（地区）</td><td></td><td>许可证/审批单号</td><td colspan="3"></td></tr>
<tr><td>起运地</td><td></td><td>到达口岸</td><td></td><td>生产单位注册号</td><td colspan="3"></td></tr>
<tr><td colspan="8">集装箱规格、数量及号码</td></tr>
<tr><td colspan="2">合同订立的检验检疫条款
或特殊要求</td><td colspan="3">标记及号码</td><td colspan="3">随附单据（画“√”或补填）</td></tr>
</table>

续

<table>
<tr><td></td><td></td><td>□ 合同
□ 信用证
□ 发票
□ 换证凭单
□ 装箱单
□ 厂检单</td><td colspan="2">□ 包装性能结果单
□ 许可/审批文件
□
□
□
□</td></tr>
<tr><td colspan="2">需要证单名称（画“✓”或补填）</td><td colspan="3">* 检验检疫费</td></tr>
<tr><td rowspan="3">□ 品质证书　_正_副
□ 重量证书　_正_副
□ 数量证书　_正_副
□ 兽医卫生证书 _正_副
□ 健康证书　_正_副
□ 卫生证书　_正_副
□ 动物卫生证书 _正_副</td><td rowspan="3">□ 植物检疫证书　_正_副
□ 熏蒸/消毒证书　_正_副
□ 出境货物换证凭单
□ 出境货物通关单
□
□</td><td colspan="2">总金额
（人民币元）</td><td></td></tr>
<tr><td colspan="2">计费人</td><td></td></tr>
<tr><td colspan="2">收费人</td><td></td></tr>
<tr><td colspan="2" rowspan="3">报检人郑重声明：
1. 本人被授权报检。
2. 上列填写内容正确属实，货物无伪造或冒用他人的厂名、标志、认证标志，并承担货物质量责任。
签名：____________</td><td colspan="3">领取证单</td></tr>
<tr><td colspan="2">日期</td><td></td></tr>
<tr><td colspan="2">签名</td><td></td></tr>
</table>

6.5 能力扩展

根据 2.5 节能力扩展中的外贸合同（见素材 2-2）和相应信用证（见素材 4-4）和拟定好的商业发票（见素材 4-5）及装箱单（见素材 4-6），填写出境货物报检单和出境货物通关单。出境货物报检单框架如素材 6-3 所示，出境货物通关单框架如素材 6-4 所示。

素材 6-4　出境货物通关单框架

<table>
<tr><td colspan="2">中华人民共和国出入境检验检疫
出境货物通关单
编号：</td></tr>
<tr><td>1. 发货人</td><td>5. 标记及号码</td></tr>
</table>

续

<table>
<tr><td colspan="3">2．收货人</td><td></td></tr>
<tr><td>3．合同/信用证号</td><td colspan="2">4．输往国家或地区</td><td></td></tr>
<tr><td>6．运输工具名称及号码</td><td colspan="2">7．发货日期</td><td>8．集装箱规格、数量及号码</td></tr>
<tr><td>9．货物名称</td><td>10．H.S. 编码</td><td>11．申报总值</td><td>12．数/重量、包装数量及种类</td></tr>
<tr><td colspan="4">13．证明
上述货物业经检验检疫，请海关予以放行。
本通关单有效期至　　年　月　日。
年　月　日</td></tr>
<tr><td colspan="4">14．备注</td></tr>
</table>

项目 7

缮制与申领原产地证

学习目标

知识目标：了解原产地证的申领手续和原产地证申请书的内容，掌握一般原产地证和普惠制原产地证的内容与缮制要求。

能力目标：能够根据相关资料缮制原产地证申请书、一般原产地证和普惠制原产地证。

7.1 工作任务

大连思念纺织品进出口公司原产地注册登记手续已于 2010 年在大连出入境检验检疫局办理，企业注册号为 380000031，手签人员为蔡平。2012 年 7 月 16 日，单证员蔡平开始办理合同 PG1061 原产地证的制作与申领手续。

在本业务中，出口方单证员蔡平需要根据合同和信用证的要求，完成以下工作任务。

任务 1 分析信用证中关于原产地证的条款。

任务 2 准确缮制原产地证签证所需要的文件。

任务 3 在规定的时间到相应部门申领原产地证。

7.2 操作步骤

7.2.1 第一步：分析信用证中关于原产地证的条款

单证员蔡平根据合同 PG1061 和信用证的相关条款分析，进口方国家为波兰，属于普惠制给惠国；根据信用证 DCTBT123456 条款 46A“G.S.P. CERTIFICATE OF ORIGIN FORM A IN 1 DUPLICATE STATING THAT THE GOODS ARE OF CHINESE ORIGIN.”，确定需要填制与申领普惠制原产地证。

7.2.2 第二步：缮制原产地证签证所需文件

单证员蔡平根据合同及信用证条款，按规范填写普惠制原产地证申请书、普惠制原产地证 FORM A 并盖章签字。

（1）缮制的普惠制原产地证申请书如表 7-1 所示。

表 7-1 普惠制原产地证申请书

<table>
<tr><td colspan="8">普惠制原产地证申请书
注册号：380000031
申请单位（盖章）：大连思念纺织品进出口公司　　证书号：123800000310020
申请人郑重声明：　　组织机构代码：__________
本人是被正式授权代表出口单位办理和签署本申请书的。
本申请书及普惠制原产地证 FORM A 所列内容正确无误，如发现弄虚作假、冒充 FORM A 所列货物、擅改证书，自愿接受签证机关的处罚及负法律责任。现将有关情况申报如下。</td></tr>
<tr><td>生产单位</td><td colspan="3">辽宁海城创新制衣厂</td><td colspan="2">生产单位联系人</td><td colspan="2">李　力</td></tr>
<tr><td>商品名称
（中英文）</td><td colspan="3">女士针织开衫
(LADIES'S KNITTED CARDIGAN)</td><td colspan="2">H.S.税目号
（以六位数码计）</td><td colspan="2">6110.12</td></tr>
<tr><td colspan="3">商品（FOB）总值（以美元计）</td><td colspan="3">81032.039 美元</td><td>发票号</td><td>12GEP329
8</td></tr>
<tr><td>最终销售国</td><td colspan="2">波兰</td><td colspan="3">证书种类（画“√”）</td><td colspan="2">加急证书
普通证书</td></tr>
<tr><td colspan="3">货物拟出运日期</td><td colspan="5">2012.7</td></tr>
<tr><td colspan="8">贸易方式和企业性质（请在适用处画“√”）</td></tr>
<tr><td>正常贸易
C</td><td>来/进料加工
L</td><td>补偿贸易
B</td><td>中外合资
H</td><td>中外合作
Z</td><td>外商独资
D</td><td>零售
Y</td><td>展卖
M</td></tr>
<tr><td>√</td><td></td><td></td><td></td><td></td><td></td><td></td><td></td></tr>
<tr><td colspan="2">包装数量或毛重或其他数量</td><td colspan="6">235 CTNS　　9 400PCS</td></tr>
<tr><td colspan="8">原产地标准
本项商品系在中国生产，完全符合该给惠国方案规定，其原产地情况符合以下第（　）条；
（1）“P”（完全国产，未使用任何进口原材料）
（2）“W”，H.S.税目号为__________（含进口成分）</td></tr>
</table>

续表

<table>
<tr><td colspan="2">(3)“F”(对加拿大出口产品，其进口成分不超过产品出厂价的 40%)
本批产品系：1．直接运输，从 DALIAN 到 GDANSK
2．转口运输，从 ××× 中转国（地区）＿＿＿到＿＿＿</td></tr>
<tr><td>申请人说明：×××</td><td>领证人（签名）：
电话：
日期：　　年　月　日</td></tr>
<tr><td colspan="2">现提交中国出口商业发票副本一份，普惠制原产地证格式 A（FORM A）一正二副，以及其他附件份，请予审核签证。
注：凡含有进口成分的商品，必须按要求提交《含进口成分受惠商品成本明细单》。</td></tr>
<tr><td>检验检疫局联系记录</td><td></td></tr>
</table>

普惠制原产地证申请书填写规范如下。

1）申请单位。填写申请原产地证的企业并加盖申请单位公章。

2）注册号。填写申请单位在出入境检验检疫局原产地证签证部门注册的注册号。

3）证书号。根据签证当局的编号规则，对应于每批申证货物的编号。不得重号或跳号。

4）生产单位。填写该批出口商品的生产企业。

5）生产单位联系人。填写生产单位的联系人。

6）商品名称。填写商品品名的中英文，并且与商业发票上的商品名称一致。

7）H.S.税目号。填写商品的 H.S. 6 位数编码的前 6 位。

8）商品（FOB）总值。根据申报的出口货物发票上所列的金额以 FOB 价格填写（以美元计）。如果出口货物不是以 FOB 价格成交的，应换算成 FOB 价格。

9）发票号。填写商业发票的号码，并与随附发票相一致。

10）最终销售国。填写货物即将运抵的最终销售国。

11）证书种类。在证书种类前画“√”。

12）货物拟出运日期。如实准确填写货物离开起运口岸的当天日期（年、月、日）。

13）贸易方式和企业性质。根据实际情况选择画“√”。

14）包装数量或毛重或其他数量。填写该批出口货物的箱数、毛重或个数等。

15）原产地标准。根据提示及货物实际情况如实填写。

16）本批产品系。根据货物运输路线的起运港、中转港及目的港填写本批商品运输路线，无转运港的填写“×××”。

17）申请人说明。填写具体说明，如果没有,则填“×××”。

18）领证人。填写领证人签名、电话及日期。

（2）缮制的普惠制原产地证 FORM A 如表 7-2 所示。

表 7-2 普惠制原产地证 FORM A

ORIGINAL

<table>
<tr>
<td>1. Goods consigned from(Exporter's business name, address, country)
DALIAN SINIAN TEXTILES IMP. &EXP. Co. ,LTD
53 ZHIGONG STREET, DALIAN,
P.R. CHINA</td>
<td rowspan="2">Reference No. G123800000310020

GENERALIZED SYSTEM OF PREFERENCE
CERTIFICATE OF ORIGIN
(Combined declaration and certificate)
FORM A
Issued in <u>THE PEOPOE'S REPUBLIC OF CHINA</u>
(Country)
See Noted Overleaf</td>
</tr>
<tr>
<td>2. Goods consigned to (Consignee's name, address, country)
POLISH PULICI TEXTILE GROUP Co.,LTD
UL. KILIŃSKIEGO 57, 27-400 OSTROWIEC ŚW.
POLAND</td>
</tr>
<tr>
<td>3. Means of transport and route(as far as known)
SHIPPED FROM DALIAN TO GDANSK BY SEA</td>
<td>4. For official use</td>
</tr>
</table>

5. Item Number	6. Marks and number of packages	7. Number and kind of packages; description of goods	8. Origin criterion (see notes overleaf)	9. Gross weight or other quantity	10. Number and date of invoices
1	POLISH PG1061 GDANSK C/N：1-235	TWO HUNDRED AND THIRTY FIVE (235) CARTONS OF LADIES’S KNITTED CARDIGAN ******************** ********************	“P”	9 400PCS	12GEP3298 JUN. 25, 2012

续表

11．Certification	12．Declaration by the exporter
It is hereby certified, on the basis of control carried out, the declaration by the exporter is correct. （出入境检验检疫局盖章） DALIAN JUL.16，2012 --- Place and date. signature and stamp of certifying authority	he undersigned hereby declares that the above detail and statements are correct that the goods were produce in -------------------CHINA-----------------------------and that they comply with the original requirements specified_for those goods in the Generalized System of Preferences for goods exported to （大连思念纺织品进出口公司盖章） --------------POLAND------------------- (import country) （蔡平手签） ----DALIAN JUL. 16, 2012---------------------------- Place and date, signature of authorized signatory

普惠制原产地证的右上角是标题栏，填写签证当局所规定的证书号。证书号为 16 位，依次为证书识别代码[FORM A 证书为 G（1 位）]、年份末二位数（2 位）、企业注册号（9 位）、企业自编流水号（4 位）。例如，证书号 G123800000050045 是注册号为 380000005 的单位 2012 年办理的第 45 票 FORM A 证书。除标题栏外，普惠制原产地证 FORM A 共有 12 栏各栏的填写规范如下。

1）出口商的名称、地址、国别[Goods consigned from（Exporter's business name, address, country）]。此栏是带有强制性的，应填明在中国境内的出口商详细地址，包括街道名、门牌号码等。出口商必须是已办理原产地注册的企业，且公司英文名称应与在出入境检验检疫局注册备案的名称一致。此栏切勿出现香港、台湾地区的中间商。

2）收货人的名称、地址、国别[Goods consigned to （Consignee's name, address, country）]。一般应填写给惠国最终收货人名称（信用证上规定的提单通知人或特别声明的收货人）。此栏不能填香港、台湾地区其他中间商的名称。在特殊情况下，此栏也可填上“TO ORDER”或“TO WHOM IT MAY CONCERN”。

3）运输路线及方式（已知）[Means of transport and route（as far as known）]。运输路线始发地应填中国大陆最后一个离境地，如是转运货物，应加上转运港，如“FROM NINGBO TO PIRAEUS，GREECE VIA HONGKONG BY SEA”。运输方式有海运、陆运、空运、海空联运等。一般情况下，目的国跟进口商国家是一致的。特殊情况下，如进口商国家和目的国都是欧盟成员国，则可以不一致，即进口商国别跟运输路线目的国不一致。

4）供签证当局使用（For official use）。此栏由签证当局填写，申请单位应将此栏留空。签证当局根据实际情况，填写如下内容。

① 如属“后发”证书，签证当局会在此栏加打“ISSUED RETROSPECTIVELY”；如

属签发“复本”（重发证书），签证当局会在此栏注明原发证书的编号和签证日期，并声明原发证书作废，其文字是“THIS CERTIFICATE IS IN REPLACEMENT OF CERTIFICATE OF ORIGIN No.… DATED…WHICH IS CANCELLED”，并加打“DUPLICATE”。

② 出口日本产品采用日本原料的，签证当局会在此栏加打“SEE THE ANNEX No.…”。

③ 出口欧盟国家或挪威、瑞士的产品采用上述国家原料的，签证当局会在此栏加打“EC CUMULATION”、“NORWAY CUMULATION”或“SWITZERLAND CUMULATION”。

5）项目编号（Item number）。在收货人、运输条件相同的情况下，如同批出口货物有不同品种，则可按不同品种分列“1”、“2”、“3”……

6）唛头及包装数量（Marks and number of packages）。此栏按实际货物和发票上的唛头，填写完整的图案文字标记及包装号。唛头中处于同一行的内容不要换行打印。货物无唛头时，应填“N/M”。如唛头过多，可填在第 7 ~10 栏的空白处。注意：唛头不得出现“HONGKONG”、“MACAO”、“TAIWAN”、“R.O.C.”等中国大陆以外字样。

7）商品名称、包装数量及种类（Number and kind of packages; description of goods）。商品名称应填写具体，应详细到可以准确判定该商品的 H.S.号。如果信用证中商品名称笼统或拼写错误，则必须在括号内加注具体描述或正确品名。商品名称等项列完后，应在末行加上截止线，以防止他人加填伪造内容。国外信用证有时要求填写合同、信用证号码等，可加在此栏截止线下方，并以“REMARKS:”作为开头。请勿忘记填写包装数量及种类，并在包装数量的英文数字描述后用括号加上阿拉伯数字。

8）原产地标准[Origin criterion（see notes overleaf）]。此栏用字最少，却是国外海关审证的核心项目。含有进口成分的商品，因为其情况复杂，国外要求严格，因此极易弄错而造成退证，应认真审核。一般情况说明如下。

① 完全原产的，填写“P”。

② 含有进口成分，但符合原产地标准，输往下列国家和地区时，填写如下。

a. 输往挪威、瑞士、欧盟、日本、土耳其。填“W”，其后填明出口产品在《商品名称和编码协调制度》中的 4 位数税则号（如“W”96.18）；但属于给惠国成分的进口原料部分可视为本国原料，所以，如果产品的进口成分完全采用给惠国成分，则该产品的原产地标准仍填“P”。

b. 输往加拿大。进口成分占产品出厂价的 40%以下，填“F”。

c. 输往俄罗斯、白俄罗斯、乌克兰、哈萨克斯坦。进口成分不得超过产品离岸价的 50%；填“Y”，其后填明进口原料和部件的价值在出口产品离岸价中所占百分比（如“Y”35%）。

d. 输往澳大利亚和新西兰。本国原料和劳务不低于产品出厂成本的 50%，第 8 栏留空。

9）毛重及数量（Gross weight or other quantity）。此栏应以商品的正常计量单位填，如“只”、“件”、“匹”、“双”、“台”、“打”等。以重量计算的则填毛重，只有净重的，填净重也可以，但要标上“N.W.”（NET WEIGHT）。

10）发票号及日期（Number and date of invoices）。发票内容必须与正式商业发票一致，此栏不得留空。为避免误解，月份一般用英文缩写“JAN.”、“FEB.”、“MAR.”等表示。发票日期年份要填全，如“2008”不能为“08”。发票号太长需换行打印，应使用折行符“-”。发票日期不能迟于提单日期和申报日期。

11）签证当局证明（Certification）。此栏填写签证地址和日期，一般情况下与出口商申报日期、地址一致。签证当局授权签证人员在此栏手签，并加盖签证当局印章。

如果进口国为俄罗斯，则需在此栏加注直属检验检疫局的英文全称，如“NINGBO ENTRY-EXIT INSPECTION AND QUARANTINE BUREAU OF THE PEOPLE'S REPUBLIC OF CHINA”。

注意：签证当局只在普惠制原产地证正本加盖印章。

12）出口商声明（Declaration by the exporter）。生产国的横线上应填上“CHINA”(普惠制原产地证上已印制)。进口国横线上的国名一定要填写正确，进口国必须是给惠国，一般与最终收货人或目的港的国别一致。凡货物发往欧盟国家的，进口国不明确时，进口国可填“E.U.”。

申请单位的申报员应在此栏签字，加盖已注册的中英文合璧签证章，填上申报地点、时间。印章应清晰，如“NINGBO, CHINA MAY 24, 2013”。

注意：申报日期不要填法定休息日，日期不得早于发票日期，一般也不要迟于提单日期，如迟于提单日期，则要申请后发普惠制原产地证。在普惠制原产地证正本和所有副本上盖章签字时避免覆盖进口国名称、生产国名称、申报地址和申报时间。更改证申报日期一般与原证一致，重发证申报日期应为当前日期。

7.2.3 第三步：办理原产地证申领手续

蔡平携带缮制好的《普惠制原产地证申请书》1 份、《普惠制原产地证 FORM A》1 套（1 正 2 副）、正式的出口商业发票副本 1 份，在大连出入境检验检疫局办理普惠制原产地证签证业务并领取证书。

7.3 知识扩展

7.3.1 原产地证

1. 原产地证的定义

原产地证是出口商应进口商要求而提供的，由公证机构、政府或出口商出具的证明货物原产地或制造地的一种证明文件。

2. 原产地证的作用

原产地证的作用如下。

(1) 原产地证是用于确定货物“国籍”的一种特定格式的有效证明文件。

(2) 原产地证是出口国享受配额待遇，体现货物享有关税和非关税待遇的国别政策的凭证。

(3) 原产地证是进口国通关验收、征收关税的有效凭证。

(4) 原产地证是海关统计的主要依据之一。

(5) 原产地证是贸易关系人交接货物、结算货款、索赔理赔的主要依据之一。

3. 原产地证的分类

(1) 一般原产地证。一般原产地证（Certificate of Origin）（简称“产地证”，又称“CO”）是证明货物原产于某一特定国家或地区，享受进口国正常关税（最惠国）待遇的证明文件。它的适用范围包括征收关税、贸易统计、保障措施、歧视性数量限制、反倾销和反补贴、原产地标记、政府采购等。

在我国，一般原产地证可由出口商自行签发，或由出入境检验检疫局签发，或由中国国际贸易促进委员会签发。实际业务中，应根据买卖合同或信用证的规定，提交相应的一般原产地证。在缮制一般原产地证时，应按《中华人民共和国出口货物原产地规则》及其他规定办理。

(2) 普惠制原产地证。普惠制原产地证（Generalized System of Preferences Certificate of Origin）简称“GSP 产地证”，又称“FORM A”。目前，世界上给予我国产品普惠制优惠待遇的国家有 39 个，它们是欧盟 27 国（奥地利、比利时、丹麦、芬兰、法国、德国、希腊、爱尔兰、意大利、卢森堡、荷兰、葡萄牙、西班牙、瑞典、英国、匈牙利、波兰、捷克、斯洛文尼亚、斯洛伐克、爱沙尼亚、立陶宛、马耳他、塞浦路斯、拉脱维亚、罗马尼亚和保加利亚）、瑞士、挪威、列支敦士登、土耳其、日本、加拿大、澳大利亚、新西兰、俄罗斯、乌克兰、白俄罗斯和哈萨克斯坦。

凡向给惠国出口受惠商品，均须提供普惠制原产地证，才能享受关税减免的优惠，所以不管来证是否要求提供这种原产地证，我国出口商均应主动提交。

在我国，普惠制原产地证由出入境检验检疫局签发。

(3) 区域性经济集团互惠原产地证。区域性经济集团互惠原产地证目前主要有《中国–东盟自由贸易区》优惠原产地证、《亚太贸易协定》原产地证、《中国与巴基斯坦自由贸易区》优惠原产地证、《中国–智利自由贸易区》原产地证等。这种原产地证是具有法律效力的在协定成员国之间就特定产品享受互惠减免关税待遇的官方凭证。在我国，区域性经济集团互惠原产地证由出入境检验检疫局签发。

《中国–东盟自由贸易区》优惠原产地证（2004 年 1 月 1 日开始签发）包括的国家有文

莱、柬埔寨、印度尼西亚、老挝、马来西亚、缅甸、菲律宾、新加坡、泰国、越南。

《亚太贸易协定》原产地证（2002 年 10 月 1 日开始签发）包括的国家有韩国、印度、斯里兰卡、孟加拉国。

(4) 专用原产地证。专用原产地证是国际组织和国家根据政策和贸易措施的特殊需要，针对某一特殊行业的特定产品规定的原产地证，主要有输往欧盟蘑菇罐头原产地证、烟草真实性证书等。

7.3.2 一般原产地证的申请与制作

1. 一般原产地证的申请

申请一般原产地证时，需要递交原产地证申请书，如表 7-3 所示。

表 7-3 原产地证申请书

<table>
<tr><td colspan="8">原产地证申请书</td></tr>
<tr><td colspan="8">申请人盖章：（盖章） 注册/登记号： 证书号：
申报员郑重声明：
本人是被正式授权代表申请人申请办理原产地证和签署本申请书的。
本人所提供原产地证及所附单据内容正确无误，如有弄虚作假、冒充证书所列货物、擅改证书等行为，自愿按照有关规定承担法律责任。现将有关情况申报如下。</td></tr>
<tr><td colspan="2">证书种类</td><td colspan="3"></td><td colspan="2">发票号码</td><td></td></tr>
<tr><td colspan="2">最终目的国/地区</td><td></td><td>中转国/地区</td><td colspan="2"></td><td>出运日期</td><td></td></tr>
<tr><td colspan="2">贸易方式</td><td colspan="3">商品 FOB 总值（美元）</td><td colspan="3"></td></tr>
<tr><td>序号</td><td>H.S.税目号（6~10 位）</td><td>货物名称</td><td>进口成分</td><td>生产企业/联系人/电话</td><td>数（重）量</td><td>单位</td><td>FOB 值（美元）</td></tr>
<tr><td></td><td></td><td></td><td></td><td></td><td></td><td></td><td></td></tr>
<tr><td></td><td></td><td></td><td></td><td></td><td></td><td></td><td></td></tr>
<tr><td colspan="8">随附单证</td></tr>
<tr><td colspan="4">备注：</td><td colspan="4">申报员（签名）：
电话：
日期： 年 月 日</td></tr>
</table>

注：① 贸易方式包括一般贸易、进料加工贸易、来料加工贸易、零售贸易、其他贸易方式等。② 进口成分是指产品含非原产成分（包括进口成分和来源地不明的成分）的情况，如果该产品不含非原产成分，则填 0；若含非原产成分，则填非原产成分占产品 FOB 总值的百分比。

2. 一般原产地证的缮制

一般原产地证样本如表 7-4 所示。

表 7-4　一般原产地证

<table>
<tr><td colspan="2">1．Exporter</td><td colspan="3" rowspan="2">Certificate No.
CERTIFICATE OF ORIGIN
OF THE PEOPLE'S REPUBLIC OF CHINA</td></tr>
<tr><td colspan="2">2．Consignee</td></tr>
<tr><td colspan="2">3．Means of transport and route</td><td colspan="3" rowspan="2">5．For certifying authority use only</td></tr>
<tr><td colspan="2">4．Country/region of destination</td></tr>
<tr><td>6．Marks and numbers</td><td>7. Number and kind of packages; description of goods</td><td>8．H.S. code</td><td>9．Quantity</td><td>10．Number and date of invoices</td></tr>
<tr><td colspan="2">11．Declaration by the exporter
The undersigned hereby declares that the above details and statements are correct; that all the goods were produced in china and that they comply with the rules of origin of the people's republic of china.
……………………………………………………
Place and date, signature and stamp of certifying authority</td><td colspan="3">12．Certification
It is hereby certified that the declaration by the exporter is correct.
……………………………………………………
Place and date, signature and stamp of certifying authority</td></tr>
</table>

一般原产地证（以下简称 CO 证书）的右上角是标题栏，填写签证当局所规定的证书号。证书号为 16 位，依次为证书识别代码[CO 证书为 C（1 位）]、年份末二位数（2 位）、企业注册号（9 位）、企业自编流水号（4 位）。例如，证书号 C073800000050045 是注册号为 380000005 的单位 2007 年办理的第 45 票 CO 证书。除标题栏外，CO 证书共有 12 栏，各栏的填写规范如下。

（1）出口商（Exporter）。此栏是带有强制性的，应填明在中国境内的出口商详细名称和地址，包括街道名、门牌号码等。出口商必须是已办理原产地证注册的企业，且公司英文名称应与在出入境检验检疫局注册备案的名称一致。若中间商要求显示其名称，可按如下方式填写："出口商名称 VIA 中间商名称"。

（2）收货人（Consignee）。一般应填写外贸合同中的买方、信用证上规定的提单通知人或特别声明的收货人的名称、地址、国别，如果最终收货人不明确，可填打发票抬头人。为方便外贸需要，此栏也可填上 TO ORDER 或 TO WHOM IT MAY CONCERN。

（3）运输方式及路线（Means of transport and route）。运输路线始发地应填中国大陆最后一个离境地，如系转运货物，应加上转运港，如"FROM NINGBO TO PIRAEUS, GREECE VIA HONG KONG BY SEA"。运输方式有海运、陆运、空运、海空联运等。

（4）目的地国家（地区）（Country/region of destination）。填写货物最终运抵目的地国家或地区，即最终进口国（地区），一般与最终收货人所在国家（地区）一致，不能填写中间商国家名称。

（5）仅供签证当局使用（For certifying authority use only）。此栏由签证当局填写，申请单位应将此栏留空。签证当局根据实际情况，填写如下有关内容。

1）如属“后发”证书，签证当局会在此栏加打“ISSUED RETROSPECTIVELY”。

2）如属签发“复本”（重发证书），签证当局会在此栏注明原发证书的编号和签证日期，并声明原发证书作废，其文字是“THIS CERTIFICATE IS IN REPLACEMENT OF CERTIFICATE OF ORIGIN NO…DATED…WHICH IS CANCELLED”，并加打“DUPLICATE”。

（6）唛头及包装号（Marks and numbers）。此栏按实际货物和发票上的唛头，填写完整的图案文字标记及包装号。唛头中处于同一行的内容不要换行打印。注意内容如下。

1）唛头不得出现“HONG KONG”、“MACAO”、“TAIWAN”、“R.O.C.”等中国大陆以外其他产地制造字样。

2）此栏不得留空。货物无唛头时，应填“N/M”。如唛头过多，可填在第 7～10 栏的空白处。如为图文等较复杂的唛头或内容过多，则可在该栏填上“SEE ATTACHMENT”，并另加附页。附页需一式四份，附页上方填上“ATTACHMENT TO THE CERTIFICATE OF ORIGIN No.…（CO 证书号码）”，附页下方两边分别打上签证地点、签证日期和申报地点、申报日期，左下方盖上申报单位签证章并由申报单位申报员签名。附页应与 CO 证书大小一致。

3）此栏内容及格式必须与实际货物的外包装箱上所刷的内容一致。

（7）商品名称、包装数量及种类（Number and kind of packages; description of goods）。填写包装数量及种类，并在包装数量的英文数字描述后用括号加上阿拉伯数字。如果信用证中商品名称、笼统或拼写错误，则必须在括号内加注具体描述或正确商品名称。商品名称等项列完后，应在末行加上截止线，以防止他人加填伪造内容。国外信用证有时要求填写合同、信用证号码等，可加在此栏截止线下方，并以“REMARKS：”作为开头。例如：

FIVE HUNDRED (500) CTNS OF SHRIMPS

****

REMARKS：

L/C: 2846905067640

（8）H.S.税目号（H.S code）。此栏要求准确填打商品的 4 位数 H.S.税目号，不得留空。

（9）数量(Quantity)。此栏应以商品的正常计量单位填制，如“只”、“件”、“匹”、“双”、“台”、“打”等。以重量计算的可填毛重，也可填净重，如为毛重须加注 G.W.（GROSS WEIGHT），净重则加注 N.W.（NET WEIGHT）。

（10）发票号及日期（Number and date of invoices）。发票内容必须与正式商业发票一致，此栏不得留空。为避免误解，月份一般用英文缩写“JAN.”、“FEB.”、“MAR.”等表示，发票日期年份要填全，如“2007”不能为“07”。发票号太长需换行打印，应使用折行符“-”。发票日期不能迟于提单日期和申报日期。

（11）出口商声明（Declaration by the exporter）。申请单位的申报员应在此栏签字，加盖已注册的中英文合璧签证章，填上申报地点、时间，印章应清晰。例如“NINGBO, CHINA, MAY 24, 2013”。

（12）签证当局证明（Certification）。此栏填打签证地址和日期，一般情况下与出口商申报日期、地址一致。签证当局授权签证人员在此栏手签，并加盖签证当局印章。

注意：签证当局一般只在 CO 证书正本上加盖印章，如客户要求，也可在副本上加盖印章。

7.3.3 出入境检验检疫局原产地证申领程序

1．办理注册登记

申请签发原产地证，必须先办理注册登记，经审核确认有申请资格后，才能按正常程序进行签发原产地证书申请。每个注册企业都有一个注册号，该注册号在申请原产地证时应填在申请书上，供计算机识别使用。自注册之日起满 2 年，需办理年审。

办理注册登记须提交以下资料。

（1）进出口经营权资格批准证书复印件或对外贸易经营者备案登记表复印件。

（2）营业执照复印件及组织机构代码证复印件。

（3）原产地证注册登记表（一式二份）。

（4）产品成本明细单。

（5）产品所用的原辅料、零部件的进料发票复印件。

2．申领原产地证

注册后出入境检验检疫局会对原产地证申请手签人员（申领人员）进行业务培训，考试合格后，签发申报证件。出入境检验检疫局不接受非申领人员办理相关业务。新注册企业的申领人员为临时申领人员。企业变更申领人员须提供情况说明，企业变更申领人员 1 年不超过 2 次。

各单位凭申领员证办理原产地证申领业务，特殊情况下，可凭单位介绍信办理。一般原产地证的申领时间为货物出运 3 日前，普惠制原产地证的申领时间为货物出运 5 日前。

申请原产地证时，申领人员需提交以下文件资料。

（1）普惠制原产地证申请书或一般原产地证申请书一份，申请书需盖申请单位公章。

（2）缮制完整的普惠制原产地证或一般原产地证一套，证书需签字、盖章。签字人员应是取得原产地证申领资格的人员。

（3）正式出口商业发票副本一份，发票需盖章，并应注明包装、数量、毛重，否则还需另附装箱单。

（4）含有进口成分的商品，需提供含进口成分受惠商品成本明细单。

（5）如果后发证书，还需提供提单。

7.4 能力实训

根据信用证（见素材 7-1）和补充信息（见素材 7-2），缮制一般原产地证申请书和一般原产地证。一般原产地证申请书框架如素材 7-3 所示，一般原产地证框架如素材 7-4 所示。

素材 7-1 信用证

RECEIVED FROM: BRITISH BANK OF THE MIDDLE EAST, JEBEL HUSSEIN, AMMAN, JORDAN.	
DESTINATION: THE HONGKONG AND SHANGHAI BANKING CORPORATION LIMITED.	
SEQUENCE OF TOTAL	*27: 1/1
FORM OF DOC. CREDIT	*40B: IRREVOCABLE
DOC. CREDIT NUMBER	*20: DCFJOM978454
DATE OF ISSUE	31: 20090520
APPLICABLE RELUES	*40E: UCP LATEST VERSION
EXPIRY	*31D: DATE 20090730 CHINA
APPLICANT	*50: INTERNATIONAL TRADING AND RE EXPORT Co. P.O.BOX1147.AMMAN-JORDAN.
BENEFICIARY	*59: GOOD FRIEND ARTS AND CRAFTS IMP.&EXP. Co. No.19 SAN TIAO XIANG CHAOZHOU, GUANGDONG CHINA
AMOUNT	*32B: CURRENCY USD AMOUNT 26160.00 CFR AQABA, JORDAN
AVAILABLE WITH/BY	*41D: ANY BANK BY NEGOTIATION
DRAFTS AT: AT SIGHT FOR FULL INVOICE VALUE, MENTIONG THIS DC No.	
DRAWEE	42D: ISSUING BANK
PARTIAL SHIPMENTS	43P: NOT ALLOWED
TRANSSHIPMENT	43T: NOT ALLOWED
PORT OF LOADING	44E: GUANGDONG CHINA
PORT OF DISCHARGE	44F: AQABA, JORDAN
LATEST DATE OF SHIP.	44C: 20090715
DESCRIPT. OF GOODS	45A:

续

24000 PAIRS "EVA"SLIPPER MODEL DO27 SIZE 36-40

24000 PAIRS "EVA"SLIPPER MODEL DO02 SIZE 30-35

ALL IN 4 ASSORTED COLORS, LIGHT BLUE, RED, PINK AND VIOLET

AS PER S/C No.97 ACX417 DATED APRIL 17, 2009

DOCUMENTS REQUIRED 46A:

20．COMMERCIAL INVOICE MANNUALLY SIGNED IN 3 ORIGINALS PLUS 3 COPY .

21．PACKING LIST IN TRIPLICATE.

22．CERTIFICATE OF ORIGIN CERTIFYING THAT THE GOODS EXPORTED ARE OF CHINESE ORIGIN TO BE DULY CERTIFIED BY THE CHINA COUNCIL FOR THE PROMOTION OF INTERNATIONAL TRADE.

ADDITIONAL COND. 47A:

+"MADE IN CHINA" MUST BE STICKED ON EACH PAIR AND THE RELATIVE INVOICES MUST CERTIFY TO THIS EFFECT.

+ INVOICE MUST CERTIFY THAT THE CARTON SIZE ASSORTMENT IS AS FOLLOWS:

FOR SIZE 36-40:36/6, 37/12, 38/15, 39/15, 40/12, EQUAL 60 PAIRS.

FOR SIZE 30-35:30/8, 31/8, 32/10, 33/10, 34/12, 35/12 EQUAL 60 PAIRS

+ALL DOCUMENTS REQUIRED UNDER THIS DOCUMENTARY CREDIT SHOULD BE ISSUED. IN ARABIC AND /OR ENGLISH.

+ALL DOCUMENTS REQUIRES UNDER THIS DOCUMENTARY CREDIT MUST MENTION THIS DC NUMBER AND THE ISSUING BANK NAME.

DETALLS OF CHARGES 71 B:

ALL BANKING CHARGES OUTSIDE JAPAN ARE FOR ACCOUNT OF BENEFICIARY'.

CONFIRMATION *49 :WITHOUT

素材 7-2 补充信息

唛头由受益人决定

商品编码：6405.2000

发票号：4646564

发票日期：2009 年 5 月 29 日

提单日：2009 年 6 月 16 日

素材 7-3　一般原产地证申请书框架

一般原产地证申请书

申请人盖章：（盖章）　　　　　　注册/登记号：　　　　　　证书号：

申报员郑重声明：

本人是被正式授权代表申请人申请办理原产地证和签署本申请书的。

本人所提供原产地证及所附单据内容正确无误，如有弄虚作假、冒充证书所列货物、擅改证书等行为，自愿按照有关规定承担法律责任。现将有关情况申报如下。

证书种类				发票号码			
最终目的国/地区		中转国/地区				出运日期	
贸易方式				商品 FOB 总值（美元）			
序号	H.S.税目号（6~10 位）	货物名称	进口成分	生产企业/联系人/电话	数（重）量	单位	FOB 值（美元）
随附单证							
备注：				申报员（签名）： 电话： 日期：　年　月　日			

素材 7-4　一般原产地证框架

1．Exporter		**Certificate No.**		
2．Consignee		**CERTIFICATE OF ORIGINOF** **THE PEOPLE'S REPUBLIC OF CHINA**		
3．Means of transport and route		5．For certifying authority use only		
4．Country/region of destination				
6．Marks and numbers	7．Number and kind of packages; description of goods	8．H.S. code	9．Quantity	10．Number and date of invoices
11．Declaration by the exporter The undersigned hereby declares that the above details and statements are correct; that all the goods were produced in china and that they comply with		12．Certification It is hereby certified that the declaration by the exporter is correct.		

续

the rules of origin of the people's republic of china. …………………………………………………… Place and date, signature and stamp of certifying authority	…………………………………………………… Place and date, signature and stamp of certifying authority

7.5 能力扩展

请根据 2.5 节能力扩展中的外贸合同（见素材 2-2）及 3.5 节能力扩展中修改后的信用证（见素材 3-5）缮制普惠制原产地证一份。补充信息如素材 7-5 所示，普惠制原产地证框架如素材 7-6 所示。

素材 7-5　补充信息

INVOICE No.: HW001 DATE：FEB.06, 2011 提单号码：BL3213314354 拟出运日期：2011.2.16 船名：SHENGLI 航次：V.945 每箱规格：MEAS: 35×45×50CM/CTN，G.W: 45KGS/CTN，N.W: 40KGS/CTN G.S.P. FORMA：原产地标准“P”

素材 7-6　普惠制原产地证框架

<table>
<tr><td>1．Goods consigned from(Exporter's business name, address, country)</td><td rowspan="2">Reference No.

GENERALIZED SYSTEM OF PREFERENCE
CERTIFICATE OF ORIGIN
(Combined declaration and certificate)
FORM A
Issued in ____________________
(Country)
See Noted Overleaf</td></tr>
<tr><td>2．Goods consigned to (Consignee's name, address,country)</td></tr>
<tr><td>3．Means of transport and route(as far as known)</td><td>4．For official use</td></tr>
</table>

续

<table>
<tr><td>5. Item Number</td><td>6. Marks and number of packages</td><td>7. Number and kind of packages; description of goods</td><td>8. Origin criterion (see notes overleaf)</td><td>9. Gross weight or other quantity</td><td>10. Number and date of invoices</td></tr>
<tr><td colspan="3">11. Certification
It is hereby certified, on the basis of control carried out, the declaration by the exporter is correct.

Place and date. signature and stamp of certifying authority</td><td colspan="3">12. Declaration by the exporter
he undersigned hereby declares that the above detail and statements are correct that the goods were produce in
----
and that they comply with the original requirements specified for those goods in the Generalized System of Preferences for goods exported to
----
(import country)

Place and date, signature of authorized signatory</td></tr>
</table>

项目 8 出口货物报关流程和报关单的填制

学习目标

知识目标：熟悉报关单的种类和用途，了解报关和报关流程。

能力目标：能准确缮制报关单及其他附属单据。

8.1 工作任务

2012 年 7 月 19 日，大连万翔国际货运代理有限公司通知大连思念纺织品进出口公司配舱成功。大连思念纺织品进出口公司外贸单证员蔡平根据相关信息马上制作和备齐出口货物报关单、出口收汇核销单等报关单证，同时与报检委托书、出境货物换证凭条一起寄给大连万翔国际货运代理有限公司，委托其办理报关手续。在本业务中，单证员蔡平需完成以下工作任务。

任务 1 制作出口货物报关单和代理报关委托书。

任务 2 整理报关单据并办理委托报关。

8.2 操作步骤

8.2.1 第一步：制作出口货物报关单

本业务中缮制的出口货物报关单如表 8-1 所示。

表 8-1　出口货物报关单

<table>
<tr><td colspan="9">中华人民共和国出口货物报关单</td></tr>
<tr><td colspan="6">预录入编号：897888789</td><td colspan="3">海关编号：15158815</td></tr>
<tr><td colspan="3">出口口岸
大连海关（0200）</td><td colspan="2">备案号</td><td colspan="2">出口日期
20120726</td><td colspan="2">申报日期
20120722</td></tr>
<tr><td colspan="3">经营单位：大连思念纺织品进出口公司（210221065）</td><td colspan="2">运输方式
水路运输（2）</td><td colspan="2">运输工具名称
JINGBI/HV300W</td><td colspan="2">提运单号
CPNE12789</td></tr>
<tr><td colspan="3">发货单位：大连思念纺织品进出口公司（210221065）</td><td colspan="2">贸易方式
一般贸易（0110）</td><td colspan="2">征免性质
一般征税（101）</td><td colspan="2">结汇方式
信用证（6）</td></tr>
<tr><td colspan="2">许可证号</td><td colspan="2">运抵国（地区）
波兰（327）</td><td colspan="3">指运港
格但斯克</td><td colspan="2">境内货源地
大连</td></tr>
<tr><td colspan="2">批准文号</td><td colspan="2">成交方式
CIF</td><td colspan="2">运费
502 /1500/3</td><td>保险费
502 /3 /1</td><td colspan="2">杂费
502 / 800/3</td></tr>
<tr><td colspan="2">合同协议号
FRJ-016</td><td colspan="2">件数
235</td><td colspan="2">包装种类
纸箱</td><td>毛重（公斤）
3 595.5</td><td colspan="2">净重（公斤）
2 961.0</td></tr>
<tr><td colspan="2">集装箱号
MANU200454 /20/2275</td><td colspan="5">随附单据
Y: 0618985642</td><td colspan="2">生产厂家
辽宁海城创新制衣厂</td></tr>
<tr><td colspan="9">标记唛头及备注
POLISH
PG1061
GDANSK
C/N：1-235</td></tr>
<tr><td>项号</td><td>商品编号</td><td>商品名称、规格型号</td><td>数量及单位</td><td>最终目的国（地区）</td><td>单价</td><td>总价</td><td>币制</td><td>征免</td></tr>
<tr><td>01</td><td>60062200</td><td>女士针织开衫
11574</td><td>2 400 件</td><td>波兰</td><td>6.50</td><td>15 600.00</td><td>EUR</td><td>照章征税</td></tr>
<tr><td></td><td>60062200</td><td>女士针织开衫
11575</td><td>3 000 件</td><td>波兰</td><td>5.50</td><td>16 500.00</td><td>EUR</td><td>照章征税</td></tr>
</table>

续表

<table>
<tr><td>60062200</td><td>女士针织开衫
11576</td><td>2 400 件</td><td>波兰</td><td>8.50</td><td>20 400.00 EUR</td><td>照章征税</td></tr>
<tr><td>60062200</td><td>女士针织开衫
11577</td><td>1 600 件</td><td>波兰</td><td>8.00</td><td>12 800.00 EUR</td><td>照章征税</td></tr>
<tr><td colspan="7">税费征收情况</td></tr>
<tr><td colspan="4">兹声明以上申报无讹并承担法律责任
录入员　录入单位
报关员
报关单位
报关单位地址
报关专用章
邮编　电话　填制日期</td><td colspan="3">海关审单批注及放行日期（签章）
审单　审价
征税　统计
查验　放行</td></tr>
</table>

出口货物报关单与进口货物报关单填写项目大致相同，填写规范如下。

（1）预录入编号。预录入编号是指申报单位或预录入单位对该单位填制录入的报关单的编号，用于该单位与海关之间引用其申报后尚未批准放行的报关单。预录入报关单及 EDI 报关单的预录入编号由接受申报的海关决定编号规则，计算机自动打印。

（2）海关编号。海关编号是指海关接受申报时给予报关单的编号。海关编号由各海关在接受申报环节确定，应标识在报关单的每联上。各直属海关对进口货物报关单和出口货物报关单应分别编号，并确保在同一公历年度内，能按进口和出口唯一地标识本关区的每份报关单。

（3）进口口岸/出口口岸。进口口岸/出口口岸是指货物实际进（出）我国关境口岸海关的名称。本栏应根据货物实际进（出）口的口岸海关选择填报《海关关区代码表》中相应的口岸海关名称及代码。《海关关区代码表》中有隶属海关关别及代码时，则应填报隶属海关名称及代码。

（4）备案号。备案号是指进出口企业在海关办理加工贸易合同备案或征、减、免税审批备案等手续时，海关给予的《进料加工登记手册》、《加工装配和中小型补偿贸易进口货物登记手册》、《中华人民共和国海关对外商投资企业履行产品出口合同所需进口料件加工复出口登记手册》（以下均简称《登记手册》）、《进出口货物征免税证明》（以下简称《征免税证明》）或其他有关备案审批文件的编号。一份报关单只允许填报一个备案号。具体填报要求如下。

1）加工贸易合同项下货物，除少量低价值辅料按规定不使用《登记手册》外，必须在报关单备案号栏目填报《登记手册》的 12 位编码。加工贸易成品凭《征免税证明》转为享受减免税进口货物的，进口货物报关单填报《征免税证明》编号，出口货物报关单填报《登记手册》编号。

2）凡涉及减免税备案审批的报关单，本栏填报《征免税证明》编号，不得为空。

3）无备案审批文件的报关单，本栏免予填报。

备案号长度为 12 位，其中第 1 位是标记代码。备案号的标记代码必须与“贸易方式”及“征免性质”栏相协调，例如，贸易方式为来料加工，征免性质也应当是来料加工，备案号的标记代码应为“B”。

（5）进口日期/出口日期。进口日期指运载所申报货物的运输工具申报进境的日期。本栏填报的日期必须与相应的运输工具进境日期一致。出口日期指运载所申报货物的运输工具办结出境手续的日期。无实际进出境的报关单填报向海关办理申报手续的日期，以海关接受报关申报的日期为准。

本栏为 8 位数，顺序为年（4 位）、月（2 位）、日(2 位)。

（6）申报日期。申报日期是指海关接受进（出）口货物的收发货人或其代理人申请办理货物进（出）口手续的日期。以电子数据报关单方式申报的，申报日期为海关计算机系统接受申报数据记录的日期。以纸质报关单方式申报的，申报日期为海关接受纸质报关单对报关单进行登记处理的日期。

本栏为 8 位数，顺序为年（4 位）、月（2 位）、日（2 位）。

（7）经营单位。经营单位是指对外签订并执行进出口贸易合同的中国境内企业、单位或个人。本栏应填报经营单位名称及经营单位编码。经营单位编码为 10 位数字，指进出口企业在所在地主管海关办理注册登记手续时，海关给企业设置的注册登记编码。

经营单位编码的结构如下。

1）第 1~4 位数为进出口单位属地的行政区划代码，其中第 1、第 2 位数表示省、自治区、直辖市；第 3、第 4 位数表示省辖市（地区、省直辖行政单位）。例如，北京西城区编码为 1102，广州市编码为 4401；如果第 3、第 4 位数用“90”，则表示未列名的省直辖行政单位。

2）第 5 位数为市内经济区划代码，具体含义为：“1”表示经济特区（深圳特区可用“0”）；“2”表示经济技术开发区和上海浦东新区、海南洋浦经济开发区；“3”表示高新技术产业开发区；“4”表示保税区；“5”表示出口加工区；“6”表示保税港区，包括已被整合到综合保税区或保税港区内的出口加工区、保税物流园区、保税区或保税物流中心；“7”表示保税物流园区；“9”表示其他。

3）第 6 位数为进出口企业经济类型代码，具体含义为：“1”表示有进出口经营权的国有企业；“2”表示中外合作企业；“3”表示中外合资企业；“4”表示外商独资企业；“5”表示有进出口经营权的集体企业；“6”表示有进出口经营权的私营企业；“7”表示有进出口经营权的个体工商户；“8”表示有报关权而没有进出口经营权的企业；“9”表示其他，包括外国驻华企事业机构、外国驻华使领馆和临时进出口货物的企业、单位和个人等。

4）第 7~10 位数为顺序编号。

特殊情况下，确定经营单位的原则如下。

1）援助、赠送、捐赠的货物，填报直接接受货物的单位。

2）进出口企业之间相互代理进出口，或没有进出口经营权的企业委托有进出口经营权的企业代理进出口的，填报代理方。

3）外商投资企业委托外贸企业进口投资设备、物品的，填报外商投资企业。

(8) 运输方式。运输方式是指载运货物进出关境所使用的运输工具的分类。本栏应根据实际运输方式按海关规定的《运输方式代码表》选择填报相应的运输方式名称或代码。

(9) 运输工具名称。运输工具名称是指载运货物进出境的运输工具的名称或运输工具编号。本栏填报内容应与运输部门向海关申报的载货清单所列相应内容一致。一份报关单只允许填报一个运输工具名称。

(10) 提运单号。提运单号是指进出口货物提单或运单的编号。本栏填报的内容应与运输部门向海关申报的载货清单所列相应内容一致。一份报关单只允许填报一个提运单号，一票货物对应多个提运单时，应分单填报。

(11) 收货单位/发货单位。收货单位指已知的进口货物在境内的最终消费、使用单位，包括自行从境外进口货物的单位，以及委托有外贸进出口经营权的企业进口货物的单位。发货单位指出口货物在境内的生产或销售单位，包括自行出口货物的单位，以及委托有外贸进出口经营权的企业出口货物的单位。

本栏应填报收（发）货单位的中文名称或其海关注册编码，没有编码的，填报其中文名称。加工贸易报关单的收（发）货单位应与《登记手册》的“货主单位”一致。

(12) 贸易方式（监管方式）。本栏应根据实际情况，按海关规定的《贸易方式代码表》选择填报相应的贸易方式简称或代码。一份报关单只允许填报一种贸易方式。

(13) 征免性质。征免性质是指海关对进出口货物实施征、减、免税管理的性质类别。本栏应按照海关核发的《征免税证明》中批注的征免性质填报，或根据实际情况按海关规定的《征免性质代码表》选择填报相应的征免性质简称或代码。征免性质共 41 种，分为法定照章征税、法定减免税、特定减免税、其他减免税和暂定税率五大类。征免性质代码由 3 位数组成，第 1 位数表示类别，第 2、第 3 位数表示该类别减免税项目的顺序号。一份报关单只允许填报一种征免性质。

(14) 征免比例/结汇方式。征免比例仅用于“非对口合同进料加工”贸易方式下（代码“0715”）进口料件的进口货物报关单，填报海关规定的实际应征税比率，如 5%填报为 5，15%填报为 15。出口报关单应填报结汇方式，即出口货物的发货人或其代理人收结外汇的方式。本栏应按海关规定的《结汇方式代码表》选择填报相应的结汇方式名称或代码。

（15）许可证号。应申领进（出）口许可证的货物，必须在此栏填报中华人民共和国商务部及其授权发证机关签发的进（出）口货物许可证的编号，不得为空。一份报关单只允许填报一个许可证号。

（16）起运国（地区）/运抵国（地区）。起运国（地区）指进口货物起始发出的国家（地区）。运抵国（地区）指出口货物直接运抵的国家（地区）。对发生运输中转的货物，如中转地未发生任何商业性交易，则起运国（地区）/运抵国（地区）不变，如中转地发生商业性交易，则以中转地作为起运国（地区）/运抵国（地区）填报。

本栏应按海关规定的《国别（地区）代码表》选择填报相应的起运国（地区）或运抵国（地区）中文名称或代码。无实际进出境的，本栏填报“中国”（代码“142”）。

（17）装货港/指运港。装货港指进出口货物在运抵我国关境前的最后一个境外装运港。指运港指出口货物运往境外的最终目的港。最终目的港不可预知的，可按尽可能预知的目的港填报。

本栏应根据实际情况按海关规定的《港口航线代码表》选择填报相应的港口中文名称或代码。无实际进出境的，本栏填报“中国境内”（代码“0142”）。

（18）境内目的地/境内货源地。境内目的地指已知的进口货物在国内的消费、使用地或最终运抵地。境内货源地指出口货物在国内的产地或原始发货地。

本栏应根据进口货物的收货单位、出口货物生产厂家或发货单位所属国内地区，并按海关规定的《国内地区代码表》选择填报相应的国内地区名称或代码。

（19）批准文号。过去进口货物报关单本栏用于填报进口付汇核销单编号。出口货物报关单本栏用于填报出口收汇核销单编号。

（20）成交方式。本栏应根据实际成交价格条款按海关规定的《成交方式代码表》选择填报相应的成交方式代码。无实际进出境的，进口填报 CIF 价，出口填报 FOB 价。

（21）运费。本栏用于成交价格中不包含运费的进口货物或成交价格中含有运费的出口货物，应填报该份报关单所含全部货物的国际运输费用。可按运费单价、运费总价或运费率三种方式之一填报，同时注明运费标记，并按海关规定的《货币代码表》选择填报相应的币种代码。运保费合并计算的，运保费填报在本栏。运费标记“1”表示运费率，“2”表示每吨货物的运费单价，“3”表示运费总价。例如，5%的运费率填报为 5，24 美元的运费单价填报为 502/24/2，7 000 美元的运费总价填报为 502/7 000/3。

(22) 保险费。成交价格中不包含保险费的进口货物或成交价格中含有保险费的出口货物，应在本栏填报该份报关单所含全部货物国际运输的保险费用。可按保险费总价或保险费率两种方式之一填报，同时注明保险费标记，并按海关规定的《货币代码表》选择填报相应的币种代码。运保费合并计算的，运保费填报在运费栏中。保险费标记“1”表示保险费率，“3”表示保险费总价。例如，3‰保险费率填报为 0.3；10 000 港元保险费总价填报为 110/10 000/3。

(23) 杂费。杂费是指成交价格以外的、应计入完税价格或应从完税价格中扣除的费用，如手续费、佣金、回扣等，可按杂费总价或杂费率两种方式之一填报，同时注明杂费标记，并按海关规定的《货币代码表》选择填报相应的币种代码。应计入完税价格的杂费填报为正值或正率，应从完税价格中扣除的杂费填报为负值或负率。杂费标记“1”表示杂费率，“3”表示杂费总价。例如，应计入完税价格的 1.5%的杂费率填报为 1.5，应从完税价格中扣除的 1%的回扣率填报为–1，应计入完税价格的 500 英镑杂费总价填报为 303/500/3。

(24) 合同协议号。本栏应填报进（出）口货物合同（协议）的全部字头和号码。

(25) 件数。本栏应填报有外包装的进（出）口货物的实际件数。特殊情况下，填报要求如下。①舱单件数为集装箱（TEU）的，填报集装箱个数。②舱单件数为托盘的，填报托盘数。

本栏目不得填报为 0，裸装货物填报为 1。

(26) 包装种类。本栏应根据进（出）口货物的实际外包装种类，按海关规定的《包装种类代码表》选择填报相应的包装种类代码。

(27) 毛重。毛重指货物及其包装材料的重量之和。本栏填报进（出）口货物实际毛重，计量单位为公斤，不足 1 公斤的填报为 1。

(28) 净重。净重指货物的毛重减去外包装材料后的重量，即商品本身的实际重量。本栏填报进（出）口货物的实际净重，计量单位为公斤，不足 1 公斤的填报为 1。

(29) 集装箱号。集装箱号是在每个集装箱箱体两侧标示的全球唯一的编号。本栏用于填报和打印集装箱编号及数量。集装箱数量四舍五入填报整数，非集装箱货物填报为 0。本栏填报方式为“集装箱号/规格/自重”。在多于 1 个集装箱的情况下，其余集装箱编号打印在备注栏或随附清单上。

(30) 随附单据。随附单据是指随进（出）口货物报关单一并向海关递交的单证或文件，合同、发票、装箱单、许可证等必备的随附单证不在本栏填报。本栏应按海关规定的《监管证件名称代码表》选择填报相应证件的代码与编号。

(31) 用途/生产厂家。进口货物填报用途，应根据进口货物的实际用途按海关规定的《用途代码表》选择填报相应的用途代码，如“以产顶进”填报“13”。生产厂家指出口货物的境内生产企业，本栏供必要时手工填写。

(32) 标记唛头及备注。本栏上部用于打印以下内容。① 标记唛头中除图形以外的文字、数字。② 受外商投资企业委托代理其进口投资设备、物品的外贸企业名称。③ 加工贸易结转货物及凭《征免税证明》转内销货物，其对应的备案号应填报在本栏，即“转至(自) ××××××××××××手册”。④ 其他申报时必须说明的事项。

本栏下部供填报随附单据栏中监管证件的编号，具体填报要求为“监管证件代码：监管证件号码”。一份报关单多个监管证件的，连续填写。

一票货物多个集装箱的，在本栏打印其余的集装箱号（最多 160 字节，其余集装箱号手工抄写）。

(33) 项号。本栏分两行填报及打印。第一行打印报关单中的商品排列序号，第二行专用于加工贸易等已备案的货物，填报和打印该项货物在《登记手册》中的项号。

(34) 商品编号。商品编号指按海关规定的商品分类编码规则确定的进（出）口货物的商品编号。加工贸易《登记手册》中商品编号与实际商品编号不符的，应按实际商品编号填报。

(35) 商品名称、规格型号。本栏分两行填报及打印。第一行打印进（出）口货物规范的中文商品名称，第二行打印规格型号，必要时可加注原文。具体填报要求如下。① 商品名称及规格型号应据实填报，并与所提供的商业发票相符。② 商品名称应当规范，规格型号应当足够详细，以满足海关归类、审价及监管的要求为准。禁止、限制进出口等实施特殊管制的商品，其名称必须与交验的批准证件上的商品名称相符。③ 加工贸易等已备案的货物，本栏填报录入的内容必须与备案登记中同项号下货物的名称与规格型号一致。

(36) 数量及单位。数量及单位是指进（出）口商品的实际数量及计量单位。本栏分三行填报及打印，具体填报要求如下。① 进出口货物必须按海关法定计量单位填报。法定第一计量单位及数量，打印在本栏第一行。② 凡海关列明第二计量单位的，必须报明该商品第二计量单位及数量，打印在本栏第二行。无第二计量单位的，本栏第二行为空。③ 成交计量单位与海关法定计量单位不一致时，还需填报成交计量单位及数量，打印在商品名称、规格型号栏下方（第三行）。成交计量单位与海关法定计量单位一致时，本栏第三行为空。加工贸易等已备案的货物，成交计量单位必须与备案登记中同项号下货物的计量单位一致，不相同时必须修改备案或转换一致后填报。

(37) 原产国（地区）/最终目的国（地区）。原产国（地区）指进出口货物的生产、开采或加工制造国家（地区）。最终目的国（地区）指已知的出口货物最终实际消费、使用或进一步加工制造的国家（地区）。本栏应按海关规定的《国别（地区）代码表》选择填报相应的国家（地区）名称或代码。

加工贸易特殊情况下的填报要求如下。① 料件结转货物，出口货物报关单填报“中国”(代码“142”)，进口货物报关单填报原料件生产国。② 深加工结转货物，进出口货物报关单均填报“中国”（代码“142”）。③ 料件复运出境货物，填报实际最终目的国；加工出口成品因故退运境内的，填报“中国”（代码“142”），复运出境时填报实际最终目的国。

(38) 单价。本栏应填报同一项号下进（出）口货物实际成交的商品单位价格。无实际成交价格的，本栏填报货值。

(39) 总价。本栏应填报同一项号下进（出）口货物实际成交的商品总价。无实际成交价格的，本栏填报货值。

(40) 币制。币制是指进（出）口货物实际成交价格的币种。本栏应根据实际成交情况按海关规定的《货币代码表》选择填报相应的货币名称或代码，如《货币代码表》中无实际成交币种，需转换后填报。

(41) 征免。征免是指海关对进（出）口货物进行征、减、免税或特案处理的实际操作方式。本栏应按照海关核发的《征免税证明》或有关政策规定，对报关单所列每项商品选择填报海关规定的《征减免税方式代码表》中相应的征减免税方式。加工贸易报关单应根据《登记手册》中备案的征免规定填报。

(42) 税费征收情况。本栏供海关批注进（出）口货物税费征收及减免情况。

(43) 录入员。本栏用于预录入和 EDI 报关单，打印录入人员的姓名。

(44) 录入单位。本栏用于预录入和 EDI 报关单，打印录入单位名称。

(45) 申报单位（报关员、报关单位、报关单位地址、邮编、电话）。本栏用于填报申报单位有关情况。申报单位指对申报内容的真实性直接向海关负责的企业或单位。自理报关的，应填报进（出）口货物的经营单位名称及代码；委托代理报关的，应填报经海关批准的专业或代理报关企业名称及代码。本栏还包括报关单位地址、邮编和电话等分项目，由申报单位的报关员填报。

(46) 填制日期。填制日期指报关单的填制日期。预录入和 EDI 报关单由计算机自动打印。本栏为 6 位数，顺序为年、月、日各 2 位。

(47) 海关审单批注及放行日期（签章）。本栏指供海关内部作业时签注的总栏目，由海关关员手工填写在预录入报关单上。其中“放行”栏填写海关对接受申报的进出口货物做出放行决定的日期。

8.2.2 第二步：制作代理报关委托书

由于在现实操作过程中，实际装运时货物数量可能发生变动，蔡平只在代理报关委托书上盖章，而没有填写详细内容，详细内容由报关员在报关时填写。代理报关委托书内容如表 8-2 所示。

表 8-2　代理报关委托书

代 理 报 关 委 托 书

编号：□□□□□□□□□□□□□□

我单位现　(A. 逐票　B. 长期)委托贵公司代理　等通关事宜(A. 填单申报　B. 辅助查验　C. 垫缴税款　D. 办理海关证明联　E. 审批手册　F. 核销手册　G. 申办减免税手续　H. 其他)。详见《委托报关协议》。

我单位保证遵守《海关法》和国家有关法规，保证所提供的情况真实、完整、单货相符。否则，愿承担相关法律责任。

本委托书有效期自签字之日起至　年　月　日止。

委托方（盖章）：

法定代表人或其授权签署《代理报关委托书》的人（签字）

年　月　日

委托报关协议及委托报关协议背面所列通用条款分别如表 8-3 和表 8-4 所示。

表 8-3　委托报关协议

委 托 报 关 协 议

为明确委托报关具体事项和各自责任，双方经平等协商签订协议如下：

委托方		被委托方				
主要货物名称		*报关单编码	No.			
H.S.编码	□□□□□□□□□□	收到单证日期	年　月　日			
货物总价		收到单证情况	合同	□	发票	□
进出口日期	年　月　日		装箱清单	□	提（运）单	□
提单号			加工贸易手册	□	许可证件	□
贸易方式			其他			
原产地/货源地		报关收费	人民币：　元			
其他要求：		承诺说明：				
背面所列通用条款是本协议不可分割的一部分，对本协议的签署构成了对背面通用条款的同意。		背面所列通用条款是本协议不可分割的一部分，对本协议的签署构成了对背面通用条款的同意。				

续表

委托方业务签章： 经办人签章： 联系电话：　　　　　　　年　月　日	被委托方业务签章： 经办报关员签章： 联系电话：　　　　　　　年　月　日
（白联：海关留存　黄联：被委托方留存　红联：委托方留存）　　中国报关协会监制	

表 8-4　委托报关协议通用条款

委托方责任　应及时提供报关、报检所需的全部单证，并对单证的真实性、准确性和完整性负责。 负责在报关企业办结海关手续后，及时、履约支付代理报关费用，支付垫支费用，以及因委托方责任产生的滞报金、滞纳金和海关等执法单位依法处以的各种罚款。 负责按照海关要求将货物运抵指定场所。 负责与被委托方报关员一同协助海关进行查验，回答海关的询问，配合相关调查，并承担产生的相关费用。 在被委托方无法做到报关前提取货样的情况下，承担单货相符的责任。 **被委托方责任**　负责解答委托方有关向海关申报的疑问。 负责对委托方提供的货物情况和单证的真实性、完整性进行“合理审查”，审查内容包括：① 证明进出口货物实际情况的资料，包括进出口货物的品名、规格、用途、产地、贸易方式等。② 有关进出口货物的合同、发票、运输单据、装箱单等商业单据。③ 进出口所需的许可证件及随附单证。④ 海关要求的加工贸易（纸质或电子数据的）及其他进出口单证。 因确定货物的品名、归类等原因，经海关批准，可以看货或提取货样。 在接到委托方交付齐备的随附单证后，负责依据委托方提供的单证，按照《中华人民共和国海关进出口货物报关单填制规范》认真填制报关单，承担“单单相符”的责任，在海关规定和本委托报关协议中约定的时间内报关，办理海关手续。 负责及时通知委托方共同协助海关进行查验，并配合海关开展相关调查。 负责支付因报关企业的责任给委托方造成的直接经济损失，以及所产生的滞报金、滞纳金和海关等执法单位依法处以的各种罚款。 负责在本委托书约定的时间内将办结海关手续的有关委托内容的单证、文件交还委托方或其指定的人员（详见《委托报关协议》“其他要求”栏）。 **赔偿原则**　被委托方不承担因不可抗力而给委托方造成损失的责任。因其他过失造成的损失，由双方自行约定或按国家有关法律法规的规定办理。由此造成的风险，委托方可以以投保方式自行规避。 **不承担的责任**　签约双方各自不承担因另外一方原因造成的直接经济损失，以及滞报金、滞纳金

续表

和相关罚款。 **收费原则** 一般货物报关收费原则上按当地《报关行业收费指导价格》规定执行。特殊商品可由双方另行商定。 **法律强制** 本《委托报关协议》的任一条款与《中华人民共和国海关法》及有关法律、法规不一致时，应以法律、法规为准，但不影响《委托报关协议》其他条款的有效性。 **协商解决事项** 变更、中止本协议或双方发生争议时，按照《中华人民共和国合同法》有关规定及程序处理。因签约双方以外的原因引起的问题或报关业务需要修改协议条款，应协商订立补充协议。双方可以在法律、行政法规准许的范围内另行签署补充条款，但补充条款不得与本协议的内容相抵触。

8.2.3 第三步：整理报关单据并办理委托报关

2012 年 7 月 21 日，大连思念纺织品进出口公司单证员蔡平将出境货物换证凭条和出口货物报关单、代理报关委托书、商业发票、装箱单寄给大连万翔国际货运代理有限公司，委托其向商检局大连分局换出境货物通关单和进行代理报关。

8.3 知识扩展

8.3.1 一般进出口货物的报关

以一般进出口货物为例，报关程序通常分为一般进出口货物申报、配合查验、缴纳税费、提取或装运货物。

1．一般进出口货物申报

（1）申报的含义。申报是指进出口货物收发货人、受委托的报关企业，依照《海关法》及有关法律、行政法规的要求，在规定的期限、地点，采用电子数据报关单和纸质报关单形式，向海关报告实际进出口货物的情况，并接受海关审核的行为。

大连思念纺织品进出口公司具有报关权，既可以选择自理报关，也可以选择委托报关企业代理报关。

（2）申报地点。一般情况下，进口货物应当由收货人或其代理人在货物的进境地海关申报；出口货物应当由发货人或其代理人在货物的出境地海关申报。

经货物收发货人申请，海关同意，进口货物收货人或其代理人可以在设有海关的货物指运地申报；出口货物的发货人可以在设有海关的起运地申报。

大连思念纺织品进出口公司出口的 LADIES'S KNITTED CARDIGAN 装运地点在大连，因此可以选择大连海关进行报关。

(3) 申报期限。进口货物申报期限为自装载货物运输工具申报进境之日起 14 天内（期限的最后一天是法定节假日或星期日的，顺延到节假日或星期日后的第一个工作日）。出口货物申报期限为货物运抵海关监管区后，装货的 24 小时以前。

经电缆、管道或其他方式进出境的货物，按照海关规定定期申报。

(4) 申报日期。申报日期指申报数据被海关接受的日期。无论以电子数据报关单方式申报，还是以纸质报关单方式申报，海关接受申报数据的日期即为申报日期。

采用先以电子数据报关单申报，后提交纸质报关单，或仅以电子数据报关单方式申报的，申报日期为海关计算机系统接受申报数据时记录的日期。

电子数据报关单被退回，重新申报的，申报日期为海关接受重新申报的日期。

海关已经接受电子数据报关单，送人工审核，需对部分内容修改，收发货人修改并重新发送的，申报日期仍为海关原接受申报的日期。

先以纸质报关单申报，后补报电子数据，或只提供纸质报关单申报的，海关工作人员在报关单上做登记处理的日期为海关接受申报的日期。

(5) 申报步骤。

1) 准备申报单证。准备申报单证是报关员开始进行申报工作的第一步，也是整个报关工作能否顺利进行的关键一步。申报单证分为主要单证和随附单证两大类，其中随附单证包括基本单证、特殊单证和预备单证。

主要单证是指报关单，报关单是由报关员按照海关规定格式填制的申报单。

基本单证是指进口货物的货运单据和商业单据，主要有进口提货单据、出口装货单据、商业发票、装箱单等。

特殊单证主要是指进出口许可证件、加工贸易登记手册（包括电子的和纸质的）、特定减免税证明、原产地证、担保文件等。

预备单证主要是指贸易合同、进出口企业的有关证明文件等。海关提出要求时报关单位应提供这些单证，供海关在审单、征税时调阅或收取备案。

准备申报单证的原则是：基本单证、特殊单证和预备单证必须齐全、有效、合法；报关单填制必须真实、准确、完整；报关单与随附单证数据必须一致。

在办理大连思念纺织品进出口公司出口的 LADIES'S KNITTED CARDIGAN 报关手续时，需要准备的单证主要有报关单、出口装货单据、商业发票、装箱单等。

2) 申报前看货取样。进口货物收货人向海关申报前，因确定货物品名、规格、型号、归类等原因，可以向海关提出查看货物或提取货样的书面申请。海关审核同意后，派员到场监管。

由于本业务中的外贸合同只涉及大连思念纺织品进出口公司的货物出口，不涉及进口，因此省略该环节。

3）申报。

① 电子数据申报。电子数据申报是报关员通过计算机系统按照进出口货物报关单规范的要求向海关传送报关单电子数据并备齐随附单证的申报方式。电子数据申报方式有四种：终端申报方式、委托 EDI 申报方式、自行 EDI 方式和网上申报方式。

进出口货物收发货人或其代理人在委托录入或自行录入报关单数据的计算机上接收到海关发送的接收申报信息，即表示电子数据申报成功；接收到海关发送的不接受申报信息后，则应当根据信息提示修改报关单内容后重新申报。

② 提交纸质报关单及随附单证。海关审结电子数据报关单后，进出口货物收发货人或其代理人应当自接到海关"现场交单"或"放行交单"信息之日起 10 日内，持打印的纸质报关单，备齐规定的随附单证并签名盖章，到货物所在地海关提交书面单证，办理相关海关手续。

2．配合查验

（1）海关查验。海关查验是指海关为确定进出口货物收发货人向海关申报的内容是否与进出口货物的真实情况相符，或者为确定进出口货物归类、价格、原产地等，依法对进出口货物进行实际核查的执法行为。

海关查验方法分为彻底查验和抽查。查验操作分为人工查验和设备查验。海关还可以对进出口货物进行复验和径行开验。

（2）报关员配合查验。进出口货物收发货人或其代理人在接到海关查验通知后，要做好配合海关查验的工作，这也是报关员的义务之一。报关员要做好如下配合海关查验的工作。

1）按照海关的要求负责搬运货物、开箱、封箱。

2）如实回答海关提问，提供查验货物所需要的单证或其他资料。

3）协助海关提取需要做进一步检验、化验或鉴定的货样，收取海关开具的取样清单。

4）查验结束后，认真阅读查验人员填写的《海关进出境货物查验记录》，并在审核无误后签字确认。

（3）货物损坏及赔偿。海关的赔偿范围仅限于实施查验过程中（之前和之后损坏，海关不赔偿），由于海关关员的责任造成被查验货物损坏的直接经济损失。

作为报关员，在配合海关查验的过程中，既要积极配合，履行自己的职责，同时也要仔细观察查验过程，对于查验过程中的货物损坏及时提出异议，努力维护自己的正当权益。

3．缴纳税费

缴纳税费是指进出口货物收发货人或其代理人凭海关签发的税费缴税通知书，向海关指定的银行办理税费款项的缴纳手续，通过银行将有关税费款项缴入海关专门账户的工作环节。

4．提取或装运货物

（1）海关出境现场放行。海关出境现场放行是指海关接受进出口货物的申报，审核电子数据报关单和纸质报关单及其随附单证、查验货物、征免税费或接受担保以后，对出口货物做出结束海关出境现场监管的决定，允许进出口货物离开海关监管场所的工作环节。海关进出境现场放行一般由海关在进口提货凭证或出口装运凭证上加盖海关放行章。

（2）办理提取或装运货物手续。提取货物是指进口货物的收货人或其代理人，在办理了进口申报配合查验、纳税等手续，海关放行后，凭加盖海关放行章的进口提货凭证或海关通过计算机系统发送的放行通知书，向承运人或其代理人提取进口货物的工作环节。装运货物是指凭加盖有海关放行章戳记的出口装运凭证办理货物装上运输工具离境的手续。

（3）申请签发报关单证明联和办理其他证明手续。进出口货物收发货人或其代理人办理完提取进口货物或装运出口货物的手续以后，如需要海关签发有关货物的进口、出口货物报关单证明联或办理其他证明手续的，均可向海关提出申请。常见的报关单证明联主要有出口收汇证明联、出口退税证明联等。

8.3.2 报关单

1．报关单的分类

根据用途不同，报关单可分为以下四类。

（1）报关单录入凭单。报关单录入凭单是指申报单位按海关规定的格式填写的凭单，用做报关单预录入的依据（可将现行报关单放大后使用）。

（2）预录入报关单。预录入报关单是指预录入公司录入、打印，并联网将录入数据传送到海关，由申报单位向海关申报的报关单。

（3）EDI 报关单。EDI 报关单是指申报单位采用 EDI 方式向海关申报的电子报文形式的报关单及事后打印、补交备核的书面报关单。

（4）报关单证明联。报关单证明联是指海关在核实货物实际入、出境后按报关单格式提供的证明，用做企业向税务、外汇管理部门办结有关手续的证明文件。

2．报关单各联的用途

（1）海关作业联和留存联。报关单海关作业联和留存联是报关员配合海关审核、海关查验、缴纳税费、提货和装货的重要单据。

（2）企业单位留存联。报关企业留存该联作为合法出境货物的依据，它也是在海关放行货物和结关以后，凭以向海关申领进口付汇证明联、出口收汇证明联和出口退税证明联的文件。

（3）海关核销联。报关单海关核销联是口岸海关对申报进出口货物所签发的证明文件，是海关办理加工贸易合同核销、结案手续的重要凭证之一。加工贸易收发货人在货物进出口后申领海关核销联，凭以向主管海关办理加工贸易登记核销手续。

（4）进口付汇证明联和出口收汇证明联。过去进口付汇证明联和出口收汇证明联是海关对于实际申报进出口货物所签发的证明文件，是银行和国家外汇管理部门办理售汇、付汇、收汇及核销手续的重要凭证之一。对于需要出口收汇核销的货物，发货人向海关申领出口收汇证明联。对于需要进口付汇核销的货物，收货人申领进口付汇证明联。

（5）出口退税证明联。出口退税证明联是海关对已申报出口并装运出境的货物所签发的证明联，是国家税务部门办理出口货物退税手续的凭证之一。对可退税货物，出口发货人或其代理人在货物出运后，向海关申领出口退税证明联，海关核准后签发。不属于退税范围的，海关不予签发。

3．填制报关单的一般要求

进出口货物报关单由海关统一印制，共有 47 栏，除“税费征收情况”及“海关审单批注及放行日期”两栏外，其余均由收发货人或其代理人填写。

（1）申报人必须按照《海关法》、《中华人民共和国海关进出口货物申报管理规定》和《中华人民共和国海关进出口货物报关单填制规范》的有关规定，向海关如实申报，不可以伪报、瞒报、虚报和迟报。

（2）填制内容必须真实，做到“单证相符”和“单货相符”，即所填报关单各栏必须与商业发票、装箱单、批准文件和随附单据相符；必须与实际进出口货物情况相符。

（3）报关单的填报要准确、齐全、完整，字迹清楚，不得用铅笔或红色复写纸填写；若有更正，须在更正项目上加盖校对章。报关单填报项目一般用计算机打印或打字机打印。

（4）不同批文的货物，不同合同的货物，同一批货物不同贸易方式、同一批货物不同运输方式、同一批货物相同运输方式但航次不同的货物，均应分单填报。

（5）一份原产地证只能对应一份报关单。同一份报关单上的同一种商品不能同时享受协定税率和减免税。

（6）一份报关单最多填报 20 项商品。超过 20 项商品时，必须分单填报。一张纸质报关单上最多打印 5 项商品。

（7）反映进出口商品本身情况的项目中，须以相同的项号进行分栏填报。不同项号、商品名称、规格型号、数量及单位和不同的单价等，均要分行填制。

（8）对已向海关申报的报关单，如原填报内容与实际进出口货物不一致而有正当理由的，申报人应向海关递交书面更正申请，海关核准后，对原报关单进行更改或撤销。

（9）使用电子数据报关的，填写一份报关单作为录入原始单据即可。不同的贸易方式和不同性质的报关人，使用不同颜色的报关单。

8.4 能力实训

请根据所提供的素材（见素材 8-1~素材 8-3），按照报关单填制规范的要求，填制报关单（见素材 8-4）。

素材 8-1 背景资料

广州金辉造纸有限公司（海关注册编码 4401442568）委托泛太纸业（东莞）有限公司（海关注册编码 4419931142）进口废纸一批。货物于 2011 年 2 月 23 日由深圳皇岗海关（5301）进境，办理转关手续后运至广州新风海关（5101）办理进口申报手续。

进境载货清单号：100046403117

承运车辆内地车牌号：粤 ZSH90 港

废纸法定计量单位：千克

监管条件：7ABP

固体废物进口许可证编号：SEPAZ2011005846

自动进口许可证编号：11-19WN8334

入境货物通关单编号：470100111005133000

素材 8-2 商业发票

DENISON INTERNATIONAL Co.,LTD.

1302 CAC TOWER, 135 HOI BUN ROAD, KWUN TONG, KOWLOON, HONG KONG

Commercial Invoice

To:

Pan-Pac Paper(Dongguan)Co., Ltd. Invoice No,: CIGD Date: Feb-2011

He Xi Industrial Park, Hong mei, Dongguan, Guangdong, China

Tel: 86 8841×××× Trade Term: C&F Guangzhou

Contract No. :IGD1100223

VIA: BY Truck

POL: Hong Kong

POD: Guangzhou

ETD: 22-Feb-2011

ETA: 23-Feb-2011

Payment Term: L/C 90 days

续表

Country of Origin: USA

AQSIQ Number: A840042910

It is declared of that doesn't contain wood packing material.

Goods Description	Bales	Gross Weight	Net Weight	Unit Price(USD)	Amount(USD)
Waste Paper AOCC#11	55	21.013	21.013MT	291. 8000	6131.59
Total:	55	21.013	21.013MT	291.8000	6131.59

USD SIX THOUSAND ONE HUNDRED THIRTY ONE AND CENTS FIFTY NINE ONLY.

FOR & on behalf of

Denison International Co.,Ltd.

____

Authorized Signature

素材 8-3 装箱单

DENISON INTERNATIONAL Co.,LTD.

1302 CAC TOWER, 135 HOI BUN ROAD, KWUN TONG, KOWLOON, HONG KONG

PAKING LIST

Pan-Pac Paper(Dongguan)Co., Ltd.　　Invoice No.: CIGD　　Date :Feb-2011

He Xi Industrial Park, Hong mei, Dongguan, Guangdong, China

Tel: 86 8841××××　　Trade Term: C&F Guangzhou

Port of Loading :Hong Kong　　Port of Discharge: Guangzhou

ETD :________________　　ETA:__________

Contract No.	S.O.No.	P.O.No.	Price Term	Payment Term
IGD1100223	75433855	75433800	C&F Guangzhou	L/C 90 days

Product Description: Waste Paper AOCC#11

	Container No.	Container Size	No. of Bales	Gross Weight(MT)	Net Weight(MT)
1	FSCU9242766	40ft	55	21.013	21.013
Total	1×40ft		55	21.013	21.013

素材 8-4 进口货物报关单框架

中华人民共和国进口货物报关单				
预录入编号：			海关编号：	
进口口岸	备案号	进口日期	申报日期	
经营单位	运输方式	运输工具名称	提运单号	
收货单位	贸易方式	征免性质	征税比例	
许可证号	起运国（地区）	装货港	境内目的地	
批准文号	成交方式	运费	保险费	杂费
合同协议号	件数	包装种类	毛重（公斤）	净重（公斤）
集装箱号	随附单据			用途
标记唛头及备注				
项号 商品编号 商品名称、规格型号 数量及单位 最终目的国（地区） 单价 总价 币制 征免				
税费征收情况				
录入员 录入单位	兹声明以上申报无讹并承担法律责任		海关审单批注及放行日期（签章）	
报关员			审单	审价
单位地址	申报单位（签章）		征税	统计
邮编 电话	填制日期		查验	放行

8.5 能力扩展

根据 4.5 节能力扩展中涉及的商业发票（见素材 4-5）和装箱单（见素材 4-6），以及相关背景资料，填写出口货物报关单（见素材 8-5）。

素材 8-5 出口货物报关单框架

中华人民共和国海关出口货物报关单				
预录入编号：				海关编号：
出口口岸 2225	备案号		出口日期	申报日期
经营单位	运输方式		运输工具名称	提运单号
发货单位	贸易方式		征免性质	结汇方式
许可证号	运抵国（地区）		指运港	境内货源地
批准文号	成交方式	运费	保险费	杂费

续表

<table>
<tr><td colspan="3">合同协议号</td><td>件数</td><td>包装种类</td><td colspan="2">毛重（公斤）</td><td colspan="2">净重（公斤）</td></tr>
<tr><td colspan="3">集装箱号</td><td colspan="4">随附单据</td><td colspan="2">生产厂家</td></tr>
<tr><td colspan="9">标记唛码及备注</td></tr>
<tr><td>项号</td><td>商品编号</td><td>商品名称、规格型号</td><td>数量及单位</td><td>最终目的国（地区）</td><td>单价</td><td>总价</td><td>币制</td><td>征免</td></tr>
<tr><td colspan="9"></td></tr>
<tr><td colspan="9">税费征收情况</td></tr>
<tr><td colspan="5">录入员　录入单位　兹声明以上申报无讹并承担法律责任
报关员

单位地址　申报单位（签章）
邮编　电话　填制日期</td><td colspan="4">海关审单批注及放行日期（签章）
审单　审价
征税　统计
查验　放行</td></tr>
</table>

项目 9

缮制投保单和办理保险

学习目标

知识目标：了解保险单据的种类及投保流程，掌握信用证关于保险单的条款，掌握保险单填制方法。

能力目标：能办理保险，能正确填制投保单和保险单。

9.1 工作任务

大连思念纺织品进出口公司备妥货，并确定了装运日期和运输工具后，根据项目 4 中 NATIONAL BANK OF POLAND 银行开给受益人大连思念纺织品进出口公司的 DCTBT123456 号信用证（见表 4-1）中的 46A 条款的要求准备货物运输保险单。2012 年 7 月 15 日大连思念纺织品进出口公司的单证员蔡平制作投保单并传真给保险公司；保险公司回传确认件，蔡平审核无误后，在确认件上写“OK”，再传回保险公司；7 月 17 日蔡平到保险公司拿到正本保险单。

在本业务中，出口方单证员蔡平需要完成以下工作任务。

任务 1　制作投保单。

任务 2　办理保险手续。

任务 3　取回保险单。

9.2　操作步骤

9.2.1　第一步：仔细阅读合同中的保险条款

出口方单证员蔡平首先应仔细阅读合同中的保险条款及信用证中与保险有关的条款。

(1) 合同中的保险条款。本业务中保险条款如下。

INSURANCE: TO BE EFFECTED BY THE SELLER FOR 110% OF FULL INVOICE VALUE COVERING ALL RISKS AS PER OCEAN MARINE CARGO CLAUSES OF THE PEOPLE'S INSURANCE COMPANY OF CHINA DATED 1/1, 1981.

(2) 信用证中与保险有关的条款。本业务中有关条款如下。

DOCUMENTS REQUIRED 46A: 4. INSURANCE POLICY/CERTIFICATE IN DUPLICATE BLANK ENDORSED FOR 110% INVOICE VALUE COVERING ALL RISKS SHOWING CLAIMS PAYALBLE IN POLAND IN THE CURRENCY OF THE CREDIT.

9.2.2　第二步：填制投保单，向保险公司投保

出口商备妥货，并确定了装运日期和运输工具后（收到经船公司签署的配舱回单后），单证员蔡平即填制出口货物投保单，随附商业发票等单据，向保险公司投保。

投保单填制主要规范如下。

(1) 保险人。填写承保此批货物的保险公司的名称。通常，各个保险公司会在自己公司的投保单上事先印就以自身为保险人。

(2) 被保险人。除非信用证有特别规定，否则 CIF 交易中一般填写信用证受益人，即出口公司。

(3) 标记。标记即“唛头”，填写货物的装运标志。如唛头比较复杂，也可以简单填写“As per Invoice No.×××”。

(4) 包装及数量。与提单相同，填写总包装件数。以重量计价的包装货，应注明包装件数和计价重量。

(5) 保险货物项目。与提单相同，可填写货物的统称。

(6) 保险金额。保险金额是指保险人对被保险人负担损失补偿或给付约定的最高金额。它是计收保险费的基础（不要把发票金额直接填进去），一般按信用证规定的金额及加成率投保。如信用证对此未做具体规定，则按 CIF 价、CIP 价或发票金额的 110%投保。注意：投保单上的保险金额填法应该是“进一取整”，例如，如果保险金额经计算为 US$11 324.12，则在投保单上应填“US$11 325”。

(7) 开航日期。填写船公司配船资料上的货物装船日期。

（8）运输工具。填写运输工具的名称。如采用海运，则根据配舱回单填写相应的承运船名及航次。

（9）起讫地点。填写信用证规定的货物的装运港口和卸货港口。

（10）投保险别。填写信用证规定的投保险别，包括险种和相应的保险条款等。

（11）投保日期。填写出口公司投保的日期。

（12）投保人签字。盖出口公司的公章并由具体经办人签字。

本业务中缮制的投保单如表 9-1 所示。

表 9-1 投保单

货物运输保险投保单 APPLICATION FOR CARGO TRANSPORTATION INSURANCE				
被保险人（THE INSURED）：DALIAN SINIAN TEXTILES IMP.&EXP. Co., LTD. 发票号（INVOICE No.）：12GEP3298 合同号（CONTRACT No.）：PG1061 信用证号（L/C No.）：DCTBT123456 发票金额：EUR65 300.00　　投保加成（PLUS）：10 % 兹有下列物品向中国人民保险公司大连分公司投保（INSURANCE IS REQUIRED ON THE FOLLOWING COMMODITIES）。				
标记 Marks &Nos.	包装及数量 Quantity	保险货物项目 Description of Goods		保险金额 Amount Insured
POLISH PG1061 GDANSK C/N：1-235	235CTNS	LADIES'S KNITTED CARDIGAN		EUR71 830.00
开航日期 Sailing on or about　AS PER B/L			运输工具 Per Conveyance S.S.　JINGBI/HV300W	
提单号 B/L No.　CPNE12789			赔款偿付地点 Claim Payable at　POLAND IN EUR	
起讫地点 From　DALIAN, CHINA　To　GDANSK, POLAND				
投保险别 Conditions: COVERING ALL RISKS AS PER OCEAN MARINE CARGO CLAUSES OF THE PEOPLE'S INSURANCE COMPANY OF CHINA DATED 1/1, 1981.				

续表

<table>
<tr><td colspan="2">请如实告知下列情况 [如“是”，则在（ ）中画“×”](IF ANY, PLEASE MARK“×”)
1．货物种类（GOODS）
袋装（×）　散装（ ）冷藏（ ）　液体（ ）　活动物（ ）　机器/汽车（ ）　　危险品等级（ ）
BAG/JUMBO BULK　REEFER　LIQUID　LIVEANIMAL　MACHINE/AUTO　DANGEROUS CLASS
2．集装箱种类（CONTAINER）
普通（×）　开顶（ ）　框架（ ）　平板（ ）　冷藏（ ）
ORDINARY　OPEN　FRAME　FLAT　REFRIGERATOR
3．转运工具（BY TRANSIT）
海轮（×）　飞机（ ）　驳船（ ）　火车（ ）　汽车（ ）
SHIP　PLANE　BARGE　TRAIN　TRUCK
4．船舶资料（PARTICULAR OF SHIP）
船籍（ ）　船龄（ ）
RIGISTRY　AGE</td></tr>
<tr><td colspan="2">投保人声明：本投保单及所填各项内容均属事实，同意以本投保单作为保险人签发保险单的依据和保险合同的组成部分。投保人确认在填写本投保单时，保险人已就货物运输条款及附加条款（包括责任免除部分）的内容向投保人做了明确说明。
投保人签字（盖章）　　　投保日期　15-JULY-2012
DALIAN SINIAN TEXTILES IMP. &EXP. Co., LTD.
王小明
备件：被保险人确认本保险合同条款和内容已经完全了解。
THE ASSURED CONFIRMS HEREWITH THE TERMS AND CONDITIONS OF THESE INSURANCE CONTRACT FULLY UNDERSTOOD。</td></tr>
<tr><td colspan="2">本公司自用（FOR OFFICE USE ONLY）
费率
RATE　　　　保险费
PREMIUM</td></tr>
<tr><td>经办人：
日期</td><td>核保人：
日期</td></tr>
</table>

9.2.3　第三步：签发正本保险单

单证员蔡平将填制好的投保单传真给保险公司，保险公司回传确认件，蔡平审核无误后，在确认件上写“OK”，再传回保险公司；蔡平到保险公司缴清保险费后，拿到正本保险单（见表 9-2）。

表 9-2 货物运输保险单

PICC 中国人保财险	货 物 运 输 保 险 单 CARGO TRANSPORTATION INSURANCE POLICY 总公司设于北京　　一九四九年创立 Head Office Beijing　　Established in 1949
发票号（INVOICE No.）：12GEP3298 合同号（CONTRACT No.）：PG1061 信用证号（L/C No.）：DCTBT123456 被保险人： INSURED: DALIAN SINIAN TEXTILES IMP. &EXP. Co., LTD	保险单号次： POLICY No.：12-45013135

中国人民财产保险股份有限公司（以下简称本公司）根据被保险人的要求，由被保险人向本公司缴付约定的保险费，按照本保险单承保险别和背面所载条款与下列特别条款承保下述货物运输保险，特立本保险单。

THIS POLICY OF INSURANCE WITNESSES THAT PICC PROPERTY AND CASUALTY COMPANY LIMITED (HEREINAFTER CALLED "THE COMPANY") AT THE REQUEST OF THE INSURED AND IN CONSIDERATION OF THE AGREED PREMIUM PAID TO THE COMPANY BY THE INSURED, UNDERTAKES TO INSURE THE UNDERMENTIONED GOODS IN TRANSPORTATION SUBJECT TO THE CONDITIONS OF THIS POLICY AS PER THE CLAUSES PRINTED OVERLEAF AND OTHER SPECIAL CLAUSES ATTACHED HEREON.

标记 MARKS & NOS.	包装及数量 QUANTITY	保险货物项目 DESCRIPTION OF GOODS	保险金额 AMOUNT INSURED
POLISH PG1061 GDANSK C/N：1-235	235 CTNS	LADIES'S KNITTED CARDIGAN	EUR71 830.00

总保险金额： TOTAL AMOUNT INSURED:	SAY EURO SEVENTY ONE THOUSAND EIGHT HUNDRED AND THIRTY ONLY.

续表

保险费：　　　　　　　　　　　开航日期　　　　　　　　　　　运输工具：
PERMIUM:　AS ARRANGED　　DATE OF COMMENCEMENT:　　PER CONVEYANCE
AS PER B/L　　JINGBI/HV300W

自　　　　　经
FROM:　DALIAN, CHINA　　VIA　**　　To DANSK, POLAND

承保险别：
CONDITIONS:
COVERING ALL RISKS AS PER OCEAN MARINE CARGO CLAUSES OF THE PEOPLE'S INSURANCE COMPANY OF CHINA DATED 1/1, 1981.

所保货物如发生保险单项下可能引起索赔的损失或损坏，应立即通知本公司下述代理人查勘。如有索赔，应向本公司提交保险单正本（本保险单共有贰份正本）及有关文件。如一份正本已用于索赔，其余正本自动失效。

IN THE EVENT OF LOSS OR DAMAGE WITCH MAY RESULT IN A CLAIM UNDER THIS POLICY, IMMEDIATE NOTICE MUST BE GIVEN TO THE COMPANY'S AGENT AS MENTIONED HEREUNDER. CLAIMS, IF ANY, ONE OF THE ORIGINAL POLICY WHICH HAS BEEN ISSUED IN TWO ORIGINAL(S) TOGETHER WITH THE RELEVANT DOCUMENTS SHALL BE SURRENDERED TO THE COMPANY. IF ONE OF THE ORIGINAL POLICY HAS BEEN ACCOMPLISHED. THE OTHERS TO BE VOID.

赔款偿付地点：　　　　　　　　　　　　　　　　　　　　　中国人民财产保险股份
CLAIM PAYABLE AT/IN：　POLAND IN EURO　　　　　　　　有限公司大连市分公司
出单日期：
ISSUING DATE：　JUL.20.2012　　　　　　　　　　　　General Manager

保险单填写规范如下。

（1）发票号、合同号、信用证号和保险单号次。发票号填写投保货物的商业发票号码；合同号、信用证号据实填写；保险单号次由保险公司编列。

（2）被保险人。被保险人又称“抬头人”，填制规则如下。

1）被保险人通常填写出口商名称，并由出口商做空白背书（BLANK ENDORSED），以表示保险权益的转让。

2）如信用证规定被保险人为受益人以外的某公司或某银行，保险单应直接打该公司或银行名称。这个时候受益人不用背书。

3）如信用证要求保险单做成“TO ORDER”，则应在被保险人栏照打“TO ORDER”并由受益人背书。

4）如果信用证规定保险单背书给特定方，如“ENDORSED TO ORDER OF OPENING BANK”，则在本栏填出口商，并在背面背书，注明“CLAIMS, IF ANY, PAYABLE TO ORDER OF ××××（特定方）”。

（3）标记、包装及数量、保险货物项目和保险金额。这几栏与投保单填写方法一致。

（4）总保险金额。填写大写累计保险金额，大小写金额需保持一致。

（5）保险费。本栏通常不注明具体数字，而分别注明“As arranged”（按约定）。

（6）运输工具。

1）海运方式下填写船名和航次，如“Huanghe V.113”。

2）铁路运输填写“By Railway”或加上车号，如“Wagon No.12345”。

3）航空运输填写“By Air”。

4）邮包运输填写“By Parcel Post”。

（7）开航日期。开航日期也称起运日期（DATE OF COMMENCEMENT），填写提单的签发日期，或简单填写“AS PER B/L”。

（8）起讫地点。在“FROM”之后填写装运港名称，在“TO”之后填写目的港名称，并要与运输单据相符；若货物需要中转，则使用“W/T”或“VIA”，表明进行了中转。

（9）承保险别。应按 L/C（托收方式下按合同）中有关保险险别的条款填写，注意除险别外还要有保险险别适用的文本及其生效日期。

（10）保险单的份数。

1）如果信用证没有明确规定保险单的份数，保险公司一般出具一套三份正本的保险单。

2）在信用证没有特别规定交几份的情况下，必须向银行提交全套正本保险单。

3）如果保险单未注明正本份数，而信用证也没有特别规定，则银行可以接受只提交一份正本的保险单，但该保险单必须注明是唯一正本。

（11）赔款偿付地点。本栏包括保险赔款支付地点和赔付的货币两项内容。

1）应根据信用证（托收方式下按合同）规定填写。如信用证（或合同）未做规定，赔付地点应填目的港（地）名称，币别可不填列。

2）如信用证规定了赔款支付地点，保单应照打。如“CLAIMS, IF ANY, ARE PAYABLE IN JAPAN IN USD”说明赔付地在日本，货币为USD；“INSURANCE CLAIMS PAYABLE AT A THIRD COUNTRY GERMANY”，说明赔付地在德国。

（12）出单日期。出单日期指保险单的签发日期。由于保险公司提供仓至仓条款，所以保险手续应在货物离开出口方仓库前办理。保险单的出单日期不应晚于提单日期。

（13）保险公司签章。由保险公司或其代理人签章。

9.3 知识扩展

9.3.1 海洋货物运输的风险、损失和费用

1．海洋货物运输的风险

海洋货物运输的风险包括两大类：海上风险和外来风险。风险的具体种类如表 9-3 所示。

表 9-3　风险的种类

风险	海上风险	自然灾害：恶劣气候、雷电、洪水、流冰、地震、海啸
		意外事故：搁浅、触礁、沉没、失火、爆炸与流冰等其他物体的碰撞、失踪
	外来风险	一般外来风险：偷窃、雨淋、串味、破损、铁损、渗漏、沾污、受潮、受热、发霉、短量、包装破裂和钩损
		特殊外来风险：战争险、罢工险、类似战争的行为、敌对行为、武装冲突或海盗行为，以及由此引起的捕获、拘留、管制或扣押等

2．海洋货物运输的损失

海洋货物运输的损失即海上损失（Marine Losses），简称海损，是指被保险货物在海洋运输途中，因遭遇海上风险所引起的损坏或灭失，还包括在与海运连接的陆上运输和内河运输过程中遭受的损坏或灭失。海上损失的具体种类如表 9-4 所示。

表 9-4　海上损失的种类

海上损失	全部损失（按程度分）	实际全损
		推定全损
	部分损失（按性质分）	单独海损
		共同海损

3．海洋货物运输的费用

海洋货物运输的费用即海上费用，是指海上风险而造成的费用上的损失。这个费用是由保险公司承担的。

由保险公司承担的费用有施救费用和救助费用两种。所谓施救费用，是指被保险的货物在遭受承保责任范围内的灾害事故时，被保险人或其代理人与保险单的受让人为了避免或减少损失，采取各种抢救或防护措施而支付的合理费用。救助费用则有所不同，它是指被保险货物在遭受了承保责任范围内的灾害事故时，由保险人和被保险人以外的第三者采取了有效的救助措施，在救助成功后，由被救方付给救助方的一种报酬。

9.3.2 常见的货物运输保险条款

常见的货物运输保险条款有英国伦敦保险业协会货物保险条款（Institute Cargo Clauses，ICC）与中国人民保险公司海上货物保险条款（China Insurance Clause，CIC）。两者的比较如表 9-5 所示。

表 9-5 常见的货物运输保险条款的比较

ICC（英国伦敦保险业协会货物保险条款）	CIC（中国人民保险公司海上货物保险条款）
ICC（A）	ALL RISKS（一切险）
ICC（B）	WPA（水渍险）
ICC（C）	FPA（平安险）
附加险（战争险、罢工险、恶意损害险）	一般附加险、特殊附加险
仓至仓条款（W/W）	

9.3.3 保险单据的种类

1．保险单

保险单俗称大保单，是保险人与被保险人之间订立保险合同的一种正式证明，具有法律效力，对双方当事人均具有约束力。

2．保险凭证

保险凭证是一种简化的保险单，与保险单有同等的法律效力，故又称为小保单，但现实中很少使用。保险凭证只有正面，其背面是空白的，没有载明保险条款。

3．预约保险单

预约保险单又称开口保险单，一般用于经常有相同类型货物需要陆续装运的保险。它是保险人与被保险人双方预先签订的、期限较长的一篮子保险合同，规定了保险货物的范围、保险险别、保险责任、费率等，货物一经装运，保险公司自动承保。这种事先预约的保险合同在我国的货物进出口中广泛使用。

4．暂保单

暂保单又称临时保险单，是保险人签发正式保险单前所出立的临时证明。暂保单的有效期一般为 30 天。

5．保险批单

保险批单是保险公司在保险单开立后，根据投保人的需求对保险内容补充或变更而出具的一种凭证。

9.3.4　保险金额和保险费的计算

1．保险金额的计算

保险金额是指保险人承担赔偿或给付保险金责任的最高限额，也是保险人计算保险费的基础。投保人在投保货物运输保险时，应向保险人申请保险金额。保险金额一般是根据保险价值确定的。保险价值一般包括货价、运费、保险费及预期利润等。

在国际贸易中，被保险人按信用证规定的金额及加成率投保。如信用证对此未做具体规定，则按 CIF 价、CIP 价或发票金额的 110%投保。投保单上的保险金额填法应该是“进一取整”。其计算公式如下：

保险金额=CIF（CIP）价×（1+投保加成率）

注意：① 贸易合同中如果不是 CIF 或 CTP 价时，应先将该价格转换为 CIF 或 CIP 价。② 通常来说，如果发票金额含有佣金，无论是否扣佣金均应按毛额（含佣金价格）投保，而含有折扣的，则应按扣除折扣后的净额投保。

2．保险费的计算

投保人交付保险费是保险合同生效的前提条件。保险费是保险公司经营保险业务的基本收入，也是保险公司所掌握的保险基金（赔偿损失基金）的主要来源。

保险费的计算公式如下：

保险费=保险金额×保险费率

保险费= CIF（CIP）价×（1+投保加成率）×保险费率

9.4　能力实训

根据以下信用证内容（见素材 9-1）及补充资料（见素材 9-2）填写一份投保单。

素材 9-1 信用证

RECEIVED FROM: BRITISH BANK OF THE MIDDLE EAST,JEBEL HUSSEIN,AMMAN,JORDAN.	
DESTINATION: THE HONGKONG AND SHANGHAI BANKING CORPORATION LIMITED.	
SEQUENCE OF TOTAL	*27 : 1/1
FORM OF DOC. CREDIT	*40B :IRREVOCABLE
DOC. CREDIT NUMBER	*20 :DCFJOM978454
DATE OF ISSUE	31: 20090520
APPLICABLE RELUES	*40E : UCP LATEST VERSION
EXPIRY	*31D: DATE 20090730 CHINA
APPLICANT	*50: INTERNATIONAL TRADING AND RE EXPORT Co..

续

	P.O.BOX1147.AMMAN-JORDAN.
BENEFICIARY	*59: GOOD FRIEND ARTS AND CRAFTS IMP.&EXP. Co. No.19 SAN TIAO XIANG C HAOZHOU, GUANGDONGCHINA
AMOUNT	*32B: CURRENCY USD AMOUNT 26160.00 CFR AQABA, JORDAN
AVAILABLE WITH/BY	*41D: ANY BANK BY NEGOTIATION
DRAFTS AT: AT SIGHT FOR FULL INVOICE VALUE, MENTIONING THIS DC No.	
DRAWEE	42D: ISSUING BANK
PARTIAL SHIPMENTS	43P: NOT ALLOWED
TRANSSHIPMENT	43T: NOT ALLOWED
PORT OF LOADING	44E: GUANGDONG CHINA
PORT OF DISCHARGE	44F: AQABA, JORDAN
LATEST DATE OF SHIP.	44C: 20090715
DESCRIPT. OF GOODS	45A: 24000 PAIRS "EVA"SLIPPER MODEL DO27 SIZE 36-40 24000 PAIRS "EVA"SLIPPER MODEL DO02 SIZE 30-35 ALL IN 4 ASSORTED COLORS, LIGHT BLUE, RED, PINK AND VIOLET AS PER S/C No.97 ACX417 DATED APRIL 17,2009
DOCUMENTS REQUIRED	46A: 1. COMMERCIAL INVOICE MANNUALLY SIGNED IN 3 ORIGINALS PLUS 3 COPY . 2. PACKING LIST IN TRIPLICATE. 3. CERTIFICATE OF ORIGIN CERTIFYING THAT THE GOODS EXPORTED ARE OF CHINESE ORIGIN TO BE DULY CERTIFIED BY THE CHINA COUNCIL FOR THE PROMOTION OF INTERNATIONAL TRADE.
ADDITIONAL COND.	47A: +"MADE IN CHINA" MUST BE STICKED ON EACH PAIR AND THE RELATIVE INVOICES MUST CERTIFY TO THIS EFFECT. + INVOICE MUST CERTIFY THAT THE CARTON SIZE ASSORTMENT IS AS FOLLOWS: FOR SIZE 36-40:36/6,37/12,38/15,39/15,40/12,EQUAL 60 PAIRS. FOR SIZE 30-35:30/8,31/8,32/10,33/10,34/12,35/12 EQUAL 60 PAIRS +ALL DOCUMENTS REQUIRED UNDER THIS DOCUMENTARY CREDIT SHOULD BE ISSUED. IN ARABIC AND /OR ENGLISH.

续

+ALL DOCUMENTS REQUIRES UNDER THIS DOCUMENTARY CREDIT MUST MENTION THIS DC NUMBER AND THE ISSUING BANK NAME.
DETALLS OF CHARGES　　71B:
ALL BANKING CHARGES OUTSIDE JAPAN ARE FOR ACCOUNT OF BENEFICIARY.
CONFIRMATION　　*49: WITHOUT

素材 9-2　补充资料

唛头由受益人决定
发票号：4646564
发票日期：2009 年 5 月 29 日
提单日：2009 年 6 月 16 日

9.5　能力扩展

请根据 2.5 节能力扩展中拟订好的外贸合同（见素材 2-2）和相应信用证（见素材 4-4）及下列补充资料（见素材 9-3）填制一份保险单（见素材 9-4）。

素材 9-3　补充资料

商业发票号：PC05A031
时间：2011 年 3 月 15 日
提单号：BL3213314354
拟出运日期：2011.3.25
船名：SHENGLI
航次：V.945

素材 9-4　保险单框架

PICC 中国人民财产保险股份有限公司
PICC Property and Casualty Company Limited
总公司设于北京　　　　一九四九年创立
Head Office: BEIJING　　　　Established in 1949
货物运输保险单
CARGO TRANSPORTATION INSURANCE POLICY

续

发票号（INVOICE No.）：　　　　　　　　　　　保险单号次（POLICY No.）：

被保险人（INSURED）：________________________________

中国人民财产保险股份有限公司（以下简称本公司）根据被保险人的要求，以被保险人向本公司缴付约定的保险费为对价，按照本保险单列明条款承保下述货物运输保险，特订立本保险单。

THIS POLICY OF INSURANCE WITNESSES THAT PICC PROPERTY AND CASUALTY COMPANY LIMITED (HEREINAFTER CALLED "THE COMPANY") AT THE REQUEST OF THE INSURED AND IN CONSIDERATION OF THE AGREED PREMIUM PAID TO THE COMPANY BY THE INSURED UNDERTAKES TO INSURE THE UNDERMENTIONED GOODS IN TRANSPORATION SUBJECT TO THE CONDITIONS OF THIS POLICY AS PER THE CLAUSES PRINTED BELOW.

标记 MARKS & NOS.	包装及数量 QUANTITY	保险货物项目 DESCRIPTION OF GOODS	保险金额 AMOUNT INSURED

总保险金额：

TOTAL AMOUNT INSURED: ________________________

保险费：　　　　　　　　　　　　开航日期：

PREMIUM: ______________ ATE OF COMMENCEMENT: ______________

运输工具：

PER CONVEYANCE: ________________________

自：______________至：______________经：______________

FROM: ______________TO:______________VIA:______________

承保险制：

CONDITIONS：

所保货物如发生保险单项下可能引起索赔的损失，应立即通知本公司或下述代理人查勘。如有索赔，应向本公司提交正本保险单（本保险单共有____份正本）及有关证件。如一份正本已用于索赔，其余正本自动失效。

IN THE EVENT OF LOSS OR DAMANGE WHICH MAY RESULT IN A CLAIM UNDER THIS POLICY, IMMEDIATE NOTICE MUST BE GIVEN TO THE COMPANY OR AGENT AS MENTIONED. CLAIMS , IF ANY , ONE OF THE ORIGINAL POLICY WHICH HAS BEEN ISSUED IN_____ ORGINALS TOGETHER WITH THE RELEVANT DOCUMENTS SHALL BE SURRENDERED TO THE COMPANY. IF ONE OF THE ORIGINAL POLICY HAS BEEN ACCOMPLISHED, THE OTHERS TO BE VOID.

续

SURVEY TO BE CARRIED OUT BY A LOCAL COMPETENT SURVEYOR. CLAIM DOCUMENTS TO BE MAILED TO THE UNDERWRITER, WE SHALL EFFECT PAYMENT BY REMITTANCE TO THE CLAIMANT. 赔款偿付地点： CLAIM PAYABLE AT: ____________ 出单日期： ISSUING DATE: __________

项目 10

缮制附属单据

学习目标

知识目标：熟悉装船通知、受益人证明等附属单据的内容及制作。

能力目标：能根据信用证条款或合同条款要求准确缮制各种附属单据。

10.1 工作任务

2012 年 8 月 2 日，大连思念纺织品进出口公司单证员蔡平收到大连万翔国际货运代理有限公司寄来的海运提单（见表 5-5）。按照国际贸易的习惯做法，在装运货物后，发货人应立即（一般在装船后 3 天内）发送装船通知（SHIPPING ADVICE）给买方或其指定的人，从而方便买方办理保险和安排接货等事宜。如卖方未及时发送上述装船通知给买方而使其不能及时办理保险或接货，卖方就应负责赔偿买方由此而引起的一切损害及/或损失。在信用证支付方式下，若信用证有要求，则此项单据就成为卖方交单议付的单证之一。

在本业务中，单证员蔡平要根据收到的海运提单，完成以下工作任务。

任务 1 读懂外贸合同 PG1061（见表 1-1）、信用证 DCTBT123456（见表 4-1）中的有关装船通知的信息。

任务 2 缮制装船通知。

10.2　操作步骤

10.2.1　第一步：阅读信用证中有关装船通知的信息

单证员蔡平认真阅读信用证 DCTBT123456 中的有关装船通知的信息。该信用证中有关装船通知的相关条款如下："SHIPPING ADVICE SHOWING THE NAME OF THE CARRYING VESSEL, DATE OF SHIPMENT, MARKS, QUANTITY, NET WEIGHT AND GROSS WEIGHT OF THE SHIPMENT TO APPLICANT WITHIN 3 DAYS AFTER THE DATE OF BILL OF LADING." 蔡平根据要求开始缮制装船通知。

10.2.2　第二步：根据信用证条款缮制装船通知并传真给进口商

1．装船通知的内容

装运通知没有固定的格式，一般由出口企业自行设计，主要内容如下。

（1）出口企业名称和地址。据实填写出口企业全称和地址。

（2）单据名称。装船通知的单据名称是"SHIPPING ADVICE"。.

（3）抬头。可以填写买方或买方指定的人或保险公司。若抬头为买方指定的保险公司，则应同时注明预保险单合同号（COVER NOTE）。

（4）日期。填写发送装运通知的日期，一般在货物装船后 3 天内。

（5）提单号及船名。应与提单一致。

（6）预计开船日期和到达日期（ETD、ETA）。按船期表所列的日期填写。

（7）装运港、目的港、装运期。按合同或信用证的规定填写，一般与提单一致。

（8）货物描述部分。填写品名、唛头、数量、发票总值等，可以按商业发票的内容填写。

（9）出口公司签章。填写出口公司和经办人签章。

2．本业务中单证员缮制的装船通知

本业务中单证员缮制的装船通知如表 10-1 所示。

接下来，将缮制好的装船通知传真给进口商。

10.3　知识扩展

在国际贸易中，有时进口商或信用证还会要求出具一些与货物的包装、运输等有关的单据，即附属单据。这些附属单据有的是出口企业自行缮制的，有的是其他单位应出口企业的要求而出具的，以补充说明履约情况，便于进口商办理进口和销售手续。虽然这类单据在国际贸易实务中不是必备的，但一旦成为信用证要求的单据，从结汇角度来看，就与发票、提单等单据一样重要，出口企业必须按信用证要求缮制和索取这些单据。它们的名称多样，内容与格式也五花八门，常用的主要有装船通知、受益人证明、有关运输方面的证明（如船公司证明信）等。

表 10-1 装船通知

DALIAN SINIAN TEXTILES IMP.& EXP. Co., LTD.

53 ZHIGONG STREET, DALIAN, P.R. CHINA

Tel: +86 0411 54345659 Fax: +86 0411 54345659

SHIPPING ADVICE

MESSRS: POLISH PULICI TEXTILE GROUP Co., LTD. DATE: AUG.3

UL. KILIŃSKIEGO 57, OSTROWIEC ŚW. ,POLAND INV. No.: 12GEP3298

Tel: +48 41 2651326 L/C No.: DCTBT123456

WE HAVE SHIPPED THE GOODS UNDER S/C No. PG1061 , THE DETAILS OF THE SHIPMENT ARE AS FOLLOWS:

FROM DALIAN **TO** GDANSK **VIA** ********

MARKS	DESCRIPTION OF GOODS	QUANTITY	AMOUNT
Polish PG1061 GDANSK C/N: 1-235	LADIES'S KNITTED CARDIGAN	9 400PCS	EUR65 300.00

VESSEL'S NAME: JINGBI V.036/ HV300W

B/L No.: CPNE12789

G.W. 3595.5KGS

N.W. 2961.0KGS

ETD: JULY 30,2012 **ETA:** AUG.30,2012

DALIAN SINIAN TEXTILES IMP.& EXP. Co., LTD.

蔡 平

10.3.1 装船通知

装船通知是出口方在货物装船后发给进口方的电报通知，其目的是让进口方了解货物已经装船发运，可准备付款接货了。在 FOB、CFR 等条件下成交的合同，需进口方自行办理货物保险的凭证，装船通知应在装船后立即发出，以便进口方办理投保手续。装船通知也可使 CIF、CIP 条件下成交的买方了解货物装运情况、准备接货或筹措资金。买方为了避免未及时得到通知，往往在信用证中明确规定卖方必须按时发出装船通知，并规定通知的内容。而且还规定，在议付时必须提供该装船通知的副本，与其他单据一起向银行议付，因而装船通知也是提交银行结汇的单据之一。但是装船通知并无统一格式，其内容只需要符合信用证的规定。在实际业务中，应根据信用证的要求和对客户的习惯做法，将各项目适当地列明在电文中。

装船通知可采用电报、电传、传真及 E-mail 等各种形式发送。

信用证中有关装船通知的条款举例如下。

（1）“SHIPMENT ADVICE WITH FULL DETAILS INCLUDING SHIPPING MARKS, CARTON NUMBERS, VESSEL'S NAME, BILL OF LADING NUMBER, VALUE AND QUANTITY OF GOODS MUST BE SENT ON THE DATE OF SHIPMENT TO US.”其中文含义是“装船通知须有装运细节，包括唛头、箱号、船名、提单号码和数量，须在装运日通知我们”。

（2）“INSURANCE EFFECTED IN IRAN BY IRAN INSURANCE COMPANY ,THE NAME OF INSURANCE COMPANY AND THE POLICY NUMBER XXX DD.——HAVE TO BE MENTIONED ON B/L SHIPMENT ADVICE TO BE MADE TO SAID INSURANCE COMPANY VIA TLX No.×××INDICATING POLICY NUMBER AND DETAILS OF SHIPMENT,A COPY OF WHICH IS TO BE ACCOMPANIED BY THE ORIGINAL DOCUMENTS.”其中文含义是“保险由伊朗保险公司承保，装船通知必须有上述保险公司及保单号码、装运细节，一张副本必须和其他正本单据附在一起”。

（3）“BENEFICIARY’S CERTIFICATE CERTIFYING THAT SHIPMENT ADVISE AND ABOVEMENTIONED DOCUMENTS HAVE BEEN FAXED TO APPLICANT FOR INSURANCE PURPOSE BEFORE SHIPMENT, FAX COPY WITH TRANSMISSION REPORT IS REQUIRED.”其中文含义是“受益人证书证明装运通知和上述单据已经传真给开证申请人，以在装运前购买保险为目的，需要传真副本”。

10.3.2 受益人证明

受益人证明也称受益人声明，格式多种多样，是一种由受益人自己出具的证明，以便证明自己履行了信用证规定的条款。受益人证明通常是证明货物的品质、唛头、包装标识、装运及其他寄单事项的单据，由受益人根据信用证的要求来缮制；有关运输方面的证明则是卖方为满足买方对货物在运输方面的特殊要求而开立的证明文件，根据情况，它可以由受益人出具，也可以由相关的运输公司出具。

信用证中有关受益人证明的条款举例如下。

(1) "COPY OF LETTER FROM BENEFICIARY TO OUR APPLICANT EVIDENCING A NON NEGOTIABLE BILL OF LADING TOGETHER WITH COPY OF OTHER DOCUMENTS WERE SENT DIRECTLY TO THEM AFTER ONE DAYS FROM SHIPMENT DATE." 其中文含义是"一张受益人发给开证人的证明信，证明一份非议付提单和其他单据一起已经在装船后的一天直接寄给开证人了"。

(2) "A STATEMENT FROM THE BENEFICARY EVIDENCING THAT: PACKING EFFECTED IN 25KGS/CTN BOX." 其中文含义是"一份受益人证明，证明货物包装在每只25公斤的箱内"。

受益人证明样式如表10-2所示。

表10-2 受益人证明

JIAYI IMPORT AND EXPROT CORP.

187 DONGSAN ROAD, NANJING, CHINA

BENEFICIARY'S CERTIFICATE

DATE: Oct.15,2012 PLACE: NANJING

TO WHOM IT MAY CONCERN:

RE: B/L No.: CGLNKG040605 INVOICE No.: SUNJA0406

WE HEREBY DECLARE THAT GOODS UNDER ABOVE MENTIONED B/L ARE WITHOUT WOOD PACKING.

JIAYI IMPORT AND EXPORT CORP.

STAMP

10.3.3 船公司证明信

船公司证明信是船公司出具的单据，是进口商为了满足当局或为了解货物运输情况等要求出口商提供的单据。

常见的船公司证明信有以下几种。

(1) 船龄证明信（CERTIFICATE OF VESSEL'S AGE)。船龄证明信是一种船公司出具的说明载货船舶船龄的证明文件。一般船龄要求在15年之内，如在15年以上则为超龄船只。一般进口商会将此项条款规定在信用证或合同内，如信用证或合同有此条款，出口商须请船公司出具船龄证明信。

(2) 船级证明信（CERTIFICATE OF CLASSFICATION)。船籍证明信是一种船公司出具的证明载货船舶符合一定船级标准的文书。

(3) 黑名单证明信（BLACK LIST CERTIFICATE）。黑名单证明信是某些阿拉伯国家列出的一些与以色列有业务往来的船舶及公司黑名单，若公司及船舶被列入黑名单，阿拉伯国家将不允许他们与本国发生运输业务关系。在阿拉伯国家开出的信用证或合同中常常有此条款规定，因此船公司出具的证明将要满足信用证条款的要求。

(4) 船籍证明信（CETIFICATE OF SHIP'S NATIONALITY）。船籍证明信是船公司说明装载货物船舶的国籍的证明文件。信用证中如有这样的条款，船公司必须出具该证明信，以确定船舶的国籍。

(5) 船长收据（CAPTAIN'S RECEIPT）。船长收据是船长收到随船带交给收货人的单证时的收单证明。进口方为防止单据迟于货物到达或其他原因，常要求出口商将某些单据或一套副本或正本单据在装船时交给载货船舶的船长，随船带交给收货人。出口商将单据交给船长后，船长签发收单证明文件，即船长收据。

10.4 能力实训

请根据 9.4 节能力实训中如素材 9-1 所示的信用证制作下列受益人证明(见素材 10-1)。

素材 10-1 受益人证明框架

BENEFICIARY'S CERTIFICATE
DATE: PLACE:
TO WHOM IT MAY CONCERN:
RE:
STAMP

10.5 能力扩展

根据 2.5 节能力扩展中拟订好的外贸合同（见素材 2-2）和相应信用证（见素材 4-4）及补充资料（见素材 10-2），制作受益人证明。

素材 10-2 补充资料

议付单据中，必须出具一份受益人证明："证明装运后 5 天内，已经将商业发票副本、装箱单副本、正本提单复印件由快递方式直接寄送给开证人，并附快件回执。" 即 "BENEFICIARY'S CERTIFICATE STATING THAT COPY OF COMMERCIAL INVOICE, PACKING LISTS AND A COPY OF BILL OF LOADING WERE SENT DIRECT TO APPLICANT BY COURIER WITHIN 5 DAYS AFTER SHIPMENT. THE RELEATIVE COURIER RECEIPT IS ALSO REQUIRED FOR PRESENTATION."

素材 10-3 受益人证明框架

<table>
<tr><td>

BENEFICIARY'S CERTIFICATE

DATE: PLACE:

TO WHOM IT MAY CONCERN:

RE:

STAMP

</td></tr>
</table>

项目 11

缮制汇票

学习目标

知识目标：了解汇票的种类及汇票的票据行为。
能力目标：能根据合同或信用证的要求，准确缮制汇票。

11.1 工作任务

2012 年 7 月 25 日，大连思念纺织品进出口公司单证员蔡平制作好附属单据后，准备在信用证交单期要求交单之前，根据信用证和商业发票缮制符合信用证要求的汇票。汇票是信用证支付方式下常用的支付工具，一般情况下是一种由出口方开出，要求国外的开证行支付货款给国内的通知行的票据。

在本业务中，单证员蔡平要根据信用证和商业发票的要求，完成以下工作任务。

任务 1 读懂外贸合同 PG1061（见表 1-1）、信用证 DCTBT123456（见表 4-1）和商业发票（见表 4-2）中的有关汇票的信息。

任务 2 根据信用证和商业发票缮制汇票。

11.2 操作步骤

11.2.1 第一步：读懂合同和信用证中的相关信息

单证员蔡平认真阅读合同和信用证，根据合同中的信息及信用证中的条款 42C“AT 30

DAYS AFTER SIGHT”和 42D“NATIONAL BANK OF POLAND”等信息，缮制一张汇票。

11.2.2 第二步：缮制汇票

单证员蔡平根据合同和信用证，填制汇票中的每个项目。

1．汇票填写规范

（1）汇票号码（No.）。一般都以相应的发票号码兼做汇票号码，其用意是核对发票与汇票中相同和相关的内容，如金额、信用证号码等。

（2）汇票小写金额（Exchange for）。汇票小写金额由货币名称缩写和阿拉伯数字组成。金额数保留两位小数，如 USD 123.50、EUR 50 000.00。

（3）汇票大写金额（The Sum of）。汇票的大写金额由货币名称和大写货币金额组成。一般要求顶格填写，以防有人故意在汇票金额上做手脚。货币名称写在大写货币金额之前，大写货币金额后加“ONLY”（整），也可在货币名称前加“SAY”（计）。例如，USD 123.50 大写金额可表述为：“(SAY) UNITED STATES DOLLARS ONE HUNDRED TWENTY THREE AND CENTS/POINT FIFTY ONLY”。

在填制汇票金额时，应注意以下几点。

1）除非信用证另有规定，否则汇票金额应与发票金额一致。

2）如信用证规定汇票金额为发票金额的百分之几，如 97%，那么发票金额应为 100%，汇票金额为 97%，其差额 3%一般为应付的佣金。这种做法通常用于中间商代开信用证的场合。

3）如信用证规定部分信用证付款、部分托收，则分做两套汇票：信用证下支款的汇票按信用证允许的金额填制，其余部分为托收项下汇票的金额，两者之和等于发票金额。

4）如信用证要求两张汇票分别支付一笔交易额，则在两张汇票上填上信用证所要求的金额。

5）汇票金额大、小写必须一致，不得涂改，不允许更改后加盖校对章。

（4）出票日期和出票地点（Date and Place of Issue）。地点一般已印好，无须现填。出票地点后的横线填出票日期，信用证方式下，一般以议付日期作为出票日期。该日期不得早于随附的各种单据的出单日期，同时不能迟于信用证的交单/有效期。该日期一般由银行代填。

（5）汇票付款期限（At…Sight）。汇票付款期限分即期和远期两种。

1）即期汇票，这一栏的填法较简单，只需在横线上用“***”或“– – –”或“×××”表示，也可直接填上“AT SIGHT”，但不能留空。

2）远期汇票，这一栏按信用证的规定填入相应的付款期限。

① 例如，来证规定“draft at 30 days after sight”，这是见票后 30 天付款的远期汇票，

填写时，在这一栏填上“30 DAYS AFTER”。

② 例如，来证规定“draft at 45 days after date”，这是汇票出票日后 45 天付款的远期汇票，填写时，在这一栏填上“45 DAYS AFTER DATE”，并把已印的“sight”划掉。

③ 例如，来证规定“draft at 60 days after the B/L date”，B/L 日期为 AUG. 20, 2012，这是提单日后 60 天付款的远期汇票，填写时，在这一栏填上“60 DAYS AFTER THE B/L DATE，AUG. 20, 2012”，并把已印的“sight”划掉。

④ 例如，来证规定“drafts to be drawn as follows:USD 29 000.00—drafts to be drawn at sight on National Australia Bank LTD., Brisbane, Queensland, Australia USD 21 000.00—drafts to be drawn at 90 days sight on National Australia bank LTD., Brisbane, Queensland, Australia”。这是要求一笔交易分两个期限付款的信用证，需要填写两张汇票。一张在付款期限中用“***”或“– – –”或“× × ×”表示，也可直接填上“AT SIGHT”，该汇票金额为 USD 29 000.00。另一张在付款期限中填“90 DAYS”，表示见票后 90 天付款，该汇票金额为 USD 21 000.00。

(6) 年息（Payable with Interest)。这一栏由结汇银行填写，用以清算企业与银行间的利息费用，信用证若无利息则不用填。出口方不必填写此栏目。

(7) 出票依据。这一栏按信用证的规定填写开证行名称、信用证号码和开证日期。

1) 凭……出票 (Drawn under)。在信用证支付条件下，开证行是提供银行信用的一方，开证行开出的信用证最终伴随所要求的单据成为凭以向买方收款的书面证据。开证行的名称和地址填写在这一栏中，使凭以收款的依据出处一目了然。

2) 信用证号码（L/C No.)。这一栏填写信用证号码。

3) 开证日期（Dated)。这一栏填写信用证的开证日期。常见的错误是将汇票的日期填在这一栏。

(8) 受款人/收款人（Pay to the Order of)，应从信用证角度来理解这一栏的要求。在信用证支付的条件下，汇票中受款人这一栏中填写的应是银行名称和地址，一般都是议付行的名称和地址。究竟要哪家银行作为受款人，这要看信用证中是否有具体的规定。

信用证对受款人的规定通常是通过两种形式表示的。一种是限制受款人，即限制议付行；另一种是不限制受款人，即不限制议付行，可自由议付。

1) 例如，来证规定“By negotiation against the documents detailed herein and beneficiary’s drafts after sight with BANK OF CHINA, HANGZHOU BRANCH”，该证限制在中国银行杭州分行议付，即受款人是中国银行杭州分行。在填写这样要求的汇票时，应在“Pay to the Order of”之后的栏目中填上“BANK OF CHINA, HANGZHOU BRANCH”。

2) 例如，来证规定“By negotiation against the documents detailed herein and beneficiary’s drafts at 30 days after sight with ABC Banking Group LTD. 120 Wall Street, New York, USA”，

该证限制在美国纽约的 ABC 银行集团议付，即受款人是美国纽约的 ABC 银行集团。在填写这样要求的汇票时，应在“Pay to the Order of”之后的栏目中填上“ABC Banking Group LTD. 120 Wall Street, New York, USA”。但是，限制在国外银行议付的来证，受益人往往要仔细考虑是否办得到，这意味着受益人要把全套制作好的单据交到在美国的一家银行，从那里取得货款。对于限制在国外议付的信用证，我方不主张接受。

3）例如，来证规定“By negotiation against the documents detailed herein and beneficiary's drafts at 30 days after sight with any bank in beneficiary's country”，该证不限制议付行，不限制受款人，可在受益人所在国家的任何银行议付。受益人可以在自己的国家里选择任何一家合适的银行作为受款人或议付行。在填写这样要求的汇票时，应在此栏目中直接填入选择好的银行名称、地址。如选择中国银行杭州分行议付的，则在此栏目中填上“BANK OF CHINA，HANGZHOU BRANCH”。

（9）付款人（To）。在信用证方式下，应按照信用证的规定，以开证行或其指定的付款行为付款人。倘若信用证中未指定付款人，则应填写开证行。

（10）出票人（Drawer）。虽然汇票上没有出票人栏，但出票人却是汇票的必要内容，习惯上在右下角空白处盖上出票人全称印章和其负责人手签印章。一般填信用证的受益人，多数情况下为出口公司，但在可转让信用证情况下，也有可能填信用证的第二受益人。

汇票在没有特殊规定时，都打两张，一式两份。汇票一般都在醒目的位置上印着“1”、“2”字样，表示第一联和第二联。汇票的第一联和第二联在法律效力上无区别。第一联生效则第二联自动作废，第二联生效则第一联自动作废，即付一不付二，付二不付一。

2．本业务中单证员缮制的汇票

本业务中单证员缮制的汇票如表 11-1 所示。

表 11-1　汇票

BILL OF EXCHANGE
No.: 12GEP3298　　　　Date: Jul.5, 2012
Exchange for: EUR 65 300.00
DALIAN
At 30 DAYS AFTER sight of this first of exchange (second of exchange unpaid) pay to the order of BANK OF CHINA, DALIAN BRANCH the sum of SAY EURO SIXTY FIVE THOUSAND THREE HUNDRED ONLY.
Payable with interest@____% per annum
Drawn under NATIONAL BANK OF POLAND., P.O.BOX 586, GDANSK, POLAND
L/C No. DCTBT123456 　Dated JUN.28, 2012

续表

To: ATIONAL BANK OF POLAND DALIAN TEXTILES IMP.&EXP. Co.,LTD 王小明

11.3　知识扩展

11.3.1　汇票的定义

《中华人民共和国票据法》第 19 条对汇票下了如下定义："汇票是出票人签发的，委托付款人在见票时或在指定日期无条件支付确定的金额给收款人或其指定人或持票人的票据。"

11.3.2　汇票的种类

汇票可从不同角度进行分类。

1．按照出票人不同，汇票可分为银行汇票和商业汇票

银行汇票的出票人是银行。在国际结算中，银行汇票签发后，一般交付款人，由付款人寄交国外收款人向指定的付款行取款。出票行签发汇票后，必须将付款通知书寄给国外付款行，以便付款行在收款人持票取款时进行核对。银行汇票一般为光票，不随附货运单据。

商业汇票的出票人是工商企业或个人。在国际结算中，商业汇票通常由出口方开立，供国外进口方或银行收取货款时使用。商业汇票的出票人不必向付款人寄送付款通知书。商业汇票大都附有货运单据。在信用证结算中，通常使用的是商业汇票。

2．按照付款时间不同，汇票可分为即期汇票和远期汇票

见票即付的是即期汇票，将来某一时间付款的是远期汇票。远期汇票的付款日期主要有以下几种记载方法。① 规定某一个特定日期，即指定日付款。② 付款人见票后若干天付款。③ 出票日后若干天付款。④ 运输单据日后若干天付款，其中，较多用"提单日期后若干天付款"。

3．按照承兑人不同，汇票可分为商业承兑汇票和银行承兑汇票

商业承兑汇票是由工商企业或个人承兑的远期汇票。商业承兑汇票建立在商业信用的基础上，其出票人也是工商企业或个人。

银行承兑汇票是由银行承兑的远期商业汇票。银行承兑汇票通常由出口人签发，银行对汇票承兑后即成为该汇票的主债务人，而出票人则成为次债务人。所以银行承兑汇票是建立在银行信用的基础之上的。

4．按照是否附有货运单据，汇票可分为光票和跟单汇票

光票是指不附带货运单据的汇票。光票的流通全靠出票人、付款人或出让人（背书人）的信用。在国际结算中，光票除少量用于货款结算外，一般仅限于贸易从属费用、货款尾款、佣金等的托收或支付时使用。

跟单汇票是指附有货运单据的汇票。跟单汇票的付款以附交货运单据为条件，付款人要取得货运单据提取货物，必须付清货款或提供一定的担保。跟单汇票体现了钱款与单据对流的原则，对进出口双方提供了一定的安全保证。在国际结算中，大都采用跟单汇票作为结算工具。

一份汇票通常同时具备几种属性，如一份商业汇票，可以是即期的跟单汇票，或远期的银行承兑跟单汇票，或远期的商业承兑跟单汇票。

11.3.3 汇票的票据行为

汇票的票据行为随汇票是即期还是远期而有所不同。即期汇票只需经过出票、提示和付款三个步骤。远期汇票需经过承兑手续。如需流通转让，通常要经过背书。汇票遭到拒付时，还要涉及做成拒绝证明、依法行使追索权等法律问题。以下分别介绍几种常见的票据行为。

1．出票

出票（Draw/Issue）是指出票人签发票据并将其交付给收款人的票据行为。出票由两个行为组成，一是由出票人写成汇票，并在汇票上签字；二是由出票人将汇票交付给收款人。由于出票是设立债权债务的行为，所以，只有经过交付，汇票才开始生效。

出票人签发汇票后，即承担保证该汇票必然会被承兑和/或付款的责任。出票人在汇票得不到承兑或付款时，应当向持票人清偿被拒绝付款的汇票金额和自到期日或提示付款日起到清偿日止的利息，以及取得拒绝证明和发出被拒绝通知等的费用。

2．提示

提示（Presentation）是指收款人或持票人将汇票提交付款人要求付款或承兑的行为。提示可分为以下两种。

（1）提示承兑。提示承兑是指远期汇票持票人向付款人出示汇票，并要求付款人承诺付款的行为。

（2）提示付款。提示付款是指汇票的持票人向付款人（或远期汇票的承兑人）出示汇票，要求付款人（或远期汇票的承兑人）付款的行为。

3．承兑

承兑（Acceptance）是指汇票付款人承诺在汇票到期日支付汇票金额的票据行为。汇票一经承兑，付款人就成为汇票的承兑人，并成为汇票的主债务人，而出票人便成为汇票的次债务人。

4．付款

付款（Payment）是指付款人向持票人支付汇票金额的行为。即期汇票在付款人见票时照付；远期汇票于到期日在持票人作提示付款时由付款人付款。汇票一经付款，汇票上的一切债务即告结束。

5．背书

背书（Endorsement）是一种以转让票据权利为目的的行为。背书通常由持票人在汇票的背书或粘单上签上自己的名字，或者再加上受让人即被背书人的名称，并把汇票交给受让人。汇票经过背书后，收款的权利就转让给了受让人，由被背书人取得了汇票的所有权。出让人对受让人负有保证汇票必然会被承兑或付款的担保责任。

6．拒付与追索

拒付（Dishonor）包括拒绝付款和拒绝承兑两个内容。汇票被拒付时，持票人除可向承兑人追索（Recourse）外，还有权向其前手，包括所有的背书人和出票人行使追索权。持票人进行追索时，应将拒付事实书面通知其前手，并提供被拒绝承兑或被拒绝付款的证明或退票理由。持票人不能出示拒绝证明、退票理由的，丧失对其前手的追索权。追索的金额包括被拒付的汇票金额和自到期日或提示付款日起到清偿日止的利息，以及取得拒绝证明和向前手发出被拒绝通知的费用。

11.4 能力实训

实训 1 根据下列资料（见素材 11-1）填制汇票（见素材 11-2）。

素材 11-1 相关资料

(1) ISSUING BANK: BANK OF CHINA, SIGAPORE；DATED: APR.2, 2012

(2) L/C No.: 12234

(3) L/C AMOUNT: USD 9900.00

(4) EXPIRY DATE: MAY.31, 2012

(5) B/L DATED: MAY.5, 2012

(6) APPLICANT: OVERSEAS TRADE COMPANY, SINGAPORE

(7) BENEFICIARY: HUNAN TRADING Co., LTD. CREDIT AVAILABLE WITH FREELY NEGOTIABLE BY ANY BANK BY NEGOTIATION

续

(8) WE OPEN IRREVOCABLE DOCUMENTARY CREDIT AVAILABLE BY NEGOTIATION AGAINST PRESENTATION OF THE DOCUMENTS DETAILED HEREIN AND OF BENEFICIARY'S DRAFTS IN DUPLICATE AT SIGHT DRAWN ON US. (9) QUANTITY OF GOODS: 1000 KGS NET (10) UNIT PRICE: USD 9.00 PER KG CIF SINGAPORE (11) INVOICE No.: 56789

素材 11-2　汇票框架

BILL OF EXCHANGE No.　　　　　　　　　　Date: For: At_______ sight of this second of exchange (first of the same tenor and date unpaid) pay to the order of the sum of ___________. Drawn under_________ L/C No. _________Dated___________ To:

实训 2　根据下列资料（见素材 11-3）填制汇票（见素材 11-4）。

素材 11-3　相关资料

(1) ISSUING BANK: THE BANK OF TOKYOL, LTD., NAGOYA OFFICE P.O.BOX 240, NAGOYA-NAKA,NAGOYA 460-91 JAPAN (2) PLACE AND DATE OF L/C: NAGOYA OCT.6,2013 (3) L/C No.: 123A-456 (4) BENEFICIARY: ZHENJIANG KINGTEX TRADING Co., LTD. No.165 ZHONGHE ZHONG ROAD HANGZHOU CHINA (5) ADVISING BANK: BANK OF CHINA, ZHEJIANG BRANCH (6) AMOUNT: USD 66500.00 (7) CREDIT AVAILABLE WITH FREELY NEGOTIABLE BY ANY BANK BY NEGOTIATION. AGAINST PRESENTATION OF THE DOCUMENTS DETAILED HEREIN AND OF YOUR DRAFTS AT SIGHT FOR FULL INVOICE COST DRAWN ON THE BANK OF TOKYO, LTD., NEW YORK AGENCY, NEW YORK, N.Y..

续

(8) PARTIAL SHIPMENTS: ALLOWED

(9) COVERING: 100% COTTON QUILT CASE # 1234 7000 PCS AT USD4.60 # 1235 7000 PCS AT USD4.90

(10) TRADE TERMS: CFR KOBE

(11) 货物实际分三批装，第一批（# 1234 1000 件；# 1235 1000 件）于 2013 年 11 月 30 日装运完毕。出口方于 2013 年 12 月 5 日交单议付。发票号码为 ZJ200311。

素材 11-4　汇票框架

BILL OF EXCHANGE

No. ________

Exchange for________,________China________ 2012.

At________sight of this First of exchange (second of exchange being unpaid) pay to the order of the sum of ________.

Payable with interest@________% per annum

To:________

Drawn under________

L/C No. ________　　Dated________

11.5　能力扩展

请根据 3.5 节能力扩展中审核改正后的信用证（见素材 3-5）和 4.5 节能力扩展中缮制的商业发票（见素材 4-5）填制下列汇票（见素材 11-5）。

素材 11-5　汇票框架

BILL OF EXCHANGE

DRAWN UNDER

L/C No. ________DATED________

PAYABLE WITH INTEREST @________%________ No. ________

EXCHANGE FOR________,________CHINA________

AT___SIGHT OF THIS FIRST EXCHANGE(SECOND OF EXCHANGE BEING UNPAID) PAY ________

THE SUM OF________

TO____________________________

项目 12

单据审核

学习目标

知识目标：熟悉审单的原则、方法和常见的单据不符点。

能力目标：能审核商业发票、运输单据、保险单、汇票及原产地证、装箱单等单据。

12.1 工作任务

2012 年 8 月 3 日，大连思念纺织品进出口公司单证员蔡平制作信用证项下的全套单据后，在交单结汇前根据信用证及《UCP 600》反复审核，确认无误后准备到银行办理交单和押汇。

在本业务中，单证员蔡平要根据信用条款和各种单据，完成以下工作任务。

任务 1 根据信用证条款审核商业发票。

任务 2 根据信用证条款、商业发票审核装箱单。

任务 3 根据信用证条款、商业发票、装箱单审核原产地证。

任务 4 根据信用证条款、商业发票、装箱单审核海运提单。

任务 5 根据信用证条款、商业发票、装箱单和海运提单审核保险单。

任务 6 根据信用证条款、商业发票审核汇票。

12.2 操作步骤

12.2.1 第一步：阅读信用证内容

单证员蔡平首先认真阅读信用证内容。本业务中的信用证如表 12-1 所示。

表 12-1 信用证

MESSAGE TYPE: MT700	ISSUE OF A DOCUMENTARY CREDIT
SEQUENCE OF TOTAL	*27: 1/1
FORM OF DOC. CREDIT	*40B: IRREVOCABLE
DOC. CREDIT NUMBER	*20: DCTBT123456
DATE OF ISSUE	31: 120628
APPLICABLE RELUES	*40E: UCP LATEST VERSION
EXPIRY	*31D: DATE 121013 IN CHINA
ALLICANT BANK	51D: NATIONAL BANK OF POLAND
	P.O.BOX 586, GDANSK, POLAND
APPLICANT	*50: POLISH PULICI TEXTILE GROUP Co., LTD.
	UL. KILIŃSKIEGO 57,OSTROWIEC ŚW.
POLAND	
BENEFICIARY	*59: DALIAN SINIAN TEXTILES IMP. &EXP. Co., LTD.
	53 ZHIGONG STREET, DALIAN,
P.R. CHINA	
AMOUNT	*32B: CURRENCY EUR AMOUNT 65 300.00
AVAILABLE WITH/BY	*41D: ANY BANK BY NEGOTIATION
DRAFTS AT…	42C: AT 30 DAYS AFTER SIGHT
DRAWEE	42D: NATIONAL BANK OF POLAND
PARTIAL SHIPMENTS	43P: ALLOWED
TRANSSHIPMENT	43T: ALLOWED
PORT OF LOADING	44E: DALIAN IN CHINA
PORT OF DISCHARGE	44F: GDANSK, POLAND
LATEST DATE OF SHIP.	44C: 120730
DESCRIPT OF GOODS	45A:
CIFC5 GDANSK LADIES'S KNITTED CARDIGAN	

续表

AS PER PURCHASE CONTRACT No. PG1061

LADIES'S KNITTED CARDIGA PACKED IN 40PCS/CTN

Article no. 11574 2400PCS AT EUR6.50/PC

11575 3000PCS AT EUR 5.50/PC

11576 2400PCS AT EUR 8.50/PC

11577 1600PCS AT EUR 8.00/PC

DOCUMENTS REQUIRED 46A:

1．COMMERCIAL INVOICE MANNUALLY SIGNED IN 2 ORIGINALS PLUS 1 COPY.

2．PACKING LIST IN TRIPLICATE.

3．FULL SET OF ORIGINAL CLEAN ON BOARD BILL OF LADING PLUSE 3/3 NON NEGOTIABLE COPIES,MADE OUT TO ORDER OF ISSUING BANK AND BLANK ENDORSED NOTIFY THE APPLICANT, MARKED FREGHT PREPAID.

4．INSURANCE POLICY/CERTIFICATE IN DUPLICATE BLANK ENDORSED FOR 110% INVOICE VALUE COVERING ALL RISKS SHOWING CLAIMS PAYALBLE IN POLAND IN THE CURRENCY OF THE CREDIT.

5．G.S.P. CERTIFICATE OF ORIGIN FORM A IN 1 DUPLICATE STATING THAT THE GOODS ARE OF CHINESE ORIGIN.

6．PRESHIPMENT INSPECTION CERTIFICATE ISSUED BY A REPRSENTATIVE OF GOOD TRADE. LTD WITH POSITIVE RESULT.

ADDITIONAL COND. 47A:

+ALL DOCS MUST BE ISSUED IN ENGLISH.

+DOCUMENTS ISSUED PRIOR TO L/C ISSUING DATE ARE NOT ACCEPTABLE.

+SHIPMENT MUST BE EFFECTED BY FCL.

+B/L MUST SHOW SHIPPING MARKS: POLISH/PG1061/GDANSK/C/N：1-UP.

+ DOCUMENTS MUST BE PRESENTED WITHIN 14 DAYS AFTER SHIPMENT DATE BUT IN ANY EVENT NOT LATER THAN THE EXPIRY DATE OF THIS CREDIT.

+FOR DOCS WHICH DO NOT COMPLY WITH L/C TERMS AND CONDITIONS, WE SHALL DEDUCT FROM PROCEEDS A CHARGE OF EUR50.00 PAYABLE IN USD EQUIVALENT PLUS ANY INCURRED SWIFT CHARGES IN CONNECTION WITH.

DETALLS OF CHARGES 71B:

ALL CHARGES OUTSIDE POLANDARE ARE ON BENEFICIARY'S ACCOUNT.

PRESENTATION PERIOD 48: 15 DAYS AFTER B/L DATE, BUT WITHIN L/C VALIDITY.

CONFIRMATION *49 :WITHOUT

12.2.2 第二步：审核商业发票，找出不符点

对照信用证条款审核商业发票。审核的商业发票如表 12-2 所示。

表 12-2 商业发票

TWO ORIGINAL ONE COPIES

COMMERCIAL INVOICE

SELLER DALIAN SINIAN TEXTILES IMP.& EXP. Co., LTD. 53 ZHIGONG STREET, DALIAN, P.R. CHINA Tel: +86 0411 54345659 Fax: +86 0411 54345659 BUYER POLISH PULICI TEXTILE GROUP Co., LTD. UL. KILIŃSKIEGO 57,OSTROWIEC ŚW. POLAND Tel: +48 41 2651326	INVOICE NO: 12GEP3298 DATE: JULY.10,2012 S/C No.: PG1061 S/C DATE: JUN.9,2012 L/C No.: DCTBT123456 L/C DATE: JUNE 28,2012 ISSUED By: NATIONAL BANK OF POLAND

FROM: DALIAN TO: GDANSK BY SEA

MARKS	DESCRIPTION	QUANTITIES	UNIT PRICE	AMOUNT
Polish	LADIES'S KNITTED CARDIGAN			
PG1061	Article no. 11574	2 400 PCS	EUR 6.50/PC	EUR15 600.00
GDANSK	11575	3 000 PCS	EUR 5.50/PC	EUR16 500.00
C/N：1-235	11576	2 400 PCS	EUR 8.50/PC	EUR20 400.00
	11577	1 600 PCS	EUR 8.00/PC	EUR12 800.00
	PACKEDIN 40PCS/CTN, TOTALLY TWO HUNDRED AND FOURTY-FIVE CARTONS ONLY.			
TOTAL		9 400 PCS		EUR 65 300.00
TOTAL AMOUNT IN WORDS		SAY EURO SIXTY FIVE THOUSAND THREE HUNDRED ONLY.		

本业务中，通过审核，发现商业发票中存在以下不符点：商业发票没有手签；单价栏漏填贸易术语“CIF GDANSK POLAND”。

12.2.3 第三步：审核装箱单，找出不符点

对照信用证、商业发票审核装箱单。审核的装箱单如表 12-3 所示。

表 12-3 装箱单

DALIAN SINIAN TEXTILES IMP.& EXP. Co., LTD.

53 ZHIGONG STREET, DALIAN,P.R. CHINA

Tel: +86 0411 54345659 Fax: +86 0411 54345659

PACKING LIST

TO: POLISH PULICI TEXTILE GROUP Co., LTD. INVOICE No.: 12GEP3298

UL. KILIŃSKIEGO 57,OSTROWIEC ŚW. POLAND DATE：JULY.10, 2012

Tel: +48 41 2651326

Marks & No.	Number and kind of packages Description of Goods	PACKAGE (CARTON)	Weights(kgs)		Meas.(M^3)
			N.W.	G.W.	
Polish	LADIES'S KNITTED				
PG1061	CARDIGAN	60 CTNS	756.0KGS	918.0KGS	5.670 M^3
GDANSK	Article no. 11574	75 CTNS	945.0KGS	1 147.5KGS	7.088 M^3
C/N：1-235	11575	60 CTNS	756.0KGS	918.0KGS	5.670 M^3
1-60	11576	40 CTNS	504.0KGS	612.0KGS	3.780 M^3
61-135	EACH PIECE IN A				
136-195	POLYBAG, 40 POLYBAGS				
196-235	TO ONE EXPORT				
	STANDARD CARTON.				
TOTAL		235 CTNS	2 961.00kgs	3 595.50kgs	22.208 M^3

SAY TOTAL: TWO HUNDRED AND THIRTY-FIVE CARTONS ONLY.

DALIAN SINIAN TEXTILES IMP. & EXP. Co., LTD.

蔡平

通过审核，发现装箱单存在以下不符点：商品描述栏漏填货号“11577”。

12.2.4 第四步：审核原产地证，找出不符点

对照信用证、商业发票和装箱单审核原产地证。审核的原产地证如表 12-4 所示。

表 12-4 原产地证

1．Goods consigned from(Exporter's business name, address, country) DALIAN SINIAN TEXTILES IMP. &EXP. Co.,LTD. 53 ZHIGONG STREET, DALIAN, P.R. CHINA	Reference No. **G123800000310020** **GENERALIZED SYSTEM OF PREFERENCE** **CERTIFICATE OF ORIGIN** (Combined declaration and certificate) FORM A Issued in **THE PEOPOE'S REPUBLIC OF CHINA** (Country) See Noted Overleaf
2．Goods consigned to (Consignee's name, address, country) POLISH PULICI TEXTILE GROUP Co., LTD. UL. KILIŃSKIEGO 57, 27-400 OSTROWIEC ŚW. POLAND	
3．Means of transport and route(as far as known) SHIPPED FROM DALIAN TO GDANSK BY SEA	4．For official use

5．Item number	6．Marks and number of packages	7．Number and kind of packages; description of goods	8．Origin criterion(see note overleaf)	9．Gross weight or other quantity	10. Number and date of invoices
1	POLISH PG1061 GDANSK C/N：1-235	TWO HUNDRED AND THIRTY FIVE (235) CARTONS OF LADIES'S KNITTED CARDIGAN		9 400 PCS	12GEP3298 JUNE. 25, 2012

11．Certification It is hereby certified,on the basis of control carried out, the declaration by the exporter is correct. （出入境检验检疫局盖章） DALIAN JUL.16，2012 -- Place and date. signature and stamp of certifying authority	12．Declaration by the exporter The undersigned hereby declares that the above detail and statements are correct that the goods were produce in------------------CHINA----------------------------------- and that they comply with the original requirements specified for those goods in the Generalized System of Preferences for goods exported to **（大连思念纺织品进出口公司盖章）**
	-------------POLISH-- (import country)（蔡平手签）---- DALIAN JUL. 16, 2012------------------------------ Place and date, signature of authorized signatory

通过审核，发现原产地证存在以下不符点：货物描述栏漏打结束符；原产地标准栏漏填“P”。

12.2.5 第五步：审核海运提单，找出不符点

对照信用证、商业发票、装箱单审核海运提单。审核的海运提单如表 12-5 所示。

表 12-5 海运提单

<table>
<tr><td colspan="2">SHIPPER
DALIAN SINIAN TEXTILES IMP. &EXP. Co.,LTD.
53 ZHIGONG STREET, DALIAN,
P.R. CHINA</td><td rowspan="6">B/L No. CPNE12789
COSCO
中国远洋运输（集团）总公司
CHINA OCEAN SHIPPING (GROUP) Co.
ORIGINAL
Combined Transport Bill of Lading</td></tr>
<tr><td colspan="2">CONSIGNEE
POLISH PULICI TEXTILE GROUP Co., LTD.
UL. KILIŃSKIEGO 57, 27-400 OSTROWIEC Ś W. POLAND</td></tr>
<tr><td colspan="2">NOTIFY PARTY
POLISH PULICI TEXTILE GROUP Co., LTD.
UL. KILIŃSKIEGO 57, 27-400 OSTROWIEC Ś W. POLAND</td></tr>
<tr><td>PLACE OF RECEIPT</td><td>OCEAN VESSEL
JINGBI</td></tr>
<tr><td>VOY. No.
HV300W</td><td>PORT OF LOADING
DALIAN,CHINA</td></tr>
<tr><td>PORT OF DISCHARGE
GDANSK,POLAND</td><td>PLACE OF DELIVERY</td></tr>
</table>

MARKS	NOS. & KINDS OF PKGS	DESCRIPTION OF GOODS	G.W.(KG)	MEAS(M^3)
POLISH PG1061 GDANSK C/N：1-235	235CTNS	LADIES'S KNITTED CARDIGAN	3 595.50KGS	22.208M^3

TOTAL NUMBER OF CONTAINERS OR PACKAGES(IN WORDS)
SAY TWO HUNDRED AND THIRTY FIVE CARTONS ONLY

续表

<table>
<tr><td>FREIGHT & CHARGES
FREIGHT COLLECT</td><td>REVENUE TONS</td><td>RATE</td><td>PER</td><td>PREPAID</td><td>COLLECT</td></tr>
<tr><td>PREPAID AT</td><td>PAYABLE AT</td><td colspan="4">PLACE AND DATE OF ISSUE
DALIAN, JUL. 30,2012</td></tr>
<tr><td>TOTAL PREPAID</td><td>NUMBER OF ORIGINAL B(S)L
THREE(3)</td><td colspan="4" rowspan="4">SIGNED FOR THE CARRIER

中国远洋运输（集团）总公司
CHINA OCEAN SHIPPING (GROUP) Co.
×××</td></tr>
<tr><td colspan="2">LOADING ON BOARD THE VESSEL</td></tr>
<tr><td>DATE

JUL.30, 2012</td><td>BY：中国远洋运输（集团）总公司
CHINA OCEAN SHIPPING (GROUP) Co.
×××</td></tr>
<tr><td colspan="2">Endorsement：
POLISH PULICI TEXTILE GROUP Co., LTD.
蔡平
JUL.30, 2012</td></tr>
</table>

通过审核，发现海运提单中存在以下不符点：收货人为进口商不妥，应做成指示提单“TO ORDER OF ISSUING BANK”；运费的支付方式“FREIGHT COLLECT”错误，正确的是“FREIGHT PREPAID”。

12.2.6 第六步：审核保险单，找出不符点

根据信用证、商业发票、装箱单和海运提单审核保险单。审核的保险单如表 12-6 所示。

表 12-6 保险单

<table>
<tr><td colspan="2">PICC
中国人保财险</td><td colspan="3">货 物 运 输 保 险 单
CARGO TRANSPORTATION INSURANCE POLICY
总公司设于北京　　　一九四九年创立
Head Office Beijing　　　Established in 1949</td></tr>
<tr><td>发票号（INVOICE No.)：</td><td>12GEP3298</td><td>保单号次</td><td></td><td></td></tr>
<tr><td>合同号（CONTRACT No.)：</td><td>PG1061</td><td>(POLICY No.)：</td><td>12-45013135</td><td></td></tr>
<tr><td>信用证号（L/C No.)：</td><td>DCTBT123456</td><td></td><td></td><td></td></tr>
</table>

续表

<table>
<tr><td colspan="4">被保险人：
INSURED: DALIAN SINIAN TEXTILES IMP.&EXP. Co. LTD</td></tr>
<tr><td colspan="4">中国人民财产保险股份有限公司（以下简称本公司）根据被保险人的要求，由被保险人向本公司缴付约定的保险费，按照本保险单承保险别和背面所载条款与下列特别条款承保下述货物运输保险，特立本保险单。
THIS POLICY OF INSURANCE WITNESSES THAT PICC PROPERTY AND CASUALTY COMPANY LIMITED (HEREINAFTER CALLED “THE COMPANY”) AT THE REQUEST OF THE INSURED AND IN CONSIDERATION OF THE AGREED PREMIUM PAID TO THE COMPANY BY THE INSURED, UNDERTAKES TO INSURE THE UNDERMENTIONED GOODS IN TRANSPORTATION SUBJECT TO THE CONDITIONS OF THIS POLICY AS PER THE CLAUSES PRINTED OVERLEAF AND OTHER SPECIAL CLAUSES ATTACHED HEREON.</td></tr>
<tr><td>标　记
MARKS & NOS.</td><td>包装及数量
QUANTITY</td><td>保险货物项目
DESCRIPTION OF GOODS</td><td>保险金额
AMOUNT INSURED</td></tr>
<tr><td>POLISH
PG1061
GDANSK
C/N:1-235</td><td>235 CTNS</td><td>LADIES'S KNITTED CARDIGAN</td><td>EUR71 830.00</td></tr>
<tr><td colspan="4">总保险金额
TOTAL AMOUNT INSURED:
SAY EURO SEVENTY ONE THOUSAND EIGHT HUNDRED AND THIRTY ONLY.
保险费：　开航日期：
PERMIUM: AS ARRANGED DATE OF COMMENCEMENT: AS PER B/L
运输工具：
PER CONVEYANCE: JINGBI/HV300W
自　经　至
FROM: DALIAN, CHINA　VIA ***　TO:GDANSK,POLAND A
承保险别：
CONDITIONS:
COVERING ALL RISKS AND WAR RISKS AS PER OCEAN MARINE CARGO CLAUSES OF THE PEOPLE'S INSURANCE COMPANY OF CHINA DATED 1/1, 1981.
所保货物，如发生保险单项下可能引起索赔的损失或损坏，应立即通知本公司下述代理人查勘。如有索赔，应向本公司提交保险单正本（本保险单共有贰份正本）及有关文件。如一份正本已用于索赔，其余正本自动失效。</td></tr>
</table>

续表

IN THE EVENT OF LOSS OR DAMAGE WITCH MAY RESULT IN A CLAIM UNDER THIS POLICY, IMMEDIATE NOTICE MUST BE GIVEN TO THE COMPANY'S AGENT AS MENTIONED HEREUNDER. CLAIMS, IF ANY, ONE OF THE ORIGINAL POLICY WHICH HAS BEEN ISSUED IN**TWO** ORIGINAL(S) TOGETHER WITH THE RELEVANT DOCUMENTS SHALL BE SURRENDERED TO THE COMPANY. IF ONE OF THE ORIGINAL POLICY HAS BEEN ACCOMPLISHED. THE OTHERS TO BE VOID.		
赔款偿付地点 CLAIM PAYABLE AT/IN	POLAND IN EURO	中国人民财产保险股份有限公司大连市分公司 PICC Property and Casualty Company Limited, DALIAN BRANCH
出单日期 ISSUING DATE	AUG. 2, 2012	GENERAL MANAGER

通过审核，发现保险单中存在以下不符点：保险单日期晚于装运日期，投保的险别应仅有一切险，而无战争险。

12.2.7　第七步：审核汇票，找出不符点

根据信用证和商业发票审核汇票。审核的汇票如表 12-7 所示。

表 12-7　汇票

BILL OF EXCHANGE	
No.: 12GEP3298	Date: AUG.4, 2012
For: USD 65 300.00	DALIAN
At ******* sight of this first of exchange (second of exchange unpaid) pay to the order of BANK OF CHINA, DALIAN BRANCH the sum of SAY U.S.DOLLARS SIXTY FIVE THOUSAND THREE HUNDRED ONLY.	
Payable with interest@____% per annum	
Drawn under NATIONAL BANK OF POLAND., P.O.BOX 586, GDANSK, POLAND	
L/C No. DCTBT123456 Dated JUN.28, 2012	
To. NATIONAL BANK OF POLAND	DALIAN TEXTILES IMP.&EXP. Co.,LTD. 王小明

通过审核，发现汇票中存在以下不符点：币制应该是欧元，而不是美元；付款期限应是“at 30 days after sight”，而非“at sight”。

综上所述，全套结汇单据存在下列不符点：

（1）商业发票没有手签，且单价栏漏填贸易术语“CIF GDANSK POLAND”。

（2）装箱单商品描述栏漏填货号“11577”。

(3) 原产地证中的货物描述栏漏打结束符；原产地标准栏漏填“P”。

(4) 海运提单中收货人栏填写错误，应填写“TO ORDER OF ISSUING BANK”；运费支付方式错误，应填写“FREIGHT PREPAID”。

(5) 保险单中的出单日期晚于装运日期，且投保险别多选了“战争险”。

(6) 汇票中的币制错误，应是欧元；付款期限错误，应是“at 30 days after sight”。

12.3 知识扩展

12.3.1 单证审核的基本方法

单证审核的基本方法包括纵向审核法和横向审核法。

纵向审核法是指以信用证或合同（在非信用证付款条件下）为基础对规定的各项单据进行一一审核，要求有关单据的内容严格符合信用证的规定，做到“单证相符”。

横向审核法在纵向审核法的基础上，以商业发票为中心审核其他规定的单据，使有关的内容相互一致，做到“单单相符”。

12.3.2 单证审核的要点

1. 综合审核的要点

单证的综合审核包括如下要点。① 检查规定的单证是否齐全，所需单证的份数也要检查。② 检查所提供的文件名称和类型是否符合要求。③ 检查需要认证的单证是否按规定进行了认证。④ 检查单证之间的货物描述、数量、金额、重量、体积、运输标志等是否一致。⑤ 检查单证出具或提交的日期是否符合要求。

2. 分类审核的要点

(1) 汇票审核要点。

1）汇票的付款人名称、地址应正确。

2）汇票上金额的大、小写应一致。

3）付款期限应符合信用证或合同（非信用证付款条件下）规定。

4）汇票金额不应超出信用证金额，如信用证金额前有“大约”一词，可按10%的增减幅度掌握。

5）出票人、收款人、付款人应符合信用证或合同（非信用证付款条件下）的规定。

6）币制名称应与信用证和发票相一致。

7）出票条款应正确；出票所根据的信用证或合同的号码应正确。

8）应按需要进行背书。

9）汇票应由出票人进行签字。

10）汇票份数应正确，如“只此一张”或“汇票一式二份，有第一汇票和第二汇票”。

（2）商业发票审核要点。

1）抬头人应符合信用证规定。

2）签发人必须是受益人。

3）商品的描述应完全符合信用证的要求。

4）商品的数量应符合信用证的规定。

5）单价和价格条件应符合信用证的规定。

6）提交的正副本份数应符合信用证的要求。

7）信用证要求表明和证明的内容不得遗漏。

8）发票的金额不得超出信用证的金额，如数量、金额均有“大约”，可按 10%的增减幅度掌握。

（3）保险单审核要点。

1）保险单必须由保险公司或其代理出具。

2）投保加成应符合信用证的规定。

3）保险险别应符合信用证的规定且无遗漏。

4）保险单的类型应与信用证的要求相一致。除非信用证另有规定，否则保险经纪人出具的暂保单银行不予接受。

5）保险单的正副本份数应齐全，如保险单注明出具一式多份正本，除非信用证另有规定，否则所有正本都必须提交。

6）保险单上的币制应与信用证上的币制相一致。

7）包装件数、唛头等应与发票和其他单据相一致。

8）运输工具、起运地及目的地应与信用证及其他单据相一致。

9）如转运，保险期限必须包括全程运输。

10）除非信用证另有规定，否则保险单的签发日期不得迟于运输单据的签发日期。

11）除信用证另有规定，否则保险单一般应做成可转让的形式，以受益人为投保人，由投保人背书。

（4）运输单据审核要点。

1）运输单据的类型应符合信用证的规定。

2）起运地、转运地、目的地应符合信用证的规定。

3）装运日期/出单日期应符合信用证的规定。

4）收货人和被通知人应符合信用证的规定。

5）商品名称可使用货物的统称，但不得与发票上货物说明的写法相抵触。

6）运费预付或运费到付应正确表明。

7）正副本份数应符合信用证的要求。

8）运输单据上不应有不良批注。

9）包装件数应与其他单据相一致。

10）唛头应与其他单据相一致。

11）全套正本都须盖妥承运人的印章及签发日期章。

12）应加背书的运输单据，须加背书。

（5）其他单据审核要点。

其他单据如装箱单、重量单、原产地证、商检证书等，均须先与信用证的条款进行核对，再与其他有关单据核对，求得单证一致、单单一致。

12.4 能力实训

2012 年 3 月，大连思念纺织品进出口公司出口业务部业务员赵进代表公司与法国某公司签订了一批女式手提包的出口合同，付款方式是 D/P AT SIGHT，销售确认书如素材 12-1 所示。2012 年 6 月 15 日货物装船后，从船公司取得提单。单证员蔡平需完成的工作任务是制作所有相关单证，根据销售确认书审核各种单据，并找出不符点进行修改。请审核以下各种单据（见素材 12-2~素材 12-7），找出不符点。

素材 12-1 销售确认书

SALES CONFIRMATION

THE SELLER:

DALIAN SINIAN TEXTILES IMP.&EXP. Co.,LTD. No.: 03CAN-1108

53 ZHIGONG STREET, DALIAN,P.R.CHINA DATE: Mar.02,2012

TEL: +86 0411 54345659

FAX: +86 0411 54345659

THE BUYER:

SHEMSY NEGOCE ID CORP.

75 ROUTE 96570 DARDILLY, FRANCE

FAX:33-56-12345678

TEL: 33-56-12345678

BUYER'S ORDER No.: FE021G

THIS SALES CONFIRMATION IS HEREBY MUTUALLY CONFIRMED, TERMS AND CONDITIONS ARE AS FOLLOWS:

续

NAME OF GOODS AND SPECIFICATIONS	QTY	UNIT PRICE	AMOUNT
WOMEN'S HANDBAGS			CIF MARSEILLES
ITEM No. SL100	1 000 PCS	USD 2.00/PC	USD 2 000.00
ITEM No. SG120	2 000 PCS	USD 1.50/PC	USD 3 000.00
ITEM No. SF200	3 000 PCS	USD 3.00/PC	USD 9 000.00
TOTAL	6 000 PCS		USD 14 000.00
SAY US DALLARS FOURTEEN THOUSAND ONLY			

PACKING: ONE BAG IN A POLYBAG,100 BAGS IN A EXPORT STANDARD CARTON.

SHIPPING MARKS: AS PER BUYER'S OPTION

SHIPMENT: NOT LATER THAN THE END OF JUNE,2012

PAYMENT: 100% OF INVOICE VALUE D/P AT SIGHT

INSURANCE: TO BE EFFECTED BY THE SELLER FOR 110% OF INVOICE VALUE TO COVER F.P.A .AS PER THE OCEAN MARINE CARGO CLAUSE OF THE PEOPLE'S INSURANCE COMPANY OF CHINA.

DOCUMENTS AS FOLLOWS SHOULD BE FORWARDED THROUGH THE BANK:

7. ONE ORIGINAL COMMERCIAL INVOICE SIGNED BY THE SELLER PLUS TWO COPIES.

8. PACKING LIST IN TRIPLICATE.

9. FULL SET OF ORIGINAL CLEAN ON BOARD BILL OF LADING PLUSE 3/3 NON NEGOTIABLE COPIES,MADE OUT TO ORDER AND BLANK ENDORSED NOTIFY THE APPLICANT, MARKED FREGHT PREPAID.

10. INSURANCE POLICY/CERTIFICATE IN DUPLICATE BLANK ENDORSED FOR 110% INVOICE VALUE COVERING FPA SHOWING CLAIMS PAYALBLE IN POLAND IN THE CURRENCY OF THE CREDIT.

11. G.S.P. CERTIFICATE OF ORIGIN FORM A IN 1 DUPLICATE STATING THAT THE GOODS ARE OF CHINESE ORIGIN.

THE SELLER:	THE BUYER:
DALIAN SINIAN TEXTILES IMP.&EXP. Co.,LTD.	SHEMSY NEGOCE ID CORP.
53 ZHIGONG STREET, DALIAN,P.R. CHINA	75 ROUTE 96570 DARDILLY, FRANCE

素材 12-2 商业发票

DALIAN SINIAN TEXTILES IMP.&EXP. Co., LTD.

53 ZHIGONG STREET, DALIAN,P.R. CHINA

COMMERCIAL INVOICE

DATE: JUNE 1，2012

TO: SHEMSY NEGOCE ID CORP. No.: A2400A/98

75 ROUTE 96570 DARDILLY, FRANCE S/C No.: 03CAN-1108

FAX: 33-56-12345678 TEL: 33-56-12345678 PAYMENT: D/P AT SIGHT

FROM DALIAN TO MARSEILLES BY VESSEL

NAME OF GOODS AND SPECIFICATIONS	QTY	UNIT PRICE	AMOUNT
WOMEN'S HANDBAGS			CIF MARSEILLES
ITEM No. SL100	1 000 PCS	USD 2.00/PC	USD 2000.00
ITEM No. SG120	2 000 PCS	USD 1.50/PC	USD 3000.00
ITEM No. SF200	3 000 PCS	USD 3.00/PC	USD 9000.00
TOTAL	6 000 PCS		USD14 000.00
SAY US DALLARS FORTY THOUSAND ONLY			

素材 12-3 装箱单

DALIAN SINIAN TEXTILES IMP.&EXP. Co., LTD.

53 ZHIGONG STREET, DALIAN,P.R. CHINA

PACKING LIST

DATE：JUNE 1，2012

TO: SHEMSY NEGOCE ID CORP. No.: A2400A/98

75 ROUTE 96570 DARDILLY, FRANCE S/C No.: 03CAN-1108

FAX: 33-56-12345678 TEL: 33-56-12345678 PAYMENT: D/P AT SIGHT

FROM DALIAN TO MARSEILLES BY VESSEL

续

MARKS & NOS.	NAME OF GOODS AND SPECIFICATIONS	PACKAGES	N.W.	G.W.	MEAS.
SNI	WOMEN'S				
MARSEILLES	HANDBAGS	10 CTNS	@26 KGS	@27 KGS	@67×39×58CM
C/ No.:1-60	ITEM No. SL100	20 CTNS	260 KGS	270 KGS	1.52 CBM
	ITEM No. SG120	30 CTNS	530 KGS	540 KGS	3.04 CBM
	ITEM No. SF200		780 KGS	810 KGS	4.56 CBM
	1 BAG/POLYBAG,				
	100BAGS/CTN				
TOTAL		60 CTNS	1 570 KGS	1 620 KGS	9.12 CBM
SAY PACKED IN SIXTY CARTONS					

素材 12-4 原产地证

1．Goods consigned from (Exporter's name, address, country) DALIAN SINIAN TEXTILES IMP.&EXP. Co., LTD. 53 ZHIGONG STREET, DALIAN,P.R. CHINA TEL: +86 0411 54345659 FAX: +86 0411 54345659	Reference No. **GENERALIZED SYSTEM OF PREFERENCES** **CERTIFICATE ORIGIN** (combined declaration and certificate) **FORM A** Issued in **THE PEOPLE'S REPUBLIC OF CHINA** (COUNTRY) see notes overleaf
2．Goods consigned to (Consignee's name, address, country) SHEMSY NEGOCE ID CORP. 75 ROUTE 96570 DARDILLY, FRANCE FAX: 33-56-12345678 TEL: 33-56-12345678	
3．Means of transport and route(as far as known) FROM DALIAN TO MARSEILLES BY VESSEL	4.For official use

续

5. Item number	6. Marks and numbers	7. Number and kind of packages; description of goods	8. Origin criterion (see notes overleaf)	9. Gross weight or other Quantity	10. Number and date of invoices
1	SNI MARSEILLES C/ No.:1-60	SIXTY（60） CARTONS OF WOMEN'S HANDBAGS	P	1 620 KGS	A2400A/98 JUNE1, 2012

11. Certification It is hereby certified, on the basis of control out, that the declaration by the exporter is correct. DALIAN, JUNE 8, 2012 ………………………………………………… Place and date, signature and stamp of certifying authority	12. Declaration by the exporter The undersigned hereby declares that the above details and statements are correct; that all the goods were produced in ____CHINA____ and that they comply with the origin requirements specified for those goods in the generalized system of preferences for goods exported to FRANCE …………………………………………………… (importing country) DALIAN，JUNE 8，2012 …………………………………………………… Place and date, signature and stamp of certifying authority

素材 12-5 海运提单

BILL OF LADING

SHIPPER (Principal or Seller licenses and full address)	BOOKING NUMBER	B/L NUMBER
DALIAN SINIAN TEXTILES IMP.&EXP. Co.,LTD. 53 ZHIGONG STREET, DALIAN,P.R. CHINA TEL: +86 0411 54345659 FAX: +86 0411 54345659		APL123
	EXPORT REFERENCES	

续

CONSIGNEE(Name and Full Address) SHEMSY NEGOCE ID CORP. 75 ROUTE 96570 DARDILLY, FRANCE FAX: 33-56-12345678 TEL: 33-56-12345678		FORWARDING AGENT (References, F.M.C. No.)
NOTIFY PARTY (Name and Full Address) SHEMSY NEGOCE ID CORP. 75 ROUTE 96570 DARDILLY, FRANCE FAX: 33-56-12345678 TEL: 33-56-12345678		POINT AND COUNTRY OF ORIGIN OF GOODS
INITIAL CARRIAGE (MODE)	PLACE OF RECEIPT	ALSO NOTIFY (Name and Full Address)/ DOMESTIC ROUTING/ EXPORT INSTRUCTIONS/ PIER TERMINAL/ ONWARD ROUTING FROM POINT OF DESTINATION
EXPORT CARRIER (Vessel voyage &nag) LIBETY V.32	PORT OF LOADING DALIAN,CHINA	
PORT OF DISCHARGE MARSEILLES	PLACE OF DELIVERY	
Excess Valuation Please refer to Clause 7 iii) on Reverse Side		PARTICULARS FURNISHED BY SHIPPER

MKS&NOS/CONTAINER NOS.	No. OR PKGS	DESCRIPTION OF PACKAGES AND GOODS	GROSS WEIGHT	MEASURE-MENT
SNI MARSEILLES C/ No.:1-60	60 CTNS CFS-CFS	WOMEN'S HANDBAGS FREIGHT COLLECT	1 620 KGS	9.12 CBM

TO BE RELEASED AT			OCEAN FREIGHT PAYABLE AT			THE CARRIER:	
FREIGHT RATES CHARGES. WEIGHTS AND/OR MEASUREMENTS (SUBJECT TO CORRECTION)			PREPAID U.S$	COLLECT U.S$	Local Currency	By: Authorized Signature: Date and Place issued: APL AS CARRIER DALIAN, JUN.12,2012	
Vessel	Voyage	Office	TOTAL PREPAID				
			TOTAL COLLECT				
FCC	FORWARDER	SHIPPER	CONSIGNEE	LD PORT	DISPORT	DEST.	NOTIFY

APPLICABLE ONLY WHEN USED AS MULTIMODAL BILL OF LADING

素材 12-6　保险单

中国平安保险股份有限公司

PING AN INSURANCE COMPANY OF CHINA，LTD.

No. 1000005959　　货 物 运 输 保 险 单

CARGO TRANPORTATION INSURANCE POLICY

被保险人：DALIAN SINIAN TEXTILES IMP.&EXP. Co.,LTD.

Insured

中国平安保险股份有限公司根据被保险人的要求及其所交付约定的保险费，按照本保险单背面所载条款与下列特款，承保下述货物运输保险，特立本保险单。

This Policy of Insurance witnesses that PING AN INSURANCE COMPANY OF CHINA, LTD., at the request of the Insured and in consideration of the agreed premium paid by the Insured, undertakes to insure the undermentioned goods in transportation subject to the conditions of Policy as per the clauses printed overleaf and other special clauses attached hereon.

COPY

保单号
Policy No.: 1000005959

赔款偿付地点
Claim Payable at:

发票或提单号
Invoice No. or B/L No.: A2400A/98

运输工具
per conveyance S.S.: LIBETY V.32

查勘代理人
Survey By：

起运日期
Slg. on or abt.: JUN.12,2012

自　　至
From: DALIAN　　To: MARSEILLES

保险金额
Amount Insured USD 15 400.00 (US DOLLARS FIFTEEN THOUSAND FOUR HUNDRED ONLY.)

续

保险货物项目、标记、数量及包装 Description, Marks, Quantity & Packing of Goods：	承保条件 Conditions：COVER FPA
签单日期 Date: JUN.13,2012	
	For and on behalf of **PING AN INSURANCE COMPANY OF CHINA，LTD.** *authorized signature*

素材 12-7 汇票

BILL OF EXCHANGE

No.: SI1207　　　　Date: JUN.13,2012

For: USD 14 000.00

At *******sight of this second of exchange (first of the same tenor and date unpaid) pay to the order of BANK OF CHINA，DALIAN BRANCH the sum of US DALLARS FORTY THOUSAND ONLY

Drawn under AS PER S/C 03CAN-1108

To. CREDIT INDUSTRIAL ET COMMERCIAL (CIC PARIS)　　　　DALIAN SINIAN TEXTILES IMP.&EXP. CO

ZHAOJIN

12.5 能力扩展

A 食品进出口公司向国外出口一批野禽。3 月 9 日，A 食品进出口公司接到买方开来的一张电开信用证，证中关于商品条款规定："100M/T of frozen partridge, packing in cartons, each containing 20-24brace."（100 公吨冷冻鹧鸪，纸箱包装，每箱 20~24 对。）A 食品进出口公司根据对方开来的信用证要求，于 3 月 13 日进行装运，14 日备妥所有单据向议付行交单办理议付。但 3 月 29 日开证行提出拒付，指出卖方发票有不符点，未表明商品规格"Fresh feathers-on, neat and intact, with viscera, without distinction as to sex, a grade, 0.5kg, per brace"（新鲜、羽毛整洁、带内脏、不分雌雄、一级、每对净重 0.5 千克以上）。开证申请人不接受上述单据。A 食品进出口公司查对留底单据与信用证，发现没有规定商品规格，随即发电反驳："你方 3 月 9 日开立的信用证条款并没有规定上述规格，因此我方是相符交单。"开证行答复："关于商品规格事宜，我方 3 月 9 日电开信用证注明'证实书后寄'，后于 3 月 10 日邮寄证实书，在证实书中规定了上述商品规格。”并提出，根据《UCP 600》，“如电开信用证中声明以邮寄的证实书为有效信用证，则电讯不应视为有效信用证，应以规定有商品规格的证实书为有效信用证，所以你方是不符交单”。请问 A 食品进出口公司应如何处理此事？

项目 13

交单收汇与单证归档

学习目标

知识目标：熟悉信用证结算方式下交单收汇的规定；熟悉 T/T 结算方式下交单收汇的规定；了解在规定的时间内及时催收报关单、场站收据等单据的重要性；了解各类单据移交所规定的时间。

能力目标：能按信用证指示或合同条款交单；能检查收回单据的准确性、完整性和一致性；能处理有问题的收回单据，并按业务要求将各类单据归档。

13.1 工作任务

2012 年 8 月 5 日，大连思念纺织品进出口公司单证员蔡平通过审核全套单据，认为各单据都单证一致、单单一致，就将信用证项下的全套单据及原信用证正本（如修改的，还需提交修改通知书）向中国银行大连分行国际业务部进行交单。在交单时需要填写交单联系单。

2012 年 8 月 6 日，中国银行大连分行国际业务部工作人员通知蔡平，开证行 NATIONAL BANK OF POLAND 来电拒绝付款，拒付理由是“没有提交装运前检验证书”。

大连思念纺织品进出口公司马上采取拒付的救济措施。2012 年 8 月 8 日，中国银行大连分行国际业务部工作人员通知蔡平，开证行 NATIONAL BANK OF POLAND 已经在当日对远期汇票承兑。

收汇之后，单证员尚需做好出口收汇核销、出口退税、业务善后工作。为了能够更顺利地办理出口收汇核销和退税手续，必须要注意催促货运代理公司尽快把相关报关单据退回和进行单据归档工作。

在本业务中，单证员蔡平要在交单收汇和单证归档阶段完成以下工作任务。

任务 1 填写交单联系单。

任务 2 处理开证行拒付事件。

任务 3 业务结束后，进行单据归档处理。

13.2 操作步骤

13.2.1 第一步：填写交单联系单

单证员应根据信用证和合同的指示，填写交单联系单。本业务中的交单联系单如表 13-1 所示。

表 13-1 交单联系单

交单联系单					
致：中国银行大连分行					
兹随附下列出口单据一套，信用证业务请按国际商会现行《跟单信用证统一惯例》办理，跟单托收业务请按国际商会现行《托收统一规则》办理。					
信用证	开证行：NATIONAL BANK OF POLAND		信用证号：DCTBT123456		
	通知行号：******	提单日期：120730	效期：121013	交单期限 15 天	
无证托收	付款人全名及详址：				
	代收行名称及详址：				
	交单方式：（ ）D/P （ ）D/A		付款期限：		
发票编号：12GEP3298				金额：EUR65 300.00	
单据					
2	汇票 DRAFT		原产地证 CERTIFICATE OF ORIGIN	2	保险单 INSURANCE POLICY/CERTIFICATE
2+1C	商业发票 COMMERCIAL INVOICE	2	普惠制原产地证 G.S.P FORM A	3+3N	运输单据 BILL OF LADING/C.R / A.W.B

续表

	海关发票 CUSTOM INVOICE		质量证明 QUANLITY CERTIFICATE		船公司证明 SHIPPING Co. CERTIFICATE
3	装箱单/重量单 PACKING/WEIGHT LIST	**1**	检验/分析证书 INSPECTION CERTIFICATE	**1**	装船通知 SHIPMENT ADVICE
	受益人证明 BENEFICIARY CERTIFICATE		电传回执 FAX REPORT		邮递收据 POST RECEIPT
单据：					

委办事项：（打"×"者）	
	（ ）上述单据请按我司与贵行签订之总质押书办理押汇。
	（ ）上述单据系代理出口项下业务，收妥后请原币划______________
	（ ）开户行：________账号：______________
	（ ）若付款人拒绝付款/承兑，不必做成拒绝证书，但须以电传通知我司。
	（×）附信用证及修改书共__2__纸。
	（ ）单据中有下列不符点：（ ）请向开证行寄单，我司承担一切责任。
	（ ）请电询开证行同意后再寄单。
	（ ）____

公司联系人：蔡平	联系电话：0411-54345659	公司公章：大连思念纺织品进出口公司

银行审单记录	银行接单日期：		
（ ）单证相符。	索汇金额：		BP No.
（ ）存在下列不符点：	寄单日期：		OC No.
	银行 费用	通知/修改通知	/
		议付/托收	
		邮　费	
		电报费	
		合　计：	由　　　　　承担
	索汇方式：		寄单方式：
经询，受益人确认不符寄单。	银行经办：		银行复核：
退单记录：			

13.2.2　第二步：处理开证行拒付事件

1．分析开证行拒付理由是否成立

针对开证行 NATIONAL BANK OF POLAND 的拒付进行分析，根据《UCP 600》的规定，提交的单据需要齐全，因此，“没有提交装运前检验证书”构成了不符点。

2．采取拒付的救济措施

针对这一不符点，单证员蔡平可以采取补交单据的救济措施，即马上将装运前检验证书在信用证规定的交单期内向议付行中国银行大连分行补交，要求转交给开证行，从而完成交单手续。

13.2.3　第三步：进行单据归档处理

单证员必须要注意催促货运代理公司尽快退回场站收据等相关单据。重要单据的移交要用专门的本子登记，由接收人签收。

对于每票业务，单证员需归档的单据一般包括信用证、商业发票、装箱单、订舱委托书、报检单、报关单、报关委托书、原产地证、运输单据、保险单据、其他结汇单据等。

13.3　知识扩展

13.3.1　信用证结算方式下的交单收汇

信用证交易是纯粹的单据买卖。出口人想要及时、安全地收回货款，在按信用证要求发运完毕货物后，应随即缮制信用证规定的全套单据，开立汇票与发票，连同信用证正本（如经修改，还需连同修改通知书）在信用证规定的交单期和信用证的有效期内递交信用证限定的银行、通知行或自己有往来的其他银行请求议付，该过程被称为交单。

1．交单时间的限制

受益人制单后，应在规定的交单期内向信用证指定的银行交付全套单据。若信用证没有规定交单期限，银行将不接受自装运日起 21 天内提交的单据，但在任何情况下，单据的提交不得迟于信用证的有效期。若信用证到期日或交单日的最后一天适逢接受单据的银行的终止营业日，则规定的到期日或交单期的最后一天将延至该银行开业的第一个营业日。但若该银行中断营业是因为天灾、暴动、骚乱、叛乱、战争、罢工、停工或银行本身无法控制的任何其他原因，则信用证规定的到期日或交单期的最后一天不能顺延。对交单期产生影响的时间包括生产及包装所需的时间，内陆运输或集装箱运输所需的时间，进行必要的检验（如法定商检或客检）所需的时间，申领出口许可证、原产地证所需的时间（如果需要），报关查验所需的时间，船期安排时间，到商会和/或领事馆办理认证或出具有关证明所需的时间（如果需要），制造、整理、审核信用证规定的文件所需的时间，将单据提交银行所需的时间（包括单据提交银行后经审核发现有误退回更正的时间）等。

2．交单地点的限制

所有信用证必须规定一个付款或承兑的交单地点，或在议付信用证的情况下规定一个交单议付的地点，但自由议付信用证除外。若开证行将信用证的到期地点定在本国或自己的营业柜台，而不是受益人国家，这对受益人极为不利，因为受益人必须保证于信用证的有效期内在开证行营业柜台前提交单据。

3．议付行对单据的处理

议付行审核单据，若单证相符、单单相符，就会办理议付（或押汇），并向开证行寄单请求付款。议付行对有不符点的单据主要采取以下处理办法。

（1）凭保函议付。如果单据有非实质性的不符点，且受益人信誉较好，银行可凭受益人出具的保函议付，并向开证行寄单索汇。在这种情况下，有的议付行会表提不符点（在面函上注明单据的所有不符点），通知开证行此信用证凭受益人出具的担保议付，请求开证行接受不符点。我国国内大多数银行则将受益人出具的保函存档，不表提不符点，与处理相符单据一样，向开证行寄单索汇。

（2）电提不符点。如果单据金额较大、不符点较严重，为保证收汇安全，银行可以采取电报、电传、SWIFT 等方式把不符点告知开证行，要求其回电授权付款、承兑或议付不符点单据。在取得开证行同意并授权付款、承兑或议付时，议付行可按单据相符的方式，直接议付单据并照常索汇。采取电提不符点，可较快地明确开证人是否接受不符点，有利于受益人及时处理。受益人应配合议付行与开证行联系，加快沟通速度。不过，即使开证行授权议付，在偿付时，仍可能从偿付货款中扣除不符点费（Discrepancy Fee）和电报费（Cable Charges）。

（3）托收寄单或征求意见寄单。若单据中含有严重不符点，在受益人征得进口商同意，且进口商资信较好的情况下，寄单行可将单据寄给开证行作托收处理，并在寄单面函上列明不符点。这种托收寄单方式可减少业务手续和费用，但也使得受益人完全失去开证行的付款保证，单据是否被接受取决于开证申请人的商业信用。寄单行也可向开证行寄单，征求其意见。在远期交易的情形下，如开证行通知单据已被接受，则应负到期付款的责任。

（4）退单。若单据严重不符，受益人或受益人所在地银行不愿做托收处理，议付行可将单据退回。

4．信用证项下不符单据的处理与救济

（1）审核开证行提出不符点的前提条件是否成立。开证行提出不符点的前提条件包括如下几点。

1）在合理的时间内提出不符点，即在开证行收到单据次日起计算的 5 个工作日之内向单据的提示者提出不符点。

2）无延迟地以电讯方式将不符点通知单据的提示者。

3）不符点必须一次性提出，即如果第一次所提不符点不成立，即使单据还存在实质性不符点，开证行也无权再次提出。

4）通知不符点的同时，必须说明单据代为保管、听候处理，或径退交单者。

以上条件必须同时满足，否则开证行便无权声称单据有不符点而拒付。

（2）审核开证行所提的不符点是否成立。单证员应根据信用证条款、《UCP 600》和《ISBP》认真审核开证行所提的不符点，判断其是否成立。若不成立，应通过议付行与开证行据理力争，直至开证行付款。

（3）若不符点成立，且条件允许，可补交相符单据，采取救济措施。信用证项下不符单据的救济措施是指当单据由于具有不符点而遭开证行拒付之后，受益人可在规定的时间内及时将替代或更正后的相符单据补交给银行。根据《UCP 600》的规定，单据经审核存在不符点，且银行决定拒付时，则开证行所承担的信用证项下的付款责任得以免除；但如果受益人在规定时间内补交了符合信用证规定的单据，则开证行必须承担其付款责任。如果受益人在前期操作过程中浪费了大量时间，就会丧失补交单据时间。

（4）若不符点成立，且无法补交相符单据，要积极与开证申请人洽谈。开证行拒付并不意味着开证申请人拒付，如果开证申请人最终放弃不符点，尽管开证行并不受开证申请人决定的约束，但一般会配合开证申请人付款。所以开证行拒付后，如果不符点确实成立，且无法补交相符单据，应分析与开证申请人之间的关系及此笔交易的实际情况，以决定怎样与其交涉，说服开证申请人接受不符点并付款。只要货物质量过关，商品市场价格较好，开证申请人一般不会以此为借口拒绝接受单据。另外，也可以采取降价的方式，使开证申请人能付款赎单。

（5）若不符点成立，且开证申请人拒绝接受单据，则可在进口国另寻买主。若开证申请人拒绝接受具有不符点的单据，受益人可以设法在进口国另寻买主，毕竟受益人拥有对单据的处理权。但其前提是信用证要求递交全套正本提单，若 1/3 正本提单已寄给开证申请人，2/3 正本提单提交给银行，则可能会面临钱货两失的困境。

（6）退单退货。如果受益人无法在进口国寻找到新买主，就只有退单退货了。不过在做出此决定之前，一定要仔细核算运回货物所需的费用和货值之间是否有利可图。有利益，即迅速安排退运，因为时间拖得越久，费用（港杂、仓储等）就越高；若运回货物得不偿失，还不如将货物放在目的港，由目的港海关处理。

13.3.2 T/T 结算方式下的交单收汇

如果采取装运前 T/T 的结算方式，出口商在装运前已全部收到进口商电汇的合同金额，则在装运之后，就直接把包括海运提单在内的所有单据寄给进口商，或指示船公司把提单电放给进口商。如果采取装运后凭提单传真件 T/T 的结算方式，出口商在装运后，把海运提单传真给进口商，等进口商把合同金额电汇到出口商银行账户之后，才把包括海运提单在内的所有单据寄给进口商。如果采取后 T/T 的结算方式，出口商在装运后就把包括海运提单在内的所有单据寄给进口商，等进口商收到货物之后的一段时间内采用电汇方式把合同款项付给出口商。

13.3.3　托收结算方式下的交单收汇

选择托收结算方式时，出口商装运货物后，应及时将有关托收单据交托收行办理托收。托收交单较灵活，单据种类、单据内容、交单时间由出口商根据合同和进口商情况决定。交单时，出口商应向托收行提供明确的托收指示书。值得注意的是，托收行没有审核单据的义务，只能根据委托人的指示和国际商会托收统一规则办理，不能擅自超越、修改、疏漏、延误委托人的指示。代收行是指接受托收行（或中间行）的委托，向付款人办理收款并交单的银行。在进口商没有付款或承兑的情况下，代收行未得到出口商授权擅自交单，将由其承担损失责任。

13.3.4　出口收汇核销单

出口收汇核销单是我国特有的国际商务单据。它是由外汇管理部门印制，出口企业凭以向海关出口报关，通过指定外汇银行办理收汇，向外汇管理部门办理收汇核销的有统一编号的凭证。其主要当事人包括出口企业、海关、外汇管理部门和指定外汇银行。

为大力推进贸易便利化，进一步改进货物贸易外汇服务和管理，根据国家外汇管理局、海关总署、国家税务总局的决定，2012 年 8 月 1 日起在全国实施货物贸易外汇管理制度改革，并相应调整出口报关流程，优化升级出口收汇与出口退税信息共享机制。这一改革是贸易便利化的又一次实践。企业从此不再办理出口收汇核销手续，出口报关和申报出口退税时也不再提供核销单，收汇时间显著缩短，资金周转速度加快，最终取得出口退税的时间也较以前普遍提前 10 天左右。

13.3.5　单证归档

单证是外贸活动的重要资料，是商品流通的原始凭证。它反映了整个商品流转过程，是业务档案资料的主要组成部分，具有重要的分析参考价值。因此，单证归档是一项非常重要的工作。

1．单证归档的意义

(1) 为完成履约提供保证。在外贸活动中，通过对单证的缮制交付、登记整理、统计分析，可以使有关人员做到心中有数，可以顺利组织货源、衔接生产出运，保证安全及时地收汇。单证归档对于企业控制工作进程、完成贸易任务有着重要意义。

（2）为统计分析提供原始资料，提高外贸工作管理水平。要检查分析外贸企业各项业务工作质量和效率，均可从单证资料中提取数据。如果平时累积了合同履约率、客户付款天数、费用指标及流通费用、资金周转率等各项指标的资料，通过分析这些数据，就可以促进外贸企业经营和管理的改善。

（3）为查询和处理业务差错事故提供资料。在外贸活动中，难免会出现一些由于操作不当而引发的工作失误。当有商品数量溢缺、品名规格（等级）不符、国别（地区）错运、多装、少装等差错事故发生时，必须查明原因、分清责任、吸取教训、加强教育、采取措施、防范今后，以达到安全优质，不断提高外贸工作质量的要求。这些均需要必要的单证归档资料。

2．单证归档的要求

（1）要建立完备的单证档案管理制度。每套单证都应有一套副本留存备查。单证副本的归档方法可分为分散归档和集中归档两种。分散归档由各分管环节各自将本环节缮制和经营的副本单证分类归档。例如，提单由办理运输的环节按运输日期归档，商业发票按发票号码分别由制单环节归档等。集中归档在交单后将全套副本集中起来进行保管。一般来说，业务量大、部门多、分工细的单位适宜分散归档；业务量不大、工作线条比较简单的单位适宜集中归档。单证编排以查找方便为原则。如采取集中归档的方式，可以按合同号码编组，也可以按发票号码排列，各企业可以视情况自行设计，保存期以 2～3 年较为恰当。因为与贸易有关的某些国际条约规定，诉讼时效自货到后算起 2 年有效，所以档案保管的时限应与之相适应。另外，除保留必要的书面资料以外，还要充分利用计算机存储电子单证信息，以加强单证工作的管理。

（2）要经常分析单证工作，以提高单证工作的质量和效率。结合对外履约情况、客户发展等方面的考察，应经常分析单证工作，研究该如何进一步提高单证工作的质量和效率，为企业实现目标发挥更大的作用。例如，可以从审核督促、人员分工、工作考核、流程重组等多方面加以改进，使单证工作趋于完善。

13.4 能力实训

以 12.4 节涉及的各单据为背景资料，2012 年 6 月 20 日，大连思念纺织品进出口公司外贸单证员蔡平通过审核，认为各单据与合同一致、单单相符。然后，就把准备好的结汇单据及合同正本向中国银行大连分行国际业务部进行交单。交单时，单证员需填写客户交单业务委托书（交单联系单）并支付托收费用。请以单证员蔡平的身份填写以下交单联系单（见素材 13-1），并办理交单手续。

素材 13-1 交单联系单框架

客户交单业务委托书

COLLECTION ORDER

致：中国银行广东分行　　　　　　　　　　　　　　　　　　日期：

兹随附下列出口托收单据/票据，请贵行根据国际商会托收统一规则及/或贵行有关票据业务处理条例予以审核，并办理寄单/票索汇：

托收行（Remitting Bank）：	代收行（Collecting Bank）：
名称：中国银行	名称：HSBC FRANCE
地址：大连市沙河口区黄河路 721 号	地址：8th ARRONDISSEMENT IN PARIS IN FRANCT

委托人（Principal）：	付款人（Drawee）：

付款交单 D/P （　　） 承兑交单 D/A （　　） 无偿交单 FREE OF PAYMENT （　　）	期限/到期日：
发票号码/票据编号：	国外费用承担人：□ 付款人　□ 委托人
金额：	国内费用承担人：□ 付款人　□ 委托人

单据种类	汇票	商业发票	海运提单	航空运单	保险单	装箱单	数量（重量）证书	原产地证	品质证书	健康证	公司证明	普惠制产地证	原产地证		
份数															

特别指示：

1．邮寄方式　　□ 快邮　□普邮　□ 指定快邮

2．托收如遇拒付，是否需代收行做成拒绝证书（PROTEST）　□ 是　□ 否

3．货物抵港时是否代办存仓保险　□ 是　□ 否

4．如付款人拒付费用及／或利息，是否可以放弃　□ 是　□ 否

付款指示：

请将收汇款以原币（　）或人民币（　）划入我司下列账户：

开户行：中国银行　　　　　　　　　　账号：

公司联系人姓名：

续表

电话：	传真：	年 月 日
银行签收人：	签收日期：	
改单/退单记录：		

13.5 能力扩展

请思考，为什么每笔业务完毕后，单证的归档工作非常重要？

项目 14

业务综合技能训练

学习目标

知识目标：掌握进出口贸易核心单据的缮制。

能力目标：能够根据外贸合同审核信用证、缮制外贸单据和审单。

工作任务

任务 1

1．根据外贸合同 GP1288（见素材 14-1），审核信用证（见素材 14-2），找出问题条款并提出修改意见。

2．根据修改后的信用证和相关资料（见素材 14-3），制作需提交的相关单据。

3．审核制作的全套单据，找出不符点并修改。

素材 14-1　外贸合同

SALES CONTRACT	
Date：JULY 1,2012	S/C No：GP1288
THE SELLER: YINGLI TOOLS MANUFACTURE Co.,LTD. 26 ANZHONG ROAD, SHANGHAI,	**THE BUYER:** SODA INDUSTRIES Co. ,LTD. 5 CAT ROAD,NEW YORK,U.S.A

续

P.R CHINA Tel: 0086-21- 58766688 Fax: 0086-21- 58766688	Tel: 001-212-2337891 Fax: 001-212-2337891

THE SELLER AGREES TO SELL AND THE BUYER AGREES TO BUY THE UNDERMENTIONED GOODS ON THE TERMS AND CONDITIONS STATED BELOW.

品名及规格 COMMODITY&SPECIFICATION	数 量 QUANTITY	单 价 UNIT PRICE	总 值 AMOUNT
CLAW HAMMER		CIF NEW YORK, U.S.A	
ARTICLE No. 92306	8 000 PCS	USD 9.00/PC	USD 72 000.00
ARTICLE No. 92307	8 000 PCS	USD 10.00/PC	USD 80 000.00
ARTICLE No. 92308	8 000 PCS	USD 12.00/PC	USD 96 000.00
合计（**TOTAL**）	24000 PCS		USD 248 000.00

TOTAL CONTRACT VALUE:SAY U.S.DOLLARS TWO HUNDRED AND FORTY EIGHT THOUSAND ONLY

Packing: 8 PIECES PACKED IN ONE BOX, TEN BOXES PACKED IN ONE EXPORT CARTON.

Marks:

SODA
GP1288
NEW YORK
C/N：1-300

SHIPMENT: SHIPPDE FROM SHANGHAI, CHINA TO NEW YORK,U.S.A NOT LATER THAN SEPT. 26,2012; PARTIAL SHIPMENT AND TRANSSHIPMENT ARE ALLOWED.

INSURANCE:TO BE EFFECTED BY THE SELLER FOR 110% OF INVOICE VALUE COVERING ALL RISKS AS PER OCEAN MARINE CARGO CLAUSES OF THE PEOPLE'S INSURANCE COMPANY OF CHINA DATED 01/01, 1981.

PAYMENT: BY IRREVOCABLE LETTER OF CREDIT AT 30 DAYS AFTER SIGHT, REACHING THE SELLER NOT LATER THAN JULY 15 2012 AND REMAINING VALID FOR NEGOTIATION IN CHINA FOR FURTHER 15 DAYS AFTER THE EFFECTED SHIPMENT.

SIGNED BY:

THE SELLER	**THE BUYER**
YINGLI TOOLS MANUFACTURE Co.,LTD.	SODA INDUSTRIES Co., LTD.
方 勇	JACK SMITH

素材 14-2 信用证

MESSAGE TYPE: MT700	
SEQUENCE OF TOTAL	*27: 1/1
FORM OF DOC. CREDIT	*40A : IRREVOCABLE
DOC. CREDIT NUMBER	*20: LC35576
DATE OF ISSUE	31C : 120711
APPLICABLE RELUES	*40E: UCP LATEST VERSION
EXPIRY	*31D: DATE 121015 PLACE IN NEW YORK
ALLICANT BANK	51D: BANK OF CHINA NEW YORK
APPLICANT	*50: SODA INDUSTRIES Co. ,LTD. 5 CAT ROAD,NEW YORK,U.S.A
BENEFICIARY	*59: YINGLI TOOLS MANUFACTURE Co.,LTD 26 ANZHONG ROAD, SHANGHAI,CHINA
AMOUNT	*32B: CURRENCY USD AMOUNT 248 000.00
AVAILABLE WITH/BY	*41D: ANY BANK BY NEGOTIATION
DRAFTS AT…	42C: 30 DAYS AFTER B/L DATE
DRAWEE	42D: BANK OF CHINA NEW YORK
PARTIAL SHIPMENTS	43P: ALLOWED
TRANSSHIPMENT	43T: ALLOWED
PORT OF LOADING	44E: CHINESE PORT
PORT OF DISCHARGE	44F: NEW YORK,U.S.A
LATEST DATE OF SHIP	44C: 120926
DESCRIPT. OF GOODS	45A: 24 000 PIECES OF CLAW HAMMER, AS PER S/C No. GP1288 ARTICLE No. 92306 8 000 PCS USD 9.00/PC ARTICLE No. 92307 8 000 PCS USD10.00/PC ARTICLE No. 92308 8 000 PCS USD12.00/PC
AT CFR NEW YORK,U.S.A	
DOCUMENTS REQUIRED	46A:

1．COMMERCIAL INVOICE SIGNED IN TRIPLICATE.

2．PACKING LIST IN TRIPLICATE.

续

3. FULL SET OF CLEAN ON BOARD OCEAN BILL OF LADING MARKED FREGHT COLLECT MADE OUT TO ORDER OF ISSUING BANK AND BLANK ENDORSED NOTIFY APPLICANT.	
4. CERTIFICATE OF CHINESE ORIGIN CERTIFIED BY ANY BANK.	
5. INSURANCE POLICY IN DUPLICATE BLANK ENDORSED FOR 130 PERCENT OF THE INVOICE VALUE COVERING ALL RISKS&WAR RISK OF CIC OF PICC (1/1/1981) INCL.	
ADDITIONAL COND.	47A:
+ALL DOCUMENTS MUST INDICATE THE NUMBER OF THIS CREDIT.	
+DOCUMENTS ISSUED PRIOR TO L/C ISSUING DATE ARE NOT ACCEPTABLE.	
+ DOCUMENTS MUST BE PRESENTED WITHIN 15 DAYS AFTER SHIPMENT DATE BUT IN ANY EVENT NOT LATER THAN THE EXPIRY DATE OF THIS CREDIT.	
+ALL PRESENTATIONS CONTAINING DISCREPANCIES WILL ATTRACT A DISCREPANCY FEE OF USD60.00 PLUS TELEX COSTS OR OTHER CURRENCY EQUIVALENT. THIS CHARGE WILL BE DEDUCTED FROM THE BILL AMOUNT WHETHER OR NOT WE ELECT TO CONSULT THE APPLICANT FOR A WAIVER.	
DETALLS OF CHARGES	71B: ALL CHARGES ARE ON BENEFICIARY'S ACCOUNT..
PRESENTATION PERIOD	48: 5DAYS AFTER B/L DATE, BUT WITHIN L/C VALIDITY.
CONFIRMATION	*49: WITHOUT

素材 14-3 相关资料

(1) INVOICE No.: YL12900

(2) B/L No.: JH-YL702

(3) H.S. CODE: 82052000

(4) 公司向中国远洋运输总公司订 2012 年 9 月 20 日的船期，船名为 LONGGANG，航次为 S312。

(5) 40'集装箱号码：MIDU7251255

(6) 运费 3 400 美元，保险费 550 美元，杂费 400 美元。

(7) 货物规格如下表。

规　格	PACKAGE	N.W.(KGS)	G.W.(KGS)	MEAS
ARTICLE No. 92306	100 CTNS	3 000	3 800	35.675M^3
ARTICLE No. 92307	100 CTNS	3 500	4 300	35.675M^3
ARTICLE No. 92308	100 CTNS	4 000	4 800	35.675M^3

任务 2

1. 根据外贸合同 LY2012-006（见素材 14-4），审核信用证（见素材 14-5），找出问题条款并修改。

2．根据修改后的信用证和相关资料（见素材 14-6），制作需提交的相关单据。

3．审核制作的全套单据，找出不符点并修改。

素材 14-4 外贸合同

SALES CONTRACT

S/C No.: GP1288　　　　Date: JULY 1,2012

THE SELLER:	THE BUYER:
GUANGZHOU FUSHENG IMP. &EXP. Co., LTD. 136 WUXING ROAD, GUANGZHOU P.R CHINA Tel: +86-20-5369778 Fax: +86-20-5369778	FCY TRADING Co., LTD. 1-15 AZA SHINBO,OSAKA,JAPAN Tel: +81 66 5395162 Fax: +81 66 5395162

THE SELLERS AGREES TO SELL AND THE BUYER AGREES TO BUY THE UNDERMENTIONED GOODS ON THE TERMS AND CONDITIONS STATED BELOW.

品名及规格 COMMODITY&SPECIFICATION	数　量 QUANTITY	单　价 UNIT PRICE	总　值 AMOUNT
MOUNTAIN BIKE		CIF OSAKA,JAPAN	
ARTICLE No.			
AUT 660	500 SETS	USD 110.00/SET	USD 55 000.00
AUT 770	500 SETS	USD 125.00/SET	USD 62 500.00
合计（**TOTAL**）	1 000 SETS		USD 117 500.00

TOTAL CONTRACT VALUE: SAY U.S.DOLLARS ONE HUNDRED AND SEVENTEEN THOUSAND FIVE HUNDRED ONLY.

ASSORTMENT：

ARTICLE No.	XS(SETS)	S(SETS)	M(SETS)	L(SETS)	XL(SETS)
AUT 660	100	100	100	100	100
AUT 770	100	100	100	100	100

PACKING：TO BE PACKED IN CARTONS OF ONE SET EACH,TOTAL 1000 CARTONS.

续

MARKS:

FCY
LY2012-006
OSAKA
C/N：1-1000

SHIPMENT: SHIPPED FROM GUANGZHOU, CHINA TO OSAKA, JAPAN NOT LATER THAN MAY 31,2012; PARTIAL SHIPMENT AND TRANSSHIPMENT ARE ALLOWED.

INSURANCE:TO BE EFFECTED BY THE SELLER FOR 110% OF FULL INVOICE VALUE COVERING ALL RISKS AND WAR RISKS AS PER OCEAN MARINE CARGO CLAUSES OF THE PEOPLE'S INSURANCE COMPANY OF CHINA DATED 01/01, 1981.

PAYMENT：30% OF PROCEEDS PAID BY T/T IN ADVACE. THE BALANCE 70% OF PROCEEDS PAID BY IRREVOCABLE L/C AT SIGHT.

SIGNED BY:

THE SELLER	**THE BUYER**
GUANGZHOU FUSHENG IMP. &EXP. Co.,LTD.	FCY TRADING Co., LTD.
向岩	JOHN

素材 14-5　信用证

MESSAGE TYPE: MT700	
SEQUENCE OF TOTAL	*27: 1/1
FORM OF DOC. CREDIT	*40A: REVOCABLE
DOC. CREDIT NUMBER	*20: LCS67506579
DATE OF ISSUE	31C: 120420
APPLICABLE RELUES	*40E: UCP LATEST VERSION
EXPIRY	*31D: DATE 120615 PLACE IN OSAKA
ALLICANT BANK	51D: SUMITOMO MITSUI BANK OSAKA
APPLICANT	*50: FCY TRADING Co., LTD. 1-15 AZA SHINBO, OSAKA, JAPAN
BENEFICIARY	*59: GUANGZHOU FUSHENG IMP. &EXP. Co., LTD. 136 WUXING ROAD, GUANGZHOU, P.R CHINA
AMOUNT	*32B: CURRENCY USD AMOUNT 82 250.00
AVAILABLE WITH/BY	*41D: ANY BANK

续

	BY NEGOTIATION
DRAFTS AT…	42C: 30 DAYS AFTER SIGHT
DRAWEE	42D: SUMITOMO MITSUI BANK OSAKA
PARTIAL SHIPMENTS	43P: ALLOWED
TRANSSHIPMENT	43T: ALLOWED
PORT OF LOADING	44E: GUANGZHOU, CHINA
PORT OF DISCHARGE	44F: OSAKA, JAPAN
LATEST DATE OF SHIP	44C: 120431
DESCRIPT. OF GOODS	45A: MOUNTAIN BIKE AS PER S/C No. LY2012-006 Article no. AUT 660　500 SETS AT USD110.00/SET AUT 770　500 SETS AT USD125.00/SET AT CIF OSAKA, JAPAN PACKED IN 1 000 CTNS
DOCUMENTS REQUIRED	46A:

1. SIGNED COMMERCIAL INVOICE IN QUADRUPLICATE MENTIONING L/C No. AND VESSEL'S NAME, TOGETHER WITH BENEFICIARIES' DECLARATION CONFIRMING THAT ONE SET OF NON-NEGOTIABLE DOCS. HAS TO BE SENT TO THE APPLICANT.

2. PACKING LIST IN TRIPLICATE.

3. FULL SET OF ORIGINAL CLEAN ON BOARD BILL OF LADING MADE OUT TO APPLICANT AND BLANK ENDORSED NOTIFY THE APPLICANT, MARKED FREGHT PREPAID.

4. INSURANCE POLICY IN DUPLICATE BLANK ENDORSED FOR 120 PERCENT OF THE INVOICE VALUE COVERING ALL RISKS&WAR RISK OF CIC OF PICC (1/1/1981) INCL.

5. G.S.P. CERTIFICATE OF ORIGIN FORM A IN DUPLICATE, ISSUED AND SIGNED BY THE COMMODITY INSPECTION BUREAU IN GUANGZHOU.

6. SHIPPING ADVICE SHOWING THE NAME OF VESSEL, VOYAGE NO, L/C NO, B/L NO,QUANTITY SHIPPED WITHIN 2 DAYS AFTER THE DATE OF BILL OF LADING.

ADDITIONAL COND.　　47A:

+ THIS L/C COVERS 80% OF THE INVOICE VALUE, 30% HAS BEEN DOWN BY T/T IN ADVANCE.

+DOCUMENTS ISSUED PRIOR TO L/C ISSUING DATE ARE NOT ACCEPTABLE.

+ DOCUMENTS MUST BE PRESENTED WITHIN 15 DAYS AFTER SHIPMENT DATE BUT IN ANY EVENT NOT LATER THAN THE EXPIRY DATE OF THIS CREDIT.

续

+ALL PRESENTATIONS CONTAINING DISCREPANCIES WILL ATTRACT A DISCREPANCY FEE OF USD60.00 PLUS TELEX COSTS OR OTHER CURRENCY EQUIVALENT. THIS CHARGE WILL BE DEDUCTED FROM THE BILL AMOUNT WHETHER OR NOT WE ELECT TO CONSULT THE APPLICANT FOR A WAIVER.	
DETALLS OF CHARGES	71B: ALL CHARGES ARE ON BENEFICIARY'S ACCOUNT..
PRESENTATION PERIOD	48: 15DAYS AFTER B/L DATE, BUT WITHIN L/C VALIDITY.
CONFIRMATION	*49: WITHOUT

素材 14-6 相关资料

（1）INVOICE No.: FS12018

（2）B/L No.：JH-FCY06

（3）H.S. CODE：87120030

（4）公司向中国远洋运输总公司订 2012 年 5 月 25 日的船期，船名为 LONGXIANG，航次为 V206。

（5）40'集装箱号码：JMISU7234121、MISU7234122

（6）运费 700 美元，保险费 320 美元，杂费 500 美元。

（7）公司产品的原材料都由中国制造，属于法定检验商品。规格如下表。

规格	体积（台）	N.W.(KGS)	G.W.(KGS)
AUT 660	0.261M^3	15	19
AUT 770	0.261M^3	15	19

参考文献

[1] 全国国际商务单证专业培训考试办公室．国际商务单证理论与实务（2008 年版）[M]．北京：中国商务出版社，2008.
[2] 章安平．外贸单证操作[M]．北京：高等教育出版社，2008.
[3] 祝卫，等．出口贸易模拟操作教程（第三版）[M]．上海：上海人民出版社，2008.
[4] 屈韬．外贸单证处理技巧（第三次修订）[M]．北京：中国海关出版社，2008.
[5] 杨静．国际商务单证实训教程[M]．大连：东北财经大学出版社，2012.
[6] 李秀华．国际物流单证实务[M]．北京：清华大学出版社，2011.
[7] 姜宏．国际贸易单证实训[M]．北京：机械工业出版社，2009.
[8] 曾鸣．UCP600 的主要变化及对实务的影响[M]．大连：东北财经大学出版社，2007.
[9] 杨晓明，张晓辉．新编国际贸易实务教程[M]．杭州：浙江大学出版社，2008.
[10] 张晓明，刘文广．国际贸易实训[M]．北京：高等教育出版社，2009.

反侵权盗版声明